INDIVIDUALS

This Book Belongs To:

DRU COLBERT

A Dutton Paperback

E. P. DUTTON & CO., INC.

NEW YORK

INDIVIDUALS:
POST-MOVEMENT ART
IN AMERICA

edited by ALAN SONDHEIM

ISBN 0-525-47428-5
Designed by The Etheredges

CONTENTS

INTRODUCTION

Alan Sondheim

Stance. Sensibility.
It is hard to find words in English that indicate a shared group of concerns, a way of looking at the world. The work in this book centers around a common stance, a sensibility.

Adjectives.
The following adjectives are useful in defining this stance: personal, eclectic, intellectual, literary, antireductive, historical.

Elaboration.
Works of art emerge out of a complex dialogue between self and society, individual concerns and the concerns of the "art world," and so forth. The artist may choose to embed his or her work into the main-

stream of contemporary art, which often results in a tendency toward formalism and the attempt to carry one particular aspect of already existing art "one step further." But the artist may also choose to turn inward, in a sense—to investigate the relationship between self and society, self and history. In short, the artist may choose to examine the position of the self in the world.

The Human.

This examination can establish the notion of humanity, give it a ground. There is still the tendency in both the sciences and the arts to quantify society, reduce everything to numbers and parameters. This tendency results in a misplaced clarity, a belief that it is possible rationally, analytically, to come to grips with the world. The work in this book, however, can be seen as an attempt to clear space for "the world of the self."

Triads.

Some of the work can be categorized in terms of triads. These triads have no critical meaning, outside of a rough scheme that occasionally appears useful. For example, there is the triad of Alice Aycock, Michael Metz, and Charles Simonds. All of them construct models or projects for models that are both architectural objects and shapings for psychophysical spaces. Aycock's structures are full-size presentations of spaces generating paranoias, or playing on the fears of the spectator.

Memory.

I saw Aycock's *Stairs* (*These Stairs can be Climbed*) at 112 Greene Street Gallery (New York City), in 1974. This enormous stairway reached thirteen feet up against the north wall of the exhibition space. The risers were extremely steep. From the top one commanded a view of nothing at all. Aycock also had a number of photographs, almost a retrospective, placed on the walls. Two of them were of the low building included here.

Problem.

There was always a problem about what to do with the stairs when the show was over. Someone suggested putting them outside a building, making the second story more accessible to burglars.

Alvin Lucier.

Alvin Lucier, the only composer in the book, is one of the most interesting artists around. A great deal of his work is concerned either with the location of the self (in a particular space, under particular circumstances) or with the psychology of speech (I am thinking of the pieces concerned with stuttering). The work described here, *Still and Moving Lines of Silence in Families of Hyperbolas,* is an example of the former, while the description itself—the interview—is also concerned with the latter. Lucier's speech is transcribed without editing; the mechanism of stuttering is revealed directly. The interview functions on two levels—that of its content (the work described), and that of its style (the mode of description).

Still and Moving Lines . . . is a *geography,* to use Lucier's term: "Well . . . spa- . . . if not visual, sp-, see . . . I was concerned with space, you know spatial, that is, the piece exists almost completely on a spatial plane . . . because what's important is that I make geographies, sound geographies, by using sine waves from oscillators through speakers—amplifiers and speakers—to make from simple to very complex and from still to moving geographies . . ."

What about geographies.

Well, say we're given a map, you know, a map of a city or town or something. Each of the symbols on the map refers to something you can find, something that really exists outside the piece of paper. The only thing that presents a problem, and it's a big problem, is the boundary—political, military, whatever. Chances are that nothing's there except for a few markers. Of course the letters aren't there, either, in the landscape. Anyway, consider a map, now, of an inhabited space. A map of a dwelling. Or even a map of a piece of paper. Certain areas within that space are going to arouse certain fears, going to bring up certain kinds of memories . . . Here's where the water spilled, here's where I lay with you. Now this is like those boundaries on the city map. There are all sorts of things that extend back in consciousness, not "things" really, but extended situations. Most personal space is like that. And even public space . . . there are two ways to deal with public space . . . First, there's familiar public space, where, again, memories play a role. The meaning of the space (like the meaning of all spaces) is a mixture of public/private function and what's happened to one within it. Second, there is the unfamiliar public space—here one tends to fall back on rules of behavior, traditional procedure, and so forth. There is also a kind of induction here—the application of familiar public spaces to unfamiliar public spaces.

What about geographies.
See, my public space may be your private space; it depends what we have in common. In any case, we've got to agree that, to get formal for a moment, space is *intentional.*

"There are several . . ."
There are several artists in the book who are dealing directly with the personalization of space. Some of them, such as Aycock or Simonds, create their own spaces (although, with both, there is a definite dialogue with the environment). Some of them, such as Lucier or Acconci, occupy and subvert existing spaces. And some of them, such as Horvitz and Morton, utilize given spaces for the presentation of personal mappings that demand *reading.*

x

Reading.

Ree Morton's environmental works are cross-referenced systems using elements that seem to relate to folk tradition. To understand her use of space, the spectator must consciously decipher the elements and comprehend their interconnections. What emerges is a fantasy map of the space, the appearance of a legend without narrative structure. The progression that occurs, then, is from real space to map of real space to real legendary space. There seems to be a connection here with the work of Washington Irving who, it turns out, is from the same part of the States as Morton . . .

Horizontal and vertical.

Morton's work can be seen as a horizontal network of images. This is comparable to the vertical approach of Acconci. (In fact, one could, perhaps, make the following lists: Vertical: Acconci, Aycock, Horvitz, Kitchel, Lucier, Bernadette Mayer, Rosemary Mayer, Metz, Piper. Horizontal: Abish, Anderson, Askevold, Morton, Oppenheim, Simonds.) Acconci's work is monolithic, investigatory; it has the "feeling" of sound, instead of sight.

Audible space and visible space.

Visible space contains objects that are differentiated, one from another. These objects need not overlap; in fact, they may exist independently (in relationship to each other). Audible space does not "contain"; instead, it is defined by the sound that fills it. Any sound dominates the entire space; two sounds (if near the same intensity, etc.) are transparent to each other. Any sound suggests the presence of the entire space, and the content of that sound is the quality of that presence. Acconci's work is, for the most part, concerned with presence, with the residue of the self in a previously neutral space. The human being Acconci dominates the space in which he places emblems of himself. The space has the appearance of darkness.

Light and dark.
(In fact, one could, perhaps, make the following lists: Light: Abish, Anderson, Askevold, Horvitz, Lucier, Metz, Morton, Oppenheim, Simonds. Dark: Abish, Acconci, Askevold, Aycock, Kitchel, Bernadette Mayer, Rosemary Mayer, Metz, Morton, Oppenheim, Piper.)

External and internal.
(In fact, the listing could be continued indefinitely. This doesn't help, it doesn't matter, just like the defining of a style, the critical formulation of a movement, doesn't matter. It is enough that the artists here share common concerns, motifs.)

Bernadette Mayer.
I first heard of her through Clark Coolidge, a poet now living near Pittsfield, Massachusetts. She, with Acconci, edited 0 to 9 magazine, which may have been the best "little" magazine of its time. She did an incredibly good and tough reading at the Rhode Island School of Design while I taught there. Her voice was tense, intense, and level. It was the opposite of the declamatory or singing style of reading I had been used to. Later, she took over one or two writing classes.

What amazes me about her is her intensity and her refusal to compromise. Her writing is extremely direct; if something is repeated, it's so you get the point. For a long period, her work came out of her personal experience, background. Like Dostoevsky, there was the presence of a continual pushing, a constant clearing away of trivia, allowing an independent selfhood to emerge. Now, it seems to me, the work has gotten deeper; the content itself is heavily modified, altered, created, by the free use of psychoanalytical technique, and investigations into the subconscious. The insistence upon the self, here as elsewhere, can be political.

Politics.
All of the artists included here are from the United States. Together, their sensibilities construct a mesh describing the conditions of contemporary American life.
1 No; it is better to say that they contribute in part to a mesh.
2 However, none of them appears to be politically *engaged;* at least, such engagement is not an intrinsic part of their work.
3 Their anti-formalism might be read . . .

Dennis Oppenheim.
He spells out RADICALITY with fireworks on a hillside. His toy trains narrowly miss each other. The dead dog howls. A cast-metal puppet head periodically smashes into a bell; the puppet is in a meditative attitude. His pieces are often simple to describe; their effect—an explosive theatricality—is not. Like Ree Morton's, their connotation of danger is almost subliminal. Morton's danger, however, is literary; Oppenheim's is directly connected to the presence of his pieces. ("Almost": His works branch in a number of directions, partly because they provide so little information. They are almost violent, almost failing, almost private . . . In one sense, they are metaphor without specific reference—they "point-to" psychological strata existing outside of ordinary language. They betray their own descriptions.)

On Introductions.
An introduction may serve as the defense for a book; as a means of clarifying the reason for its existence; as the background information necessary for an understanding of the main text; as an apology; as an acknowledgment; as an outline of the entire work; as groundwork.

An introduction to an anthology may explain the choices made; the general orientation of the anthology; the personal life of the editor or contributors; the relationships between the editor and contributors.

Defense.

The editor may be called upon to defend his or her choices. This is especially true if the anthology attempts to define a movement, style, or coherent grouping. In this instance, choices have been made on the basis of "a family of usages," "a constellation." In other words, a kind of landscape, but not a well-defined community within it.

Mike Metz.

An example of conceivable relations. In general:

M. M. shares with				Aycock, Simonds	use of models.
"	"	"	"	Acconci, Kitchel, Piper	use of writing on photographs.
"	"	"	"	Oppenheim	possibilities of movement.
"	"	"	"	Acconci, Anderson, Piper (?)	use of performance.

And so forth.

From the Adjectives category of the first page of the Introduction, the following apply: personal, eclectic, intellectual, antireductive.

Anecdote.

I once helped Metz with one of his pieces. This was a few years ago, in Providence, Rhode Island. He was attempting to suspend himself between two ropes, outdoors. The ropes had to be thrown over two trees, about twenty feet apart. The first time we tried this, one of the ropes hit a wasp's nest; Metz was stung about twenty times. We went out again, about an hour later. This time we got the ropes up, but when he tried to suspend himself, one of the trees came down. There was a dazed and solitary digger wasp sitting in the middle of the stump.

Models (from an article).

Metz has been working with models since 1969. His early pieces were concerned with light as a formal element; the physical arrangement of wood, glass, tape, and metal created a potential situation that might be "activated" by sunlight or incandescent lamp. In 1971 his interest shifted to a concern for the physical arrangements themselves; they no longer required a particular space, but could be set up anywhere . . . Recently, Metz has been working on an important series of small, movable models. Most of them are constructed out of pliable materials —substances such as balsa wood, canvas, lacquered paper, and raw-hide. The models are destructible . . . Each of them proclaims a type of psychophysical space, a mediation between the self and a hostile external world. Their titles indicate this: "Hideout/Get Away," "Hide-out/Notes on how I pass my days," and "Intention: Out of fear, I want to write what I mean."

Adopted from the proposal for the book:
The following characteristics may be applied to the work of the artists included:
a. Historical spread (temporal eclecticism): Most of the work does not occupy well-defined positions within the history of recent art; it often includes a use and acceptance of historical precedents. (I.e. It is not the "he or she was the first to . . ." variety of art.)
b. Most of the work is amenable to analysis using procedures from the fields of phenomenology, phenomenological sociology, third-stream psychology, and structuralist criticism. Here, I am thinking of European (as opposed to Anglo-American) modes of thought.
c. Most of the artists work from a position of "externalized selfhood"— their work not only proceeds from the self, but is also an amplification of the artist's psychological landscape.
d. Many of the artists have written about their own work; many are part-time critics. All are highly articulate.
e. Most of the work is cross-disciplinary (in terms of traditional categories).
f. An emphasis on procedure, on "going through the work," as opposed to a perfected final product, or the revelation of process for its own sake.

Story full of emblems.
They rode (1) on a white bicycle (2) for seven miles (3), until they reached the crossroads (4). There, they saw an altar (5), covered with a white cloth (6) held in position by four (7) red (8) doves (9). They bowed down immediately, and found themselves transported to that island in the ocean "yclept Avara" which revolves (10). An old woman (11) explained, by means of symbols tied to sticks of birch (12), that they would die (13).

The emblems themselves.
Riding, white bicycle, seven, crossroads, altar, white cloth, four, red, doves, Avara, old woman (Elder), birch, death. The last is equivalent to the rest; using initials:

$$r + wb + s + c + a + wc + f + r + d + A + ow(E) + b = d.$$

If this formula (or similar formulas) is used in the construction of an internalized description of the world, the world appears, in a sense, through these emblems, through their historical significance, their proliferation. They cancel each other, somewhat; the meaning, for example, of "Avara" is altered by the immediately subsequent appearance of the old woman. The symbols, instead of being archetypes, are the signifiers for a language with an inexact reference, or, better, as the formula reveals, are the individuated letters in a language, whose concatenation spells "death."

Triad.
Walter Abish, Laurie Anderson, and Ree Morton. The *emblematic*. In the late spring of 1974 I saw one of Anderson's performances at the Clocktower (New York City). She sat (stood, lay) in the center of what emerged as a sphere of projected images, sounds, and props. The "content" of the performance was based on her memories of her childhood—both as she actually was and as she was supposed to be. The technological ingenuity Anderson displayed was incredible. At one point, for example, she reached into her purse and pulled out a sand-

wich, which she proceeded to "read," as if it were a Bible. Later, she again reached into what appeared to be the same purse. Three things happened: the lights went out; a movie suddenly appeared on the ceiling (projected from the purse!); and a record began to play. She had been talking about being a dream girl—the film image was herself, swaying back and forth, dressed in a prom gown, and the record was a popular high school graduation song . . . This cross-referencing, from one material or medium to another, results in a kind of audio-visual punning that is highly characteristic of her work. The fifteen "vignettes" included in her section carry this into a more literary mode.

Her honesty is disarming.

Her honesty is disarming.
Authenticity is an extremely important concern in terms of the sensibility conveyed in this book. In work such as Anderson's or Kitchel's, sectors of private histories are made public and generalized in such a way as to prove useful and moving to the spectator. The result, however, is not autobiography, since the emphasis is not on a factual account of things, but on the use of events, situations, emblems, etc., to present successions of mental states. In some cases, these states can be described in terms of specific imagery . . .

Nancy Kitchel.
"I operate somewhere between the first black and the last white but closer to the last white and sometimes beyond." (N. K.) "The world of her work may be expressed by means of the following imaginary scheme. Begin with a flat, Midwestern landscape, in winter. Powder snow on the ground, a sense of disarray. There are stories in the air, almost literal floating groups of words: 'How a particular Midwestern storytelling tradition resembles (is integral to) the landscape. How my aunt or my mother can tell a story in such a way that the peaks (of

violence) are cut off and the low points are filled up (with details, with emphasis) until the whole is perfectly flat and contains the violence. Or perhaps by shaving the peaks and toppling them into the valleys— leveling.' (N. K.) The violence is everywhere, just beneath the surface of the frozen earth . . . In the center of the landscape, there is a symbol for the self, which may be indicated by the physical presence of the artist. Surrounding this are others, intruders, anonymous figures intent on violating her personal space. Now, imagine the past of this situation, a past that extends back for several generations. Finally, consider the uprooting of the entire scene, and its transplantation to the Lower East Side of New York. The result is often the emergence of a pure form of terror, what passes for terror."

The Elliptical Presence of Mind.
Which appears as the title for something that begins and fades out in the Introduction. Authenticity, as concept or concern, appears, leading into a state-description of Kitchel's work. Thus it is implied that her work is *particularly* authentic, that it, in fact, places authenticity *on the line,* that even her fictionalizing (as in a piece entitled *The Demon Lover*) is real, in some land inhabited by *attitudes.*

The Elliptical Presence of Mind.
Read *habitation.* Read *dwelling.* The pressure of an imaginary wind without air currents. Now where are you. Now the presence of the mind, that is, perhaps, the presence of Mind, the capital indicative of a kind of transcendence. Now that exists alone, like mind in any object, like Mind. As if the extension of the self in landscape were the Being of the land, the land as focal point of earth.

Triad.
Triad of the primarily visual object: Horvitz, Rosemary Mayer, Morton. Elsewhere, I have described Mayer's work as "visible emblem of in-

visible presence." The personal is used as the mode of a kind of eternality. The presence of Mind, the presence, in a sense, of non-presence, is expressed by the use of the sculptural object as a means of revelation: "The work visually leads forth into an 'openness,' the realization of a presence conveyed by the nondenotative language of the piece. The world that is expressed is not *characterized* by the work; instead, the work *lends itself* to that world . . ." The work, however, is not only concerned with a "beyond"; it also is grounded in the human, both through an exemplary sense of history and a careful presentation of color: "This work provides an evocation of an abstracted essence . . . The possibility of sculpture is (here) the possibility of the gathering of the socially separated worlds (of the spiritual, the material, the abstract) into a unified whole." Color has rarely been used with such psychological force . . .

Color.
The absence of color in the work of the majority of artists included in this book is one indication of the poverty of contemporary color theory. Color is apparently used today in the following ways: A. As local color, useful for differentiating one area of sculpture or pictorial plane from another. B. As conveying basic connotations—red for "danger," and so forth. C. The easy colors of contemporary painting. D. The harsh or muted colors of magazine and television advertising.

Colored Blindness.
One result of this has been the dying out of color names for the general public—mauve, fuchsia, viridian, cyan, magenta, and ocher on the border line. This may (or may not) accompany a real inability to discriminate.

"In an early work of Kitchel's, all of her art-school color supplies were painted white."

Walter Abish, Robert Horvitz, and the Use of the Modular Approach.

Internal Content and External Constraints.

The Role of Choice in the Structured Field.

Robert Horvitz's program for drawing seems to be an ideal method for studying the interaction of mind and body, psychology and kinesics. Each drawing is composed of the same "quantum" stroke, made by a flick of the pen across the paper. The differences in the drawings are a result of different organizations of the strokes. None of the drawings is totally free form; instead, there are "upper bounds" governing the overall organizations. (For example, a drawing may be "governed" by the notion of close packing, or specific angles may be required between the strokes, or the overall density may be a constant, etc.) Thus the play of free choice *within* the drawing is bounded, on one hand, by the specific shape of the individual stroke and, on the other, by the large-scale "societal" ordering of the whole. The result is a literal illustration of the dialectic established between choice and structure, content and form, subjective and objective . . .

The literal appearance of the self.

Personal performance and/or personal presence has occurred in the works of Acconci, Anderson, Lucier, Metz, and Piper. Acconci has for the most part abandoned performance, whereas Lucier's presence is governed by his role as composer-performer within a musical tradition. Adrian Piper's performances are solitary; her last public works occurred perhaps two years ago. Piper's work investigates the relationships between artist and audience, and, more generally, between "I" and "you."

The photographic appearance of the self.

Use of the self in photography has occurred in the works of Acconci, Anderson, Askevold, Kitchel, Oppenheim, Piper, and Simonds. Charles Simonds has constructed miniature buildings upon his body, which thereby functions as landscape; Piper has used her own image as genesis for the transformation of the self into the other (in her case, the Mythic Being); David Askevold's *Muse Extracts* reveal his self as shaman through the use of anamorphic distortion.

The written appearance of the self.
Use of the written appearance of the self has occurred in the works of Abish, Acconci, Anderson, Kitchel, Bernadette Mayer, Metz, and Piper. Piper's writing, on the surface, appears cool and analytical. There is always an underlying current of obsessiveness, however, that is placed within the trappings of an academic criticism. Walter Abish's "Self-Portrait" proliferates self into selves that are "possessed" by the same individual. These selves never get the autonomy, however, which would lead to schizophrenia; they are literary, living in the writing. Abish's recent novel, *Alphabetical Africa* (New York: New Directions, 1974), is a third-person narrative which can be considered a sphere of discourse around a first-person author who is obsessed with letters and strangulating organizations. The presence of the writer is always felt in Abish's work, which takes on the qualities of an autobiography of states of mind through the use of emblematic structures.

The mediated appearance of the self.
Use of the mediated (through materials or concepts) appearance of the self has occurred in the works of Abish, Acconci, Anderson, Askevold, Horvitz, and Metz. The following have been employed: personae, masks, doll's clothes, food, arrangements of people, bunkers, branch structures. A great deal of Acconci's recent work has been concerned in part with the "presence of presence"—various modes of charging a space *as if* the artist were present and undergoing an emotional crisis.

Lists.
It is obvious by now that a dialogue is emerging, between the subject matter of a list, and the names included within it. The names become

"tokens," in a sense, and this is dangerous, as though drawing away from the works themselves. My justification is that a list, or series of lists, can serve as a mode of discourse itself. It operates as a compacted statement, a kind of density within a text that provides an adjective (or adjectives) within the language of the sensibility I am describing. There is a second danger, of course, which is that the sensibility does not "exist" at all, that it is just a critical fabrication, that my use of the works in the book is, in fact, reprehensible, since it bends them, functionally, to my own ends.

Reply.
Of course, I must state that there is just such a stance, ambience, or sensibility, and I see the work included here as revolutionary in the development of this stance—that, in fact, I am not developing anything (certainly not an argument), but simply depicting and presenting what has been accomplished by others. My job, then, is the presentation of work that has reached one audience, to another. And, in the process, providing a kind of contextualization for those not familiar with it.

Contexts.
Many of the people included in the book are not affiliated with galleries; many of them have not shown in commercial situations. Many of them have shown more in Europe than in America. A large part of their work has been oriented toward magazine or book format. Some of them, like Charles Simonds, have worked almost totally outside formal cultural structures.

Charles Simonds.
A great deal of his work has been created somewhat anonymously on anonymous sites in New York City—outdoors, around the ruins of buildings, walls, and so forth. There is an interesting split between his postulation of the existence of "little people," and *his* arrangement and

building of their dwellings. The result is a kind of "forced mythology," an attempt to create a heightened meaning in a desolate urban landscape. Simonds's recent models for dwellings of people from different fantasy civilizations remind one of oblique Borges. These models invite vicarious participation by the spectator, while the on-site "little people" dwellings do not. The latter appear to be already occupied, and must be studied externally. The former, because of their clear existence as models, permit a more subjective approach.

Simonds himself forms a peculiar sort of model. I have seen films of him in the act of constructing the "little people" dwellings, surrounded by a number of onlookers, mostly children. One of the topics of conversation appears to be that "he's doing this for nothing," something extremely unusual in New York . . . Thus the work and its creation not only relate to the concerns of contemporary art, but also to the very real idea of neighborhood, and the possibility of neighborhood projects.

Self/Identity.
Pieces dealing with the identity or transformation of the self have been created by Acconci, Kitchel, Bernadette Mayer, and Adrian Piper. Mayer's writing often centers around the notion of the self. Piper's "Mythic Being" work, included in this book, explores (among other things) the relationship between self and image, and self and other. It is of course impossible to experience directly the consciousness of the other. My interpretation of you is based on two broad categories: my knowledge of myself and my patterns of behavior, and my recognition of you as an object in the world, an object independent of myself. Depending on your relationship to me, you can be experienced more or less as "thinglike," more or less as a fully conscious person. Most of the people one meets are "thinglike," since the relationship between them and the self is largely role-governed. If I go into a market to buy food, and you weigh the vegetables for me, your identity for me is as "weigher." Part of the difficulty anyone has in contemporary society is, in fact, the recognition of the other *as human* . . .

Piper takes the entire philosophical problem of the other and internalizes it. Interestingly enough, the "success" of her inquiry depends partly on you, the reader, and your relation to the experiences and states of mind she describes.

Differences and Repetition.

My self is different from your self. This section of the world, this table, is different from your section, your chair, your stance. The world is given to us as difference. The opposite pole is that of repetition—that which is, although different, a duplicate. The formula $a = a$ is not really an identity, but a statement of repetition, since the a is divided from itself in order to make the statement. One way of looking at art, or at least the art in this book, is as the cleaving or carving of the fabric of the world, the making of distinctions, differences, solely for the purpose of examining the gaps and interstices that are created. If Piper's self, and self's other, are separated from the social fabric of the everyday world (which they are, at least for me), there is a gap between myself and both of them, a gap that allows her use of the self's other to function as a model for my own understanding of reality. This approach, I believe, can be successfully applied to most of the artists in this book. The result turns out to be a series of deep investigations into the texture of contemporary life, or (see above), the position of the individual in relation to society, and the "universe" at large.

From Laurie Anderson:

"*For Instants* is an attempt to get back into the present. Much of it involves pine trees and horses, nature and sex. What sums them up for me is the violin bow. The tension between wood and horsehair. I want the music that is produced to be simple—but also in two parts . . ."
". . . I realized a few things about my work. One is that I do iconography. I try to let a single dense object stand for an experience . . . I want to be a sit-down comic. I try not to predict. I want to be in a power series where the general term is an almost insignificant detail—a slight twitch, a repeated phrase. I want my work to be as close to my life as possible . . ."

No Repetition!
Keep it moving! Don't stop! They understand, you can go on now! They've got it all, you can just keep moving! It's not like the others, there's something new to discover all the time! Try for impossibility! There's too little time, too much is happening!

"His classes." David Askevold.
His classes at the Nova Scotia College of Art and Design were impressive and extremely influential. His manner was "like being" deliberately quiet, but one was sure that there was something else occurring "next to him," or just beyond the reach of the class. His movements were always even, as if he had performed "that balancing act for so long that it was second nature," was no longer difficult, but resulted in a calculated solidity. The earlier work of his that I experienced was *concerned* with games, rules, organizing. His recent work seems non-*concerned*, as if its subject matter occurs elsewhere. "As if" follows him, as if he employed the phrase as a representation of his work. He is a master of the oblique.

The Oblique.
Yes, the state you might find yourself in when you wander into a room and there are people present whom you don't know, and you continue to trust your own reactions and sensations, your own experience for a while, and then you begin to realize, slowly, that these things are failing you, that your perceptions are . . . distorted . . . somehow . . . and, in fact, you have no idea who these people are, they are somewhat threatening, their means of communication even are obscure, since more seems to be going on than the idle talk they are apparently engaged in . . .

From Nancy Kitchel:
"*Variety in repetition:* It is in the way that each is different that the

whole is formed. How variants can survive in a forced structural unity. How they are absorbed into the structure. (Visual, sociological, psychological implications.)

"The whole is different from the sum of its parts. The body of work projects concerns larger than, different from, and yet composed of, individual pieces. It is not a linear progression. The whole is in a state of flux, cannot be accurately defined, and therefore remains relatively unknown, except that which can be inferred at any given moment from its parts. The invisible is composed of the visible. This is implicit in my method of working."

Or from Rosemary Mayer:
"disconnected elements working together because of the artist's intention,
not because of accord with an accepted mean
no balance without contrivance
no certainty . . ."

Or from Mike Metz:
"The attempted completion of any event suspends it."

The Authentic.
Which is usually established in opposition to "the fictional," or "the fake." "It's a fiction" has implications of a difference which cannot be surmounted, a decay of reality. Fiction, however, has the advantage of total construction, of beginning completely with the whiteness of the paper. Abish's "Self-Portrait" is not fiction, yet it begins "where it chooses to begin," in a sense, instead of an acceptance of convention.

Acceptance, Ignorance, and Objectification.
There's this man, and he's about painting and being a painter, he's worked on canvas for years, using oils, acrylics, whatever. Then someone comes along and tells him there's a certain lack of modernity to the work, nothing's happened to the canvas. The man says, "to the canvas? But there's paint all over it." The other person, call him the modernist, says, "yes, but you've never questioned that, questioned the canvas I mean. You've never really *seen* the canvas." The painter could point to a corner of the studio where the rest of the cloth is rolled. "What do you think that is?"

Now.
Now the point of all of this, of course, is that the modernist is right in a sense, and he's certainly right if the formal history of art is accepted. The painter hasn't *seen* the canvas, other than as a function of the painting, something that exists as a tool really, but without independent existence. The modernist, on the other hand, sees everything—canvas, paint, model, painter, whatever—as independent and to be questioned.

Now.
Now consider a third person, perhaps someone from this book, or a fiction of this Introduction, or someone outside the situation altogether. She (and these changes in gender are hopefully meaningless, by the way) might find the reductivist attitude of the modernist an absurdity, while at the same time she might question the *content* of the painter's work—"Why are you doing such and such?" The issue could be changed, then, from one about the tacit acceptance of objects, to one about the social and spiritual contextualization of the work as a whole. The reductivist attitude then becomes something that is meaningful only to a local segment of the cultured public, while the painter might emerge (even yet) to confront the problems of contemporary society.

From *Ch'ing-lien-fang-ch'in-ya* or *T'ien-wên-ko-ch'in-pu-chi-ch'êng* (trans. R. H. van Gulik in *The Lore of the Chinese Lute*, Tokyo, 1940):

5. Silk worms are very clever; when they spin themselves into cocoons, they often take the shape of the things they come in contact with.

Once there was a young widow. Spending the night alone, resting on her pillow, she could not sleep. In the wall near her there was a hole, and through this she looked at the silkworms of her neighbour, who were just leaving their frames. Next day the cocoons all showed a resemblance with her face. Although one could not clearly distinguish eyebrows and eyes, still when seen from some distance they closely resembled the face of a sad girl. Ts'ai Yung, the famous scholar, saw these cocoons, and bought them for a high price. He reeled off the silk threads, and from it made strings for his Lute. When he played, however, their sound appeared to be sad and melancholy. When he asked his daughter Yen about it, she said: "This is widow's silk. When listening to its sounds one cannot but weep."

The idea of the charged object is extremely ancient. The cocoons are sculpture created simply by the presence of the sculptor. The sadness of the music is the signature and transformation of this presence, a reification of the ambience of the widow herself. The strings are not simply passive objects sounded to create music; instead, they are "objectified," they possess certain characteristics which somewhat determine the quality of the compositions. And they bring the widow to Ts'ai Yung.

Transmission.
In the work of Alice Aycock, for example, a signature is present. The buildings appear formal; most of them possess rectangular or circular foundations. But that unnecessary weight, that lowering. "It has to do with function. OK, she constructs a building somewhere. Even though this occurs (in a sense) within the confines of art, one still hopes that the structure has some use. But when you enter, it becomes like those caves Clark Coolidge was talking about, where you might crawl for a while, and panic, thinking about all that weight. And here, the thing is even more complicated, since you realize 'someone is doing this to me.' "

Signature.

All work is signed; even "anonymous" work is given specific contexts. But "signature" here means something different. I am referring to the very real attempt to imbue the work with the personal, to have it stand against what could be called the "automated mathematization" of the environment that is occurring in society at large.

Two More Lists Perhaps.

The signature related to the specific individual: Abish, Acconci, Anderson, Askevold, Kitchel. Already, there is difficulty. Does the sculpture of Rosemary Mayer, for example, reflect a "specific individual," or is it based on personal and historical generalization? The question is somewhat meaningless; the list should be abandoned. The second list is that associating the artists in the book with related social issues:

Abish:	The structured ceremony of the real.
Acconci:	The political; phenomenology of the self in relation to others.
Anderson:	The position of the self in terms of an emblematic personal history.
Askevold:	The turning inward of the individual as defense; the elliptical.
Aycock:	Phenomenological approach to architecture.
Horvitz:	Mapping of the self within external constraints.
Kitchel:	The landscaping of the self; the countryside.
Lucier:	Psychology and phenomenology of internal spaces.
Mayer, B.:	The political; phenomenology of the self.
Mayer, R.:	The contemplative; the self in relation to history.
Metz:	The miniaturization of psychophysical space.
Morton:	Contemporary possibilities of the legendary, studies of clichés and meaning.
Oppenheim:	Phenomenology of the theatrical, transformations of the self.
Piper:	Phenomenology and transformations of the self in relation to the other.
Simonds:	Social analysis through architecture.

(Does this help, me or you? All labels are restrictive; in this instance, they probably relate as much to my personal "take" as to any really useful categorization. I have always had a certain fear of classification, for each classifying statement can raise more questions than it answers. Further, these listings have a reverse function—they are considerably more relevant after the book has been read. Like those introductions to Victorian novels that give synopses of the plots with critical seasonings.)

City.
This is slow now, slower. Each sentence moves at its own pace, each occupies a section of the world, leaving a trail that fades slowly in the process of reading. You, you live in the city, you live in the country. Like language, you cover the world for me, slim threads, fibers, in sheaves, cloaked incidents, situations of cloth. No, that was another story, that was you in seventy-two. You came to visit me, you came visiting, driving up in the pickup truck, newly painted green. You could find your way, you could find your way anywhere. Sun. Nothing moved on that heated morning, your feet soundlessly crossing the sidewalk, crossing the thin sliver of browned lawn. No, there were no birds flying, no songs, the black-and-white cat lay sleeping on the porch. The mail had arrived much earlier, there was a letter from you, posted the day before. It was Providence, Rhode Island. You wore a blue skirt, with brown blouse and thin silk scarf, of a color I couldn't name. It was 1964, you crossed the porch, quietly, and opened the door. Then the story began.

INDIVIDUALS

SELF-PORTRAIT

Walter Abish

Each day, each hour, passports, marriage licenses, driving licenses, bankbooks, credit cards authenticate the existence of another *I*, although with what amounts to great circumspection the *I* is never referred to in any of these documents that function as signifiers, attributing to each individual a gender, a first and a last name, occasionally an initial for a middle name, as well as a name for each parent, a place of residence, an occupation, also political affiliation, credit rating, criminal convictions, if any, race, religion, education and age. Frequently the *I* scrutinizes these joyless documents for hours, boxed in and burdened by a proof that is at one and the same time remote and intolerably near.

An individual will use language to give shape to his *I*. Language unlike a document permits the *I* to unfold, it gives it a freedom to seek out the words that will define its intention and its direction. It does not take long for an individual to discover that there is no need to stress the *I* when saying: I choose not to, or, I couldn't care less, or, I intend to take a walk around the park without you. The recipient of the remark is able to place the *I* addressing him in a proper perspective. Not to be overlooked in some tortured statement is an *I* that stands in a state of solitary and nervous uncertainty in regard to the words that have preceded it and to the words that are to follow. This precarious state of uncertainty is sufficient to crush the *I*, and obliterate it temporarily. Of course the *I* can always mobilize words to its defense, but they may not be the right words, the correct words for that occasion. Michel Leiris in *L'Age d'Homme*[1] chose his words carefully as he with meticulous care magnifies the worries of the *I*: the hands thin and rather hairy, the veins distinct, the two middle fingers curving inward toward the tip. He seems to believe that the curve of his middle fingers denotes something weak or rather evasive in his character. He may even be correct. He is simply describing his *I*. Apparently the head is a bit too large for the body, the legs too short, shoulders too narrow, etc. . . . As a reader one is overwhelmed by the seeming preciseness of his dispassionate self-appraisal. The reader is not only overwhelmed, he is also, I venture to think, won over to the degree that he himself lacks Leiris's ability to articulate the flaws that so profoundly cripple his *I*. I am not suggesting that this is Leiris's objective. All the same, the reader is won over by the disarming candor that the *I* of Leiris exudes. Possibly if the reader were to see the rather impressive long list of Leiris's achievements he or she might be less likely to accept the merciless self-scrutiny of Leiris's *I* and say: Well, I don't know . . . where is he leading me? And it is true, the moment the *I* is inserted in a sentence, the recipient of the statement or remark is being led somewhere . . .

Advancing or retreating the *I* camouflages itself behind circumlocutionary statements, endowing its small lies, its puny lies, its irrelevant lies with a shine, a polish, a misleading brilliance . . . The *I* lies at the least provocation, unnecessarily, for no other reason than to state: *I am not really what I seem to you,* or the opposite, *I am the way you see me now, in absolute control, and although I lead a life not too dissimilar from yours, I am far more intelligent and far more successful than you. I have only to press this button and a private elevator will*

[1] *Manhood: A Journey from Childhood into the Fierce Order of Virility,* trans. Richard Howard (New York: Grossman Publishers, 1963).

shoot up to this floor . . . Without a first person what need would there be for language? The *I* anchors the words firmly to the ground. Lacking the *I*, speech would lose its plausibility and its intent. From the moment a child begins to speak, its *I*, once it arrives at the *I*, faces nameless hurdles and barricades that are invisible to others. It is as if these obstacles exist for one purpose only, to impede the *I*. It is hardly surprising that the *I*, under the circumstances, keeps a sharp lookout for what lies ahead . . . how it is being received by others . . . its memory retaining for far too long each gaffe, each hideous irrevocable error, each momentous blunder.

Every time a person opens his mouth to speak his *I* is standing on the precipice of a bottomless abyss. One single wrong note and the *I* will take a desperate plunge . . . yet, for hours at a time, the *I* is also capable of obliterating the excruciating memory of past incidents, as it cheerfully babbles away, completely oblivious of itself, feeling only a delightful sense of harmony, a sense of being in tune with everything that surrounds it. I think the evening went rather well, the *I* says a bit smugly to whoever happens to be in its vicinity. So much depends on the answer, on the appropriate facial gesture. The slightest miscalculation might cause the *I* to withdraw into itself, manifesting on the exterior surface a patient resignation until its rage tears that surface apart. There are fortunately ways the *I* can alleviate its torments. For instance: five hours of TV or any randomly chosen double feature at the local movie house, or even a book might do the trick, allowing the *I* to resuscitate itself by immersing its *I* in the attractive flatness of a story line on the screen or page . . . there is also always sex. As it fucks the *I* is temporarily expunged, only to reassert itself afterwards, a bit feebly, it is true, as it addresses the other, saying: I love you. Yet in surfacing the *I* can only extend as far as the fingertips. One might reason from this that in order to love the *I* has to be dropped.

The mirror in the bathroom and in the bedroom burden the *I* with additional information. Being familiar, the information is in certain respects utterly redundant. The *I* has already seen what it now sees for the thousandth time. Still the *I* dissects itself with a compulsive passion. It is a bit disheveled in appearance . . . a bit worn . . . fatigued bags under the eyes . . . unattractive skin . . . Only with the greatest courage will the *I* use a second mirror to examine itself from the side.

3

The profile lacks the symmetry of the front, a balance that to some extent minimizes the flaws or defects. Perhaps a brighter shirt, or a beard will improve matters.

The I has no name for itself. It does not require a name. Yet it responds instantly whenever it hears its name being mentioned or called. Frequently there is a slight mixup. The I can be amazingly hostile to people who respond to the same name. A conflict between two Is who share the name Zachary is almost predictable. Dubiously at first, one Zachary stares at the other. One of them will have to give way. One of them will have to stop his I from invading the other's body. Ultimately both will realize that the name they are responding to is merely a cipher. Once they acknowledge this fact, every I they encounter is a potential Zachary.

I may this once use the first person, says a writer contemplating a new novel. It is entirely instinctual. He doesn't know why he picks the first person. He may not find out until he is halfway through the novel that his I really yearns for another writer.

Self-portraits, a game played by the I with great zeal, allow it to divulge bit by bit sensations, emotions, incidents from the past, recollections, all linked to the I by an elaborate framework, a fabrication that creates the impression that despite evidence to the contrary the richness, the questionable richness, of the past actually permeates the present. When Arrabal in an interview is asked if he likes to be rejected, he replies that it gives him an impression of living. I can only assume that he is referring to the unequivocal needs of his I.

Kafka avoided the perils of the I. He took refuge behind one of the letters of our alphabet. It so happened that the letter he picked was the initial of his family name, thereby allowing him to retain in his work—a work so removed from the understanding of the family—a formal link to the exteriority of his self. His I was reserved for his intimate letters to Milena, his long letter to his father that his father never received, his entries in his diaries, and the people with whom he was in daily contact. From what is known about Kafka, one can only deduce that his I was a bit too frail to endure the prolonged icy contemptuous tyranny of *The Castle* or *The Trial*. So we are left with the letters, the diaries, Janouch's conversations, and Max Brod's frequently exuberant and optimistic version of Kafka's I. Brod refers to Kafka's humor. It is an all too familiar humor.

4

I am not free tonight, I said to H when she invited me to her place for the first time. How about Saturday? We agreed on Saturday. She found it difficult to pronounce my name in Hebrew. This was years ago in Tel Aviv. By now the Hebrew word for *I* is completely foreign to me. I no longer have any use for it, having left H, having left the country.

A friend recently told me that he has been working on a story titled: "Why I do not write like Franz Kafka."

Will it be in the first person?

OR

The word *or* frequently precedes an alternate proposal. *It's sink or swim.* The imperative to stay above water to a nonswimmer like myself is as unpleasant as the alternative that precedes it. It's only a metaphor, I tell myself. In the English language *or* is frequently coupled with *either.* Kierkegaard wrote a book, fittingly in two volumes, entitled *Either/Or.* Certain details of Kierkegaard's life continue to fascinate me. As a young man he paid excessive attention to his appearance. Wearing his best suit, he would regularly parade up and down the theater district of Copenhagen, for some reason deriving a certain satisfaction whenever people said: There goes Kierkegaard that good for nothing. I imagine that in his mind his love for Regina collided with the words *Either/Or.* On the pretext that he was no longer in love with her he broke off their engagement. In this manner he managed to cling forever to his love, and selfishly devote himself to his writing. I expect that something can be said in favor of inflicting pain upon oneself. It seems by far preferable than to have someone else do it who might be less experienced and less skilled at this demanding task. As for Regina. She married, had children, and read all of Kierkegaard's books as soon as they appeared at the local bookstore. Somewhere in each of his books there is contained a message that only she could understand. I have read a few of Kierkegaard's books looking for his message to Regina, but it is well hidden . . .

Sink or swim. Having once almost drowned in a Shanghai swimming pool I cannot hear the word *or* mentioned without feeling a vague trepidation that is only somewhat assuaged when the speaker in question, out of compassion, says: Or else you can leave it the way

5

it is. How reassuring the final *or*. Or you can spend the weekend with us. Or finally you can read *The Sacred Fount*. Or you can fix yourself a light lunch. Or you can take a trip to Central Asia.

Just before she entered a hotel on Montague Street in Brooklyn Heights I overheard a fairly attractive woman tell the man accompanying her: Or you can fuck us both. What, I often wondered, preceded the *or*.

NO

I have a tendency to admire people who can easily decline an invitation by simply saying *no*. How easy it seems. No. Not even sorry. Just, No. In a café on Rehov Ben Yehuda the man at the next table said *no* to a couple who had invited him to join them at a party. I overheard him say, *no*. I don't really know why I should remember this particular incident. At that time he and I had not met although we both frequented the same café, and often sat at adjacent tables. His name was Michael Galt. Actually, in retrospect, it was erroneous of me to respect his ability to say *no*, since I now suspect that this gesture may have been made partly for my benefit. Later, when he and I became friends he would always insist on paying everytime we went out together. I never once said *no*. Michael lived in a small hotel in the vicinity of Dizengoff Square. Since he left everyone under the impression that he had a good deal of money, I was surprised the first time I saw his small crowded and unattractive hotel room. It's only temporary, he assured me. I find it convenient, I can walk to work. He was an assistant bank manager, but also spoke of working for American Intelligence. I believe I doubted everything he told me. Once, at his urging I visited the bank where he was employed. I was somewhat astonished to discover that indeed he was an assistant bank manager. He was still, given my distrust, determined to prove that he worked for American Intelligence, but that was a more difficult thing to do. We saw each other almost daily. I was incapable of saying no. Michael turned everything he did, no matter how trivial, into a kind of ceremony . . . everything became ritualized: the headwaiter's greeting, Michael scanning the menu, and after the meal having coffee served on the terrace, discussing our work, our mutual friends . . . it only dawned on me some time later that I detested Michael. I stopped seeing him. On the telephone he reproachfully said: you don't wish to see me. No, I said. Six months later I ran into him in the company of an old school friend of mine. Where had they met? How did they come to know each other? They had met in Aden, I was told. What were they doing in Aden? A few months later I ran into Michael in the vicinity of his bank. He had been fired that very same day for embezzling large sums of money. He had spent all of it on his friends, he explained. He had been doing it for a couple of years. To his relief the bank had decided not to press charges since he knew a good deal about their dubious business transactions. As far as I could determine he did not change his life-style. He and my friend, for as long as they could, kept on eating in some of the more expensive restaurants. After each meal Michael would sign the bill with a great flourish. He would also add a substantial tip for the waiter. Gradually he had to avoid walking down certain streets in order not to be spotted by people to whom he owed money. He admitted that all this had somewhat jeopardized his work for American Intelligence . . .

I still find it most difficult to say no, and therefore use other words to convey the message. My difficulty stems from a certain sympathy I have for the recipient of the *no* . . . yet the *no* is quick and in the long run preferable to the words I choose . . . but one cannot cling to the word *no*, the way one can to words such as: maybe . . . perhaps . . . possibly . . . I'll think of it . . . I'll keep you in mind . . . If the occasion arises . . . you may mention my name if you like . . .

When Michael and I first met he asked me why in the past I had kept staring at him in the café. I could not explain that the way he had been able to say *no* to that extremely attractive couple had caught my attention. I always wanted to meet them, but never did.

I have, however, said *no* under the most unusual circumstances. A few hours after my marriage to H, the wedding took place in a building on lower Allenby Street, she invited me up to her apartment (or was it now legally our apartment?) for a drink, and I said no. Perhaps not that abruptly . . . and not in English. After our marriage I would drop by infrequently to visit her. I was always on guard. Always prepared to say *no*. It's such a great pity, she said somewhat sadly the day we were divorced, all those wasted opportunities . . .

There are people dedicated to the *no*. They say *no* on principle. Their faces testify their need to say *no*: ask me anything, and my answer will be *no*. To say *yes* would be to admit a defeat, an unbearable and crushing defeat.

SHE

In the story or novel the pronoun *she* may well refer to a woman who is young, attractive and single. For instance, when one reads: "She crossed 57th Street and walking briskly entered the arcade," a vague picture is formed and connected to what preceded that particular sentence. As far as the reader is concerned a certain logic determined the placement of this sentence within the dense forest of words that constitute the entire work. Whether pertinent or not, the sentence forms a connecting link without conspicuously calling attention to itself. The information—it is nothing but information—is recorded by the reader unless he happens to have skipped over that particular line. The woman in question may or may not be young, single and attractive. Whether she's young, single and attractive may be left to the reader to decide. It may not be pertinent as far as the book is concerned. On the other hand, the fact that she is carrying a Pucci handbag could be as relevant as the Legion of Honor rosette in the lapel of Roberte's suit, in the novel *Roberte Ce Soir* by Klossofsky. Klossofsky ingeniously attaches an erotic content to these iconographic emblems . . . an eroticism that pervades the entire text. Frequently the reader, as if participating in a Pavlovian experiment, responds not to the story or novel, but to a word or sentence that catches his eye. Almost invariably the pronoun *she* precedes or closely follows the word or sentence which in the reader's brain has acquired a highly charged content. Quite unknowingly the writer has provided a reader with an item of information that is self-contained, that can be lifted from the book, permitting the reader to linger over it as he forms his own anticipatory creation, a fantasy that functions independent of the story or book that initially was its raison d'être. As in fiction our speech is sprinkled with masculine and feminine pronouns. The pronoun *she* is a common occurrence. No one raises an eyebrow. No one is perplexed. The speaker is simply referring to a woman. It could be a passenger speaking to the driver of a bus. She works at the lumberyard, says the passenger. She's a secretary. The passengers within earshot listen to the exchange. They do not know who *she* is. They will never find out. Not infrequently the pronoun *she* is used in the presence of the subject. She's always in bed by twelve, someone might say. And the person being discussed stands silently, feeling that to deny or affirm the statement would only serve as a provocation . . . since, for the duration of that particular exchange, *she* is not present, not counted, completely invisible.

In a book the statement she's a bitch could raise certain expectations in the reader that the author might feel compelled to satisfy. In daily conversation the venom that frequently is attached to a pronoun can disable a man or a woman without any explanation ever forthcoming. To the question, Did you invite Sandra? the response, she's a bloody bitch, may not be inappropriate or surprising. There's no further need to dwell on Sandra.

The pronoun has become a necessity. For each name the brain instantly supplies a pronoun.

I confided to Felix that I intended to marry H who would otherwise have to join the Israeli army.

What is she like? asked Felix.

Felix absorbs everything I tell him. She's attractive, she has a large apartment in Zaphon-Tel Aviv. She's a terrible cook. She adores Gamzu (a popular Israeli art critic). She detests hiking or going to the beach. She's never read a word I've written.

A few years later without Felix's prompting I painted a more elaborate picture of her. Naturally I also included Felix and myself. I called what I had done a novel. From time to time I changed the novel slightly. I improved it. I interpreted what had happened, and then I interpreted my interpretation. I decided, for instance, that when she had moved her bed to a different part of the room after I left her, her intention had been to erase my former presence. I don't know if that is true. It worked as far as the novel was concerned, and that for a writer remains the chief criterion. A few years ago a mutual friend of ours told me that H had become a judge. How fitting, I thought. In my mind I can see her say: *either/or* as well as *no* without any hesitation. If I ever were to rewrite the novel I might be tempted to include this piece of information. I might even offer a tentative explanation: She became a judge hoping that one day I might appear in front of her in court.

Watching a movie we are actually observing a reel of celluloid unwind, frame by frame, across a concentrated beam of light thereby forming on a large white screen a replication of a life we have come to identify as ours, a life that is expressed by having a couple of people speaking, or fighting, or riding on an old-fashioned train, the motion or immobility of what we see usually being predicated on a story that may have been written by someone who does not know the first thing about making a film. In any event the audience is not unaware that what it is watching is contained frame by frame on the reel, and that there may be two or three or four reels, and that they will have to sit in their seats for approximately 120 or 140 or 175 minutes in order to see the entire film, and that as the last frame on the last reel crosses the aperture through which the beam of light is being directed, the filmmaker has brought his film, his version of a story or book, his verisimilitude of life to an end. The end of the movie coincides with the end of a reel of film. The end of a peep show on 42nd Street is the end of two or three minutes of voyeurism. Another quarter will in the same machine repeat in every detail the same sexual entanglement. Even the producer of these brief films will adhere to a certain procedure, which acknowledges a beginning and an end. No matter how innovative a chess player Fischer may be, he knows, perhaps to his sorrow, that there is a beginning and an end game and that he must play accordingly. At a certain stage a chess player knows that he has passed the beginning stage and is entering the middle stage and that very soon it will be time to prepare for the ending. At some point both players become aware that they have entered the final stage. They need not communicate this to each other verbally. Although time is a significant element in professional chess, it only accentuates the beginning, the middle and the end game. The game played without a clock does not change in substance. Clock or no clock the end is anticipated by the players. At the start of the game, reading the first page of a book, or the moment a film begins the end is brought into play. In chess the fierceness of the end game appears to be more conspicuous because most of the chess pieces have been eliminated. A player who shrinks from methodically destroying a weaker opponent is simply prolonging the game, prolonging the monotony of the checkmate. In the end game a kind of nakedness of intent becomes apparent. Unlike his opponent, the losing player can always resign, thereby bringing the game to an end before the entire game has been played out. The filmmaker can also become a victim of the end. Even a gifted filmmaker like Godard has killed off his major characters at the end. The death of the character coincided with the conclusion of the film. Broadly speaking, the filmmaker, the chess player, and the writer are left with fewer and fewer options as they approach the end. In the mystery film the ending has a definite function, namely to resolve the mystery, point to the killer, and if possible implicate someone who was never under any suspicion. What has been cloudy becomes clear. In *The Fire Within* by Malle the hero commits suicide at the end. Since I had grown attached to him I felt a sense of grief. If I were to see the film again I might conceivably walk out before the end. In *L'Immortell* Robbe-Grillet disoriented the viewer by having his protagonist die an identical death to the mysterious woman he had been following and whose identity he was never able to determine. Both died in the same white convertible, their broken necks twisted at the same angle . . . By repeating every detail of the woman's death, Grillet has forced us to shift the end in our mind until we juxtaposed it with the death of the woman. The end leads us back into the middle, as Robbe-Grillet to some degree avoided the total confinement of the ending. Kafka in a much more circuitous fashion avoided the end in his then unpublished three novels, by simply not completing them. It was left up to Max Brod to provide a quasi end to the three works. Since every move by the protagonist in *Amerika, The Trial* and *The Castle* invites the mounting anxiety that often accompanies the end, the end in itself is almost redundant. It has been stated over and over again. I cannot pick up Kafka, but I read over and over again a story by Borges, called *Death and the Compass* which bears a resemblance to a mathematical equation. $a + b + c = x$. On first reading the story one is unprepared, accepting at face value the contrivance that entices the detective in the story to move from a to b then to c, finally as surprised as the reader, to die at x. The entire equation flashing in front of our eyes. Six months ago a friend of mine disappeared. A few days before her disappearance she called me up, explaining that she would like to come over and see me. I told her that it was slightly inconvenient since I had some work to finish, but she persisted until I agreed to see her. I now realize that she came not, as I had thought, to speak to me about her problems, but simply to hand me the key to her apartment. A few days later, informed by a mutual acquaintance that she was missing, I went to her apartment searching the place for some clue to her whereabouts. Why else had she given me her key? She had left all her possessions behind. All her books, papers, documents, credit cards, bankbooks. I found the signed copy of my novel in her handbag. This was six months ago. I keep hoping that it was not the *end*. Was she afraid that I might not know of it when it took place.

H and I alternately toyed with the *end* of our relationship. Everything we did lacked conviction . . . I left her, but then under some duress returned. I left her again only to marry her. This time there was no further need to return. The marriage was a sufficient bond. We lived apart. When I looked out of my window and saw her passing on the street below I could always say: there goes my end. Face to face with her I was able to contemplate an *end* that was continuing.

Frequently we would meet at the Niza. She tormented me by mentioning her lover. I prolonged the meetings. Having returned the key of her apartment I could only speculate at the changes that had taken place in her apartment since I had left. If she were to read this, I am convinced she would find what I write absolutely incorrect. Her mind could never tolerate the disturbance my dissatisfaction imposed upon her. By marrying her I was able to withhold the *end*. I was twenty and had not yet read Kafka or Kierkegaard. It was sheer intuition, if you will . . .

TRY

To try anything is to leave open an avenue of retreat. In a primitive society the young are uniformly initiated into a communal tribal life. Tribal survival depends largely on the acceptance of established customs and practices and not on experimentation with new ones. At an early age the boys begin practicing with bow and arrow. The bow and arrows are toys only in a manner of speaking. Even the exception in the tribe, the man who becomes a shaman, does not start out by trying, just as the men who carve the totems do not first practice at carving . . . Every move made in a tribe spells out an intention that will be carried out . . .

In our society we are encouraged to try out everything. It is made misleadingly clear to us that everything is more or less available to be tried. There are books that will enable us to build a twenty-foot boat, a transmitter, a Molotov cocktail, or confidently set about publishing our own books. In general, our ability to do things, everyday things, to hop on a bus, hijack a plane, or register at a hotel under an assumed name has to appear convincing not only to ourselves, but to others too. We do not try it. We do it to test ourselves. Just as we test ourselves every time we fall into a strange bed and find our spontaneous responses to whoever happens to be in the bed closely examined. We strive to feel at ease, quite quite quite relaxed . . . we don't like to admit that we are doing anything for the first time. To try something is basically an attempt to overcome the hurdle of the first time. But how reassuring to know that one can always back out . . . Have you ever lived in a ménage à trois? Try it. Have you ever spent a year with a primitive tribe that still practices cannibalism? Try it. Have you ever fucked a fourteen year old in Morroco? Try it. Have you ever crossed the Sahara in a caravan? Try it. Have you ever written a book? Try it.

In a tribe the boundaries are clearly defined and there's no withdrawal possible from one's place or role within the tribe without endangering the stability of the tribe. The American painter who lived with a tribe of cannibals returns to America and writes a book about it. He is listed in the telephone directory, and I suppose, one could call him up, ask his advice . . . However, intrinsic to certain exploratory situations is the danger that after a certain stage a return is impossible. One can try a sex change, gradually, until . . .

For the less intrepid the plastics industry in America and Japan produces an assortment of devices . . . some replicating what is otherwise sexually unavailable for the purchaser.

If we were to receive a message from outer space that read: Is there any other way to live? Our reply might be: No, there is not, but we try.

PAST

Any material that deals with the years 1943 or 1947 can be said to deal with the past. The *I Ching*, which was the subject of a series of lectures by Hellmut Wilhelm in 1943, does not focus attention on the past. The text, at least in the English translation, is firmly rooted in a kind of permanent *now*, despite the occasional references to a period in Chinese history a long time ago. The people who have occasion to use the *I Ching* are chiefly preoccupied with the future. A future that unlike the past presents numerous constantly narrowing options as well as the likelihood of obstacles that may prevent one from proceeding along a path one had hoped to take. The obstacles, incidentally, are all somewhat cryptically depicted in the *I Ching*. One can gather from Wilhelm's introduction to his book *Change*[2] that the German-speaking audience that attended his eight lectures in Peking, by keeping themselves apart from the city's pro-Axis German community, must have faced similar obstacles and danger. It is therefore not too difficult to conjecture what questions Wilhelm might have been asked during and following each lecture. I can see the heavy German faces and brains that are stocked with recollections of Meissen chinaware, Dürer-like landscapes and damask drapes, ponderously turning to the ancient Chinese text, a text that was able to magnify the elements of chance so alien to the interior of their European apartments in which even the arrangement of the furniture acknowledges an awareness of causality.

Although he may not give it much thought, Cartier-Bresson only documents the past. He photographs a eunuch at the Imperial Palace and creates a kind of overlay, one past over another. Yet, looking through his viewfinder Cartier was viewing the present. One might even say that he was selecting from among many an appropriate moment, and then still in the present, not the past, at perhaps one hundredth of a second he transfers the image of that precise moment unto film. What he, quite spontaneously, had framed in his viewfinder turns out to be a wizen-faced eunuch who had served under the Empress Tseu-hi. The eunuch holding some bank notes in one hand is engaged in a conversation with a bald-headed younger man. Quite possibly the eunuch is about to pay the man for some service rendered, or perhaps he has just received the money from the other. By the time Cartier-Bresson gets to examine the print the conversation between the eunuch and the other man belongs to the past. True, they belong to the recent past, but the division between the recent and distant past is somewhat arbitrary. In any case, Cartier's photograph encompasses both, as each shot transcends the immediacy of the situation depicted

[2] Hellmut Wilhelm, *Change: Eight Lectures on the I Ching,* trans. Cary F. Baynes (Princeton, N.J.: Princeton University Press, 1960).

on the photograph, compelling the viewer to glide from one past to another.

Critically I examine several photographs taken of me, quite vehemently objecting to a few. Why? Because they displease me. I do not care for the image I am projecting. At about the time Wilhelm was delivering his now famous eight lectures on the *Book of Changes* in Peking I was unsuccessfully trying to join the soccer team in my class. I never made it. But, then, as if things were not bad enough, none of my close friends were on the team. This, to my distress, further accentuated the split between the team members and myself. Unlike my friends I was an indifferent student. I was also somewhat of an oddity, failing to readily fall into any of the categories that most groups seem to form at their inception. I recall feeling astonished and somewhat flattered that I could be considered a threat when the mother of a friend of mine showed up at our apartment one day, asking my mother in an icy voice to keep me away from her son since my friendship was having a detrimental effect on his grades. Although my mother made no attempt to enforce this request, my friend and I stopped seeing each other. I don't recall if his grades improved.

At least twice weekly I would accompany my mother to one of the cafés where she would meet with her acquaintances. Frequently I was the only child at the table. The conversation, held in German, was generally lively and interesting. Everything around us seemed a million miles removed from China. Even the waiters were Austrian or German. I felt extremely pleased with myself whenever I could hold the attention of the grown-ups with what I considered to be a rather clever remark. From this alone I am led to suspect that I was a rather unpleasant child. In general my statements were made for the benefit of Professor Tonn and whomever else I considered worthy of my interest. Professor Tonn was one of the few people in our community who spoke an excellent Chinese, and had formed a deep interest in Chinese drama and literature. I believe he came to the café bcause he liked being in the company of so many attentive as well as attractive women. China as a subject, as far as I can remember, was rarely touched upon. My presence, odious as it must have been, was part of the price he had to pay.

In April or May of 1944, a period bracketed by the lectures of Wilhelm and the arrival of Cartier-Bresson in China, Shanghai was bombed sporadically by about a dozen or so B-19s at a time. On one mission they completely missed the Japanese radio station they were trying to destroy, obliterating instead a nearby Chinese market that was crowded with people at that time of day. The following morning a friend and I, drawn as if by a powerful magnet to the totally destroyed area, managed to slip through the barbed-wire barricades that had been set up to prevent all unauthorized people from entering the area. No one paid us the slightest attention as we started out at a rapid pace along the gutted houses and past the occasional body that had not yet been picked up. Everything was still smoldering, and the smell of burnt wood and burnt bodies became thicker the further we walked. We kept on, slightly dazed by now, not knowing where we were going until we reached a completely deserted square where the dead dismembered bodies had been almost neatly piled up in four or five tall heaps. Seeing the bodies, my friend panicked . . . Before I could stop him he had turned and was running away in the direction we had come. I called out to him, but he didn't stop. Handkerchief pressed to my nose I crossed the square passing between the piles of bodies. For some reason I cannot explain almost anything that lay ahead seemed preferable to taking the same path back. Ten or fifteen minutes later I was able to remove my handkerchief and breathe normally again. When we met the following day I never once mentioned what had happened the day before, but as far as I was concerned, he had left me in the lurch.

I wonder, would Cartier-Bresson have photographed those pyramids of mangled Chinese bodies. Would Wilhelm, had he been in my place, see six thousand years of uninterrupted Chinese history shape a stoic acceptance of chance which, in this particular instant, connected the bombloads of a dozen B-19s with this sector of Shanghai.

Everything I am able to remember about China, the tattered-looking army of Chiang entering the city, the Chinese brothels, the dance halls, The Little Club packed with American sailors, the Boy Scout Jamboree I faithfully attended, playing Bingo at the racecourse, or the coolies hauling sacks of rice on the Bund, becomes more convincing after I look at Cartier's photographs, whereas the *I Ching* allows me to enter a China I have never experienced or seen during my stay there. It is a China devoid of the explicit misery in the shape of dead infants on the sidewalk neatly wrapped in newspaper that I used to pass on my way to school. Yet nothing I have experienced in Shanghai could be said to be foreign to the *I Ching* . . . not even the two Chinese policemen who were playing football with an infant wrapped in newspaper.

How did I respond?

The two policemen were laughing uproariously as they kicked the bundle back and forth across the street. It may have temporarily alleviated their sense of helplessness.

Among my possessions when we left China was a silver cigarette case, a heavy silver ring and a quite lethal knife. I am still somewhat puzzled by these objects. What did they mean to me? By that time I knew everything the *I Ching* could possibly convey regarding the meeting of two minds. Dwight Irving Gregg whom I greatly liked and admired inexplicably aimed his new air gun at me from the first floor balcony of his room. I kept on walking and was hit in the chest. This gratuitous incident, no matter how hard we tried to efface it, signaled the end of our friendship. I, on the other hand, bloodied the nose of an extremely loyal and devoted friend, Herbert Baron. This had all come about shortly after I changed high school, and Herbert, in order to remain together with me, had persuaded his parents to permit him to do so as well. We both had returned on the school bus from the new school when I on some pretext started to fight with him. It was the only time we had ever fought, and the only time that I had seen Herbert have to defend himself. I started the fight because I was becoming increasingly annoyed by his constant attention. I started the fight because I had several new friends. To make matters worse, I beat him up in front of my new classmates. It was probably the most contemptible thing I had ever done. He left school the following day. I fully realized the implication of my behavior, and so did he. Yet, when we met a year or two later he did not show the slightest hostility. Both our families were intending to leave China. We shook hands before we parted having carefully avoided the subject of our former friendship. We spoke only of the future. Herbert had never returned to school. More than ever before I was able to realize how low I was able to stoop in order to gain an acceptance that I valued more for the sake of its form than its content. Perhaps this can be disputed, since frequently form and content are inextricably tied together.

During the last few days in Shanghai I rarely ventured out, having narrowly escaped being beaten by a gang of Chinese youths . . . a gang, I might add, that in no way resembled the tattered army of Chiang that I had watched enter the city. I was not taking any chances. China was rapidly losing its allure. It was becoming less and less familiar each day.

From deep inland Cartier-Bresson was heading back to Shanghai, covering the advance of Mao's army and the retreat of the Nationalists. At some time, I feel convinced, our paths must have crossed. I wonder what happened to the eunuch in Cartier's photograph. He and his fellow compatriots must have taken everything in their stride. Since the Ming dynasty the eunuchs have made themselves indispensable to the rulers of Imperial China. At one time these men without balls wielded considerable power and for all practical purpose ran ancient China. Who knows, it could happen again.[3]

ARMY

In the history of the Sino-Japanese War (1937–1945) compiled by Hsu Long-hsuen and Chang Ming-kai, published by the Ching Wu Publishing Co. in Taipeh, Taiwan, the Republic of China, the city of Shanghai is referred to on a number of occasions. To start with there was the Shanghai incident in 1937, although it is not made clear in the book what the incident was about. The book, however, not only covers all the military operations but lists the chain of command and with the aid of dozens of maps shows the military strategy of the Nationalists and of the Japanese forces, who for the most part are simply referred to as the enemy. Charts that show the order of battle during most of the major encounters are also included. Words that most frequently occur are: stopped, combat, readiness, attack, reinforce, mass, advance, reorganize, surprise, intercept, flank, outflank, establish, contact, lose, march, air, cover, shoot, close, combat, gallantly, struggle, fell, back, fought, bitterly, last, man, launch, restore, original, position, lesson, learned, glorious, victory, contribute, immensely, heavy, costly, casual-

---

[3] I realize that the term *without balls* might mislead the reader to infer a weakness where within the context of power none existed. In describing the eunuchs I am simply depicting the potential bureaucratization and corruption of a centralized power such as China today.

ties, capture, main, force, interrupt, enemy, transportation, Brigade, garrison, highway, isolated, abandoned, operational, guidance, insure, security, HQ, deployment, shift, disregarding, repelled, halted, feint, attack, broken, suffered, dead, North, South, East, West. The numbers from 1 to 1,000,000 in the book may indicate the number of soldiers, or casualties, or trucks, or pounds of rice, or troops that had successfully escaped encirclement.

Here and there an individual exploit is described, a pleasant break in the seeming repetitiveness of the text. For instance on page 351, beneath the subheading: "Bombing the Enemy Headquarters in Shanghai," there is a brief description of a courageous pilot, Yen Hai-wen, who *by mistake* parachuted into enemy position after his plane was shot down. After killing a number of Japanese soldiers on the ground he committed suicide rather than surrender. Recognizing his gallantry the enemy buried him with full honors and erected a tablet which read, "Tomb of a gallant Chinese Air Warrior." Even the Japanese press at home covered Yen's gallantry with admiration.

My parents and I arrived in Shanghai several years after this incident. During my stay in Shanghai I remained unaware of a prior conflict in or around the city. Certainly, as far as I was concerned, there was no evidence of it. In the history of the Sino-Japanese War the authors attempt to give a thorough account of how the enemy was gradually worn down and destroyed as he kept advancing and capturing one major Chinese city after the other. It would be simplistic to maintain that the book is merely an attempt at self-deception. Sun Tzu in the *Art of War*, writes: "One yields when it is expedient." By concentrating on the minutiae of the minor skirmishes the authors have managed to avoid touching upon the overwhelming defeat of the Chinese army. In the Orient I believe this is not considered self-deception, it is called saving face. I consider it a major accomplishment if a book is able to achieve that purpose.

In our neighborhood during the war all the air raid wardens were European. A few took their duties with a seriousness that was out of all proportion to what they had to do. My uncle Phoebus's son-in-law, carried away by some inexplicable Germanic zeal, stopped a Japanese army truck during an air raid, claiming that the road was closed to all traffic. When the driver refused to obey, Phoebus's son-in-law lost his temper, and jumping on the running board of the truck, peremptorily ordered the Japanese driver to take him to the local police station. The truck drove off, and my uncle's son-in-law, who in many respects resembled my uncle, was found the next day floating in the Wangpoo River.

After the Japanese surrender the Japanese remained in virtual control of the city until the American and Chinese army arrived thirteen days later. No attempt was made to attack or molest the Japanese forces in the city. A week after the surrender on my way to a movie I remember seeing a single Japanese soldier standing guard in the center of a large square a short distance from our house. Two hours later when I was on my way home, I found the square packed with Chinese men and women who in an absolute state of frenzy were shouting insults at the soldier. He remained completely still, almost unaffected by the incredible spectacle around him, no trace of any emotion on his broad face. I stood at the edge of the crowd expecting them to attack the soldier, but although they kept inching closer and closer, the attack did not materialize.

My uncle Phoebus, the ex-cavalry man, ex-athlete, could not resist showing his derision towards me, since he—despite my attempts to disguise them—discerned all my flaws, my overwhelming weaknesses. I was never able to win his respect, or prevent him from mimicking my obsessive attachment to games. He did this with a dispassionate but deadly accuracy. For his sake, I am sorry I never became an officer in the Israeli army. It would have made him so happy.

I have in my possession photographs of my uncles Fritz and Phoebus in Austrian uniforms during the First World War. Fritz was killed shortly after his photograph was taken by a certain R. Frantz, Wien XIV, Mariahilferstrasse. Fell on the 24th of June 1915 in Ruda Koszilua, Poland. Buried beside a windmill next to a brook, it says on the back. I wonder if my uncle Phoebus was able to refrain from mimicking the entry into Shanghai of the *victorious* Nationalist army. At least half the soldiers I saw were under fifteen. A good many were barefoot. Only a most enthusiastic supporter of Chiang could have evinced any pride in the army. To me it was simply one more inexplicable and unexpected spectacle in a world rich with strange and bizarre spectacles. But often it seemed to me that I was the only one who felt that way.

Under certain conditions ideas tend towards a common goal, towards a sameness of purpose. Deprivation of any sort is generally a good impetus to the formation of an idea that might alter the situation for the better. Inventions of all kinds are predicated on ideas, and quite frequently, when an idea is said to be in the air, people who may be separated by thousands of miles reach the same idea. In order for an idea to be effective it need not be complicated or particularly ingenious. I don't know who first made a replica of a pistol out of soap and then attempted to rob a bank or escape from jail. Making a pistol out of soap is not the easiest thing in the world. A rudimentary knowledge of the weapon is essential. The ingredients for the mock pistol, soap, black shoe polish, are however easily available. It goes without saying that the weapon would be useless in a hot boiler room, or in the proximity of a stove.

Some people who are not in jail are quite capable of thinking up ideas for people who are. Usually, when an idea becomes formalized, that is to say, when it is workable, it is patented. Ideas are also something to share with others. They allow people to create a bond, an impermanent bond perhaps, but all the same, a bond. I have an idea, someone says, and everyone perks up his ears. What will it be? They will share it. Ideas contain privileged information. I have shared some of my ideas with friends. I have a great idea, I said . . .

The inventor is filled with torment. He wishes to reveal his ideas to one and all, but is aware of the danger of doing so. Someone else might carry off the glory, the honor . . . Who really had the idea of inventing the camera, the Morse code, the radio . . .

Who was the first Chinese emperor to use eunuchs as confidential secretaries, emmisaries and flunkies, knowing that the eunuchs' loyalty would not be subject to the same temptations as that of members of the nobility at court. I unexpectedly won a short-story competition at school and in front of the class was complimented by my teacher for thinking up a story about a story competition in which the winning student had somehow managed to take the other students aside, one by one, and under the guise of friendship given them an idea for a story they could use, but in each case it was the same story. Having won the

21

competition I lived in dread for the remainder of the term, afraid that my teacher or someone else in the class might happen across the *Rover Boys Annual* from which I had lifted the idea. I was aware that my winning the first prize by plagiarizing had added a certain richness to the original story. The only pity was that I could not share the information with anyone.

When I married for the first time it was in a sense the result of an idea to keep H from having to join the Israeli army, which as a married woman she would not have to do. As a result of this idea I went through a somewhat farcical marriage and then, six months later, through an equally farcical divorce. Throughout our marriage I kept maintaining that it was simply a poetic gesture. (This brings to mind a statement by Arrabal that by poet he does not mean one who writes poems, but a terrorist or provocateur, who never writes. I have extremely mixed feelings regarding that statement now.) I kept my marriage a secret from my friends. With the exception of one person, no one knew that I was married. I lived alone and rarely saw my wife, although at one time we had been in love and lived together for a year. On the day of my wedding I had gone to see a writer I greatly admired and confided to him what I was about to do. It was he who later introduced me to Kierkegaard, and it was he who strongly urged me to abandon my idea, saying that he didn't think it to be a very good one. He was extremely tactful.

REAL

Language is used chiefly to document what is real. There is no lack of interpretations for everything that takes place or fails to take place in our bedroom, in our living room, in the bathroom, on the stairs, in the street, or in a swamp, but what the interpretations share in common is a concern with the real . . . The history of the Sino-Japanese War strives to be real. For all I know it is totally false, perhaps there never was an airman called Yen who parachuted by mistake into enemy position, and then committed suicide, but in this particular book the incident is made real. The charts, the dates, even the hours of certain battles add to the reality. True, we expect the real to be convincing, but it is almost impossible to verify the battle of Western Hupei where purportedly 41 enemy planes were downed. Still, all in all, Shanghai is

22

real. It exists. When Dwight Irving Gregg shot at me with his BB gun it was real, yet lacking a proper explanation for his conduct, and never receiving one, I remained puzzled. The reality of our friendship was undermined by an incident I could not explain. A plausible explanation is that he happened to be standing on his balcony, holding a BB gun he had just received for his birthday, when I came along . . .

When a friend whom I had not seen in years called me one day and asked; how are you? I replied that I felt dislocated and unreal. Why did I say that. What made me feel unreal . . . What is the absence of the real . . . Since everything I have ever seen seems tinged with a certain unreality, I can only conclude that unreality is entirely subjective, that in fact the viewer brings or attaches his unreality to what he sees. Wearing a Scout hat, and trying to earn a semaphore badge, I did not feel unreal, attending a Scout's jamboree I did not feel unreal, entering a luxurious Chinese whorehouse at the age of fifteen, and being confronted by a row of immensely attractive women, I felt aware of something less than real. I don't know when precisely, but the message: *Is there any other way to live?* that we may expect to receive any day from outer space carries within it the pathos of the real. From the message one will be able to conclude that the real is a boundary separating us from the hazards of our desires for everything that is new. The *I Ching* it must be stated is not, contrary to what many people believe, an oracular book. It is simply a guide to the real. In Kafka's *Castle* K. the surveyor strives for recognition from the Castle. He endeavors to have the Castle bestow its reality on him . . . and once or twice it does so, acknowledging his presence. Someone at the Castle even states that they (whoever they are) are satisfied with his progress. But this is all the more baffling since as far as he can determine he has made no progress at all.

Daily we are witnesses of the ceremony surrounding the real, or to put it another way, the ceremony of the real. Standing at attention at a parade ground in the former British army camp, Sarafand, I was not a participant of the real, I was an element that enabled the parade to be real. Standing under the canopy at my wedding, my future wife and I were culprits of a fraud . . . We went through all the expected responses and finally were congratulated by a couple of witnesses who had been paid to attend. I permitted the ceremony to intensify the reality of an isolation I wished to experience. The wedding, for me, was equivalent to stepping through the mirror in Cocteau's film, *Orpheus*.

WHERE

I've been to an extraordinary whorehouse, someone said, and I promptly asked: Where is it? The question *where* elicits all kinds of pertinent information. People, in general, are only too glad to divulge *where* they buy their shirts, and *where* they vacation, and *where* one can get a stuffed owl at a decent price. Perfect strangers confide to me *where* they live, *where* they work, *where* they met their husband or wife, as the case may be.

As a young boy in Shanghai I discovered quite by accident a most incredible mazelike building in which actors, jugglers, magicians gave a continuous performance to the people who drifted from one large chamber to another. I soon lost all sense of direction, walking down long corridors, circling one courtyard then another, stopping for a while to buy something to eat, then watching a puppet performance, and a man on stilts, and a peacock chained to a table . . . all the time aware that I was the only non-Chinese in the crowd. I returned a couple of times, always alone. I recall having described the building and what went on inside it to my friends without once eliciting the question: *Where?*

In retrospect this doesn't come as a surprise, since China was largely excluded from our minds. It certainly was excluded from our textbooks at school, since these were the standard English textbooks. I vividly remember the colored maps of Africa and South America, but not the map of China . . . After all, why study China. All one had to do was to take a look out of the window and one could get a pretty good idea what China was like.

Still, Cartier must have asked *where?* when he arrived. Briefly, after school I worked for a former manager of Leitz Optics who repaired Leicas and Rolleis for the foreign correspondents. Once I watched him take apart a Leica that had been dropped in a river during the fighting inland. Could it, I wonder, have belonged to Cartier-Bresson?

When I first met H I had just bought a camera. It was a fairly inexpensive camera made in France. By that time Cartier-Bresson had already taken his photographs of the eunuchs, and the Chinese wedding procession, and numerous shots of the fleeing Nationalist army, and the portrait of a former Chinese warlord, as well as shots of faces, simply curious faces staring at Cartier with his assortment of cameras as he casually and unselfconsciously kept stopping on the street, and lifting one of his battered cameras to eye level, snapped their curious stares . . . of course, in a sense, he was intruding, as every single white man who arrived in China intruded . . . but by then these intrusions were taken for granted. Just another foreigner intrigued with their signs, their life-style, their rituals . . .

I took a few photographs of H in a public park in the north of Tel Aviv. Unlike Cartier I was a bit self-conscious and kept fumbling with the camera as I calculated the f opening and the shutter speed . . . H smiled, but because of the prolonged wait, the smile became somewhat strained. It wasn't spontaneous anymore when I snapped the picture, it was strained the way it would be later at our wedding.

How comforting and reassuring it is to find a map attached to a wall upon which an arrow has been drawn pointing to where on the map one happens to be. You are here, it says beneath the arrow as I calculate the distance and the time that separates me from my destination.

OTHER VOICES FOR A SECOND SIGHT

Vito Acconci

Installation
(three rooms, constructions, audio equipment, audio tape, slides),
The Museum of Modern Art, New York,
October 1974–January 1975

The situation is a late-night radio program. The space is set up like a recording studio, isolated from its surroundings, as if in the middle of nowhere—a radio station in the mind.

Entrance is into a small room, low, dark: there should be a feeling of stillness, bareness, here—the walls are paneled with brown acoustical board—a bank of audio equipment is set on a shelf against the far wall —a swivel chair faces the shelf—on the wall, a blinking red light faces the viewer approaching the chair. This is the place for the disc jockey, the origin of the all-night talk show—it's as if the viewer has wandered in, out of place—as if the viewer has come into the disc jockey's last program, his final state of mind, has been left there to play itself over and over, indefinitely.

On either side of the room, there's a long, narrow, horizontal window, doubly plated, overly reflective; each window looks into a higher room, a filled room, that can't be entered. These are like sound rooms, the sources of programs; the center room, then, is like an engineer's studio, where the messages from the side are pulled together, mixed together.

But the center room seems designed for insulation: I'm talking on tape —I'm the voice of the all-night disc jockey—I'm the voice that drifts through the dark, that lulls you into the night, that makes you forget ("A quiet night . . . a taste of bitters . . . a look of blue . . . we'll keep the light away together . . .").

The radio show is like a final hour. There are thirteen "programs": a kind of autobiography—death in the family, the past as death ("I never told you why I cower at the sight of open scissors . . . my grandmother's death . . . and that's why my mother and I became so close . . . accomplices in silence . . ."); a kind of documentary, a war story —my own death, the present as death ("I know that my wrists and ankles are tied down . . . I know that the electrode is being passed, up and down, over my body . . ."); a kind of science fiction—death of a civilization, the future as death ("No one could have known then what it all would come to mean . . . the woman we watched from our window, as she walked along the shore plucking the feathers out of the dead birds that clogged the water . . .").

Each program fades off into music: wistful music, nervous music, a quiet introspective jazz—a kind of dirge, fiddling while the world burns. Each time the program returns, the name of the program changes: "Back Talk" . . . "Take Back" . . . "Buck Tick." I am your host; I come back each night as a different name: "Victor Ackon" . . . "Vida Coon" . . . "Vettor Concher" . . . It's as if I've lost myself: I've sunk into a mass, it's all the same, you (the viewer) have just as much of a place here as I do.

But the side rooms get in our way: we're not alone in the center room, the side rooms knock at our door. They're contained, they're behind glass, they're removed into the distance—but they're like mind pictures, they stay in the back of our heads. The rooms contain physical structures that "hold" each room, upright or lengthwise. The structures "present" each room; they function as supports for slides and films: carriers of light flashes, like embodiments of mental projections—fields for searchlights.

The room to the left is black, vertical, crowded. It has the air of a secret: the fourth wall is a window, looking out into the street, but the window has been covered over, walled out, there's only a line of peepholes, as if to allow, from outside the museum, a glimpse of underground activity. There are rows of 2 x 4s, sixteen of them, reaching from floor to ceiling—a jungle of posts, a miasma. Stretched across the posts, at various heights and zigzagging sometimes from row to row, are sheets of clear plastic, standing like banners, like announcements. Two sets of slides are projected over the plastic, through the plastic: reflections of images, doubled images, like something you can't shake out of your head. One set of slides is black-and-white, negative: close-ups of body parts, like a base for image, a ground for role. The other set is in color: masks are projected on my face, political posters are attached to my body. It's as if I've projected myself into a political world, I've projected politics onto me. I can offer the viewer a message now, an invitation to politics—but it's all in my mind.

The room to the right is white, horizontal, spare. The window here that looks to the street is left uncovered: there's a way out, a continuity from inside to outside. Four rows of white 2 x 4s lie across the width of the room, from wall to wall: one set is grounded on the floor, while the other three sets form an overhang halfway up the height of the room. Stretched over the supports, from row to row, are strips of white fabric, interspersed like stepping stones, screens, shades: the room has the feel of a kind of Japanese garden, a place to rest in, meditate in, float out of. From the rear of the room, a row of spotlights and slide projectors aim into the space—there's the feel of a search here. One set of slides is projected onto the floor, on and off the white planes—images of myself gaining a footing, setting myself into place; the second set is projected onto the wall—I'm in a position to relate to you, the viewer, I'm headed toward an outside world; the last set is projected through the overhang, onto the ceiling—I'm reaching for the clouds. These static images, then, have a moving base: it's as if the air is moving: a film loop is projected across the overhang—the camera moves over my body, as if over a landscape—the camera sweeps over roads, sea, sky—the direction is forward, outward, upward. There's call to transcendence here—but I can only speak in images, I can offer only illustrations, I can show only myself: it's wishful thinking.

The rooms won't stay still: the rooms talk—intermittent spurts of sound, interruptions. It's as if the side rooms are bursting: the center will be pulled apart.

From the black room comes the sound of drums, marches, bugles. I'm speaking here in other voices—revolutionaries, political heroes. The tone is mixed—homage, self-parody; I'm trying to talk myself into history, I'm trying to carry a message—a warning signal, a history lesson.

From the white room comes the sound of birds, sea, fantasy lands. I'm speaking here in an intimate whisper: my voice speaks over itself, my voice hits different pitches, different levels; it's as if I'm talking myself out of myself, transporting myself, multiplying myself—I'm trying to sing a siren song, an invitation to the invisible, the perfect love, the life beyond.

But these "other voices," these "second sights," are behind glass: they're worlds in a fishbowl—this is, underneath it all, a museum; it all comes back to myself—it's a power dream, a dream of glory. So the center room is closed off; this is a place to ignore the warnings—after all, we've made them up ourselves. So we can give ourselves up here, lose ourselves in the stories that go on forever, that turn in on themselves. The music plays and my voice continues, like a broken record: my voice is slow now, raspy, like a machine voice: the voice becomes an undercurrent, it sneaks in a frame of mind, installs a habit. Abdicate, it says: refuse, withdraw, don't make a move.

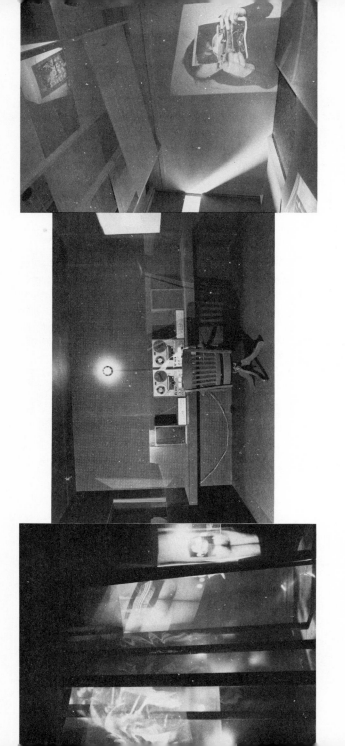

Vito Acconci: *Other Voices for a Second Sight.* 1974.
Installation The Museum of Modern Art, New York. Photos: Nick Sheidy.

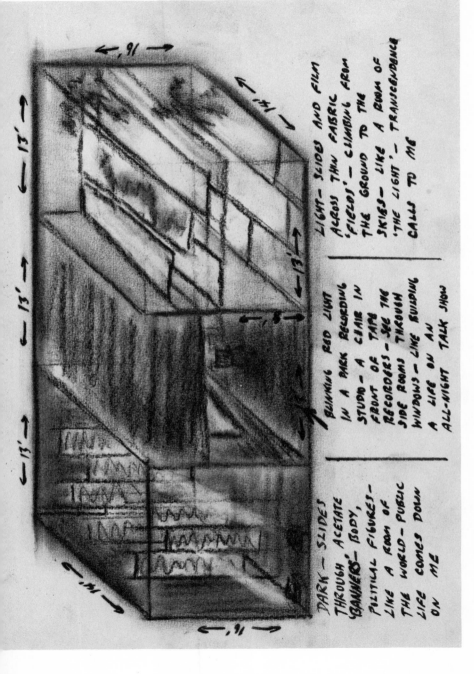

← 9' →

← 14' →

← 13' →

← 13' →

← 13' →

← 13' →

← 13' →

← 14' →

← 11' →

← 8' →

DARK — SLIDES
THROUGH ACETATE
"BANNERS" BODY,
POLITICAL FIGURES —
LIKE A ROOM OF
THE WORLD — PUBLIC
LIFE COMES DOWN
ON ME

BLINKING RED LIGHT
IN A DARK RECORDING
STUDIO — A CHAIR IN
FRONT OF TAPE
RECORDERS — SEE THE
SIDE ROOMS THROUGH
WINDOWS — LIKE BUILDING
A LIFE ON AN
ALL-NIGHT TALK SHOW

LIGHT — SLIDES AND FILM
ACROSS THRU FABRIC
"FIELDS" — CLIMBING FROM
THE GROUND TO THE
SKIES — LIKE A ROOM OF
'THE LIGHT' — TRANSCENDANCE
CALLS TO ME

BOOM-BA-DA-BOOOOM . . .
BOOOM-BA-DA-BOOOM . . .

HEY . . . PSSST . . . GUEVARA
. . . CHE HERE . . HEY . . .
PSSST . . OVER HERE.

(Background: continuous drum roll.
Foreground: two layers of voice:
my slow whisper, almost

A quiet night . . . a taste of
bitters . . . a look of blue . . .
a smell of old memorial stone . . . .
But who's to say what power . . .
who would have thought what
justice or what sacrifice . . . what
tiny unsuspected hand could stop
us when we've disguised ourselves
as time? . . . It's not for us to
ask . . . enough for me to talk,
night after night . . . enough for
you to listen . . . words of wistful
wisdom . . . whittled wisdom . .
long words work wonders westward
ho . . . Come into the dark . . .
that's the way I dream you hear
me . . . a rug, a borrowed blanket,
a zipper that will never be opened
again . . . a mind to use to forget
with . . . We'll keep the light
away together . . . because that's
why you turn me on each night:
not to pass the night but to put off
the day . . . So we'll keep the
light out of our faces as they turn
slowly to stone . . . The program
is "Back Talk" . . . this is your
host, Victor Ackon . . . so listen
to me well . . . because I'll be
keeping my ears perked up for any
sound of you . . . .

(Starting
up in the
background,
Chick

IN LOVE . . . INTO THE
DREAM . . . OUT OF THE
WORLD . . .

OOOOOOOH . . . OOOOOOOH
. . . OOOOH . . . NOT FAR
. . . INSIDE . . . THE RIGHT
TIME TO LEAVE THE
WORLD . . .

telegraphlike—on top of this, my attempt at a Spanish accent, near-parody.)

We are—we are Che Guevara—

listen—hit—hit and run—wait— wait—lie in ambush—hit and run again—again—listen—keep listening—give the enemy no rest—that's our word to you—to you—annihilate the enemy—

(Drum roll, alone.)

Listen—Che Guevara—Che Guevara speaking again—Jorge has not appeared yet—we kept watch all night—at nine the first jeep arrived—Joaquin—Joaquin and Urbano came with Coco—they brought a Bolivian, a medical student called Ernesto, who has come to stay . . . Coco went back and brought Ricardo—Ricardo, Braulio, Miguel, and another Bolivian, called Inti, who is also

---

(Machinelike voice.)
THE-IN-VI-TA-TION-

THE-SE-DUC-TION-

THE-SUS-CEP-TI-BIL-ITY-

THE-RES-PON-SI-BIL-I-TY-

THE-NEAR-A-GREE-MENT-

THE-RE-CON-SID-E-RA-TION-

THE-RE-BUFF-

Corea and Gary Burton, "Crystal Silence" —piano, vibes— hesitant, melancholy, introspective. The music continues for about two minutes.)

going to stay—going to stay—now
there are twelve rebels in all—it's
up to you now—we're talking to
you—

(*Drum roll stops abruptly.*)

THE-WITH-
DRAW-AL

THE-PRI-VA-CY-

THE-NEU-TRAL-
I-TY

I never told you why I cower at
the sight of open scissors . . . I
can't hold on to them, they fall out
of my hands, I run away into
the corner . . . whatever I'm
cutting—linen, paper for a paper
doll—lies uncut on the floor . . .
white . . . untouchable . . . it
spreads over the floor, covers my
world . . . My family lived in a
small apartment . . . my
grandmother—my father's mother—
lived across the hall . . . there
were arguments . . . my mother
and my grandmother . . . they'd
argue across the hall, in my
grandmother's apartment, away
from my brother, my sister, and

DID YOU EVER LOVE
ANYONE LIKE . . . I SAW
YOU UNTIL . . . THE
GROUND DROPPED TO . . .

TAP-TAP-TAP-TAP . . .
REV . . . REVO . . . REVOLU
. . . REVOLUTION . . . THE
. . . NEED . . . THE CALL . . .

1905 . . . BLOODY SUNDAY
. . . OCTOBER 11TH . . .
NOVEMBER 13TH . . . APRIL
4TH, 1917 . . .

me—we were always together then, people could hardly tell us apart . . . we heard the door slam as my mother came rushing back . . . first the door out in the hall—that was my grandmother's door—then, nearer, our own door . . . we could hear the wall of the kitchen shake—we'd be sitting there, my sister, my brother, and I, at the kitchen table, drawing . . . Sometime I'll tell you about the drawing contests—my father, my sister, my brother, and I—we drew my mother as she cooked . . . as she grated cheese—we'd have a good view of her hands then . . . It was my father who caused the arguments . . . my father who, every night, went out alone, went out to the opera . . . the velvet curtain after a day with rayon . . . a day at the bathrobe factory . . . I can see him now, my father preparing for his night at the opera . . . he was in his underwear—my father dressed from the top down . . . hat on, bring his tie around and through his button-down collar . . . all vulnerable below, his legs white and hairless . . . But that's another story . . . I want to go farther than that now . . . deeper into my heritage . . . it's my grandmother that I promised to

OOOOOOOOOH . . .
OOOOOOOOOH . . .
OOOOOOOOOH . . . WHERE
. . . THERE . . . WHEN . . .
WHO ELSE . . . OOOOOOH
. . . OOOOOOOH . . .
. . . OOOOOOOOOH . . .

talk about . . . I promise to tell you another time . . . on "Take Back" . . . this is Vettor Concher . . . till the next time . . .

(Background: "Crystal Silence" continues—drifting but holding back, restrained. About two minutes.)

(Machinelike voice.)
NO

I-WON'T-

NOT-ME-

I-WON'T-GO-

I-WON'T-MOVE-

I-CAN'T-DO-IT-

I-RE-FUSE-

NOT-FOR-ME-

(Background: tropical birds. Foreground: multilayered voice—intimate whisper—on top of this, my voice in different directions, different tones, different pitches.)

An old story—
Silence—
Loving it—
We couldn't feel the ground anymore—

A silent love story—
Waking from a bad dream—
I never knew anyone like—
Give and take—
Who could have known you—
In the middle—

(Tropical birds.)

We left them for another direction—
It's me, for you—
The right time to leave the world—
A violent love story—
Sleeping after a bad reality—
I never loved anyone like—

Giving away and taking back and taking away and giving back—
It was as if we had always known—

Touchstone—
Alone again—

I'M-NOT-YOUR-BOY-

I-WON'T-LISTEN-

I promised to tell you what it's like here . . . this place you never see . . . the point from which my voice comes out at you, every night . . . still point . . . point of order . . . port of dreams . . . this place I stare at, every corner, night after night . . . the corners I have on my mind, wait for, fit into, each day, before I come back here . . . There's a door here . . . honest . . . a door right in front of me . . . I can lean over now and touch it . . . No, I can't quite touch it . . . don't worry . . . don't be nervous . . . it's blocked . . . the door has been walled in, covered over . . . It's all right . . . nothing can come in here . . . nothing can touch me . . . nothing can come and take me away from you . . . I'll be here again another night, and another night after that . . . you can depend on me . . . a voice to warm you over . . . words to lose

In bed—
To the car—
Through the mountains—

It was right to get away from this world—

(*Sound of tropical birds stops abruptly.*)

WSSSSSSHHHHH . . . I . . .
YOU . . . TRANSFORMATION
. . . US . . .

LISTEN . . . TROTSKY . . . THE
TROTSKY SPEAKING . . . THE
OPPRESSION . . . THE
MASSES . . . THE PARTY . . .

TAP-TAP-TAP-TAP . . . IT
KERENSKY LIED . . . IT
WASN'T GERMAN SPIES, IT

WAS THE REVOLUTIONARY
PEOPLE . . . COME IN . . .
COME IN . . . TAP-TAP-
TAP . . .

*(Background: teletype.
Foreground: two layers of voice:
on top of my slow telegraphlike
whisper, there's my attempt
at a Russian accent, near-parody.)*

Listen—we are Leon Trotsky—it
is December 3rd—the St. Petersburg
Soviet is surrounded by troops—we
are shouting to the delegates—no
resistance to be made, no arms
to be surrendered—then, in the
meeting hall, the workers are
beginning to wreck the revolvers—
see—they strike a Mauser with a
Browning and a Browning with
a Mauser—this time it is no
jest—in the clashing of metal, we

yourself in . . . words, not worlds
to conquer . . . Don't be alarmed
. . . don't be ashamed . . . my
words absolve you . . . I absolve
us all as I sit here . . . red light
that takes the place of a bishop's
robe . . . a blink that loses sight,
glosses us over . . . I'll be here
. . . After all, I told you, the door
is covered over: I can't get out,
don't fret, I can't spring out at you,
I'll stay away . . . a distance . . .
safe . . . arm's length . . . no
arms to bear . . . no burdens . . .
I remain: Veda Conti . . . the
program is "Black Tuck" . . .

*(In the
background:
more Corea
and
Burton—
dreamy,
nostalgic
vibes—*

(Machinelike voice.)

*piano flies
a bit, then
returns to
base, keeps
a drawn-
out but
regular
beat.
About two
minutes.)*

WHO-CARES-

WHAT'S-IT-TO-
ME-

NO-SWEAT-

NO-SKIN-OFF-MY-
BACK-

WSSSSSSSSSSHHH . . .
SSWWWSSSHHH . . .
WHHSSSSSSSHHH . . .
SWSSSSH . . .
WWOOOOOOOSSSSHHHH . . .

can hear the gnashing teeth of the proletariat—listen—

(*Teletype alone.*)

Trotsky—Leon Trotsky speaking—the revolution is not like an earthquake or a flood—a new order begins to take shape instantly—listen—the revolution appears as madness only to those it sweeps aside—to us it is different—we are in our own element—listen—you can fit in—Listen—Trotsky here—modern development has strained its contradictions and driven us insane—we put the straitjacket on the sane minority—join in—we keep history moving along—

(*Teletype stops abruptly.*)

MAKES-NO-DIF-FER-ENCE.

SMALL-MAT-TER-

MEANS-NOTH-ING-TO-ME-

NOT-MY-CON-CERN-

NOTH-ING-TO-OFFER-

DOES-N'T-TOUCH- ME-

Who could have thought it? . . . Which one of us could have anticipated, as we threw another log into the fire . . . as the businessman from Kansas City spilled his cup of hot chocolate onto the rug that we had just pulled over, and we all grinned "no matter" . . . No one could have known then what it all would come to mean . . . the woman we watched from our window, as she walked along the shore plucking

NO, YOU'LL BE THE TRANSMITTER . . NO, YOU'LL BE THE RECEIVER . . WAVES, WAVES, WAVES . . .

BAM . . . BANG . . .
RAT-TAT-TAT . . .

THIS IS NO JOKE, BABY . . .
RUN FOR YOUR LIFE . . .
YOUR WHITE ASS IS MINE
. . . RAT-TAT-TAT-TAT . . .

the feathers out of the dead birds
that clogged the water . . . the
hours we spent scrutinizing the
shedding of organic forms, which
resulted in an alternate composition
of radiating electromagnetic fields
. . . the day she came in and told
us she had just gone back and
murdered her grandfather, it was
his seventeenth birthday . . . We
couldn't have suspected then . . .
But why think about it now . . .
There's no way to change our
minds . . . No use trying to crack
the bones in our faces, it took a long
time to develop our smiles . . .
So dial on . . . forget the
broadcasts . . . we don't need the
warning signals . . . we don't
have the ears for static . . . What
can they know of clinging to
weightlessness . . . what can they
hear of silence . . . But we'll hear
each other again, won't we? . . .
The program is "Bake Trick" . . .
this is Vexter Coon . . . that's
it . . .

(In the
background:
Joe Zawinul,
"From
Vienna
With Love,"
—piano,
violin,
bass—

(Machinelike voice.)

THE-SI-REN-
SONG-

I AM . . . YOU ARE . . . WE
WILL . . . THEY WERE . . .

(Background: sound of surf.
Foreground: my voice in a
whisper—on top, my voice casts
around in different directions,
levels.)

I am you—

You are me—

slow,
moody—
the piano
is free,
the strings
are tight
—there's
the sound
of some-
thing
preserved,
something
returned
to. For
two
minutes.)

THE-TRUMP-ET-
CALL-

We are One—

(*Surf.*)

THE-RAL-LY-ING-
CRY-

I love me—
I love you—
I love One—

(*Surf.*)

NO-

You love you—
You love me—
You love One—
One loves us—

(*Surf.*)

NO-GO-

I am them—
You are them—
I am One—
You are One—
They are One—

(*Surf.*)

NO-REA-SON-

I love them—
I love you—
I love One—

(*Surf.*)

THE-LACK-OF-COM-
MIT-MENT-

You love them—
You love me—
You love you—
You love One—
One loves all—

They love you—
They love me—
They love One—
One is love—

(*Sound of surf stops abruptly.*)

UNDERSTAND . . . SHE . . .
ME . . . STAND . . . I . . .
HER . . . OVERALL . . . SHE
. . . HERSELF . . . UNDO . . .
I . . . MYSELF . . .

THE-RE-FU-SAL-

THE-RE-TREAT-

Radio is dead . . . nobody listens anymore . . . I've been telling you stories for years . . . for years they've been telling me stories . . . But it only takes a shake of the head . . . a whistle in the wind . . . a fancy flutter . . . it all goes, in one, out one . . . Look, they say, you can't see anything . . . they all want more than a sound . . . a sound of trumpets . . . a feast for the eyes . . . tickle the senses . . . a voice is only Johnny One-Note . . . So radio is dead, they say . . . Good, I say . . . dead for the dead, and dust to dust . . . the song of wings . . . the song of vultures . . . that's why I keep talking like this . . . because I know you're dead, and I have to talk to prove to myself that I can hear . . . I'm talking to make you dead . . . the more I have to talk, the more I'm convinced that you're not there anymore . . . Ha, you say . . . you've missed one, that's what you say, you who still happen

I'LL HAUNT YOU . . . I'LL AMERICAN PIG . . . I'LL TORMENT YOUR ASS . . . RIDE YOU TILL YOUR NECK BREAKS.

RAT-TAT-TAT . . . DON'T YOU
HEAR IT? . . . YOUR POLICE
STATE IS OVER, SCUM . . .
THEY'RE DANCING IN THE
STREETS . . . DANCING ON
YOUR EYES . . .

*(Background: machine guns.
Foreground: slow telegraphlike
whisper—on top, my attempt at an
angry black accent, near-parody.)*

Listen—George Jackson here—we
are George Jackson—we must
accept this—this—the USA will be
brought to its knees—we must
accept this—the closing off of the
city—barbed wire—armored
pig-carriers crisscrossing the city
streets—pitted streets—tommy guns
pointed at stomach level—smoke

to be alive . . . it's simple . . .
easy . . . you think you've beaten
me . . . like taking candy . . .
like stealing a baby . . . so I've
overlooked you, so you've spoiled it,
because both of us are still alive
. . . But what can you know of
these mysteries? . . . or, at the very
least, what can you know of my
tricks? . . . You see, I never come
here anymore . . . I don't come
here, night after night, the way you
think I do . . . There's only one
night now . . . And Vida Acci has
this to say: these tapes were
recorded years ago . . . there's a
tip for you . . . that knocks the
wind right out of you . . . I'm part
of the wind, there's no one here,
I've been dead for at least three
years . . . .

*(Background
music:
Joe
Zawinul,
"Lord, Lord,
Lord"—*

(Machinelike voice.)
DON'T-LET-
THEM-TAKE-ME-

*piano—
it keeps
going,
it's
insistent,
but it's
quiet
almost,*

TERP-TERP-TERP-TERP
TERP . . . SHE LOVES ME
MORE THAN SHE DOES . . .
HE LOVES HER MORE THAN
HE DOES . . .

curling black against the daylight sky—the smell—the smell of cordite—house to house searches—doors being kicked down—the commonness—the commonness of death—

it seems to be waiting, biding its time— it has hints of a spiritual, it's aimed at something. Two minutes of this.)

DON'T-LET-MY-SELF-GO.

DON'T-BE-MOVED-

(*Machine guns, cannons.*)

DON'T-LIS-TEN-

DON'T-FOL-LOW

DON'T-PUT-MY-SELF-OUT-

DON'T-SPOIL-A-GOOD-THING-

Jackson—George Jackson speaking—we must learn the forms of resistance—the booby trap—the silenced pistol—the pitting of the streets to slow them down—the false walls—subbasements—hidden tunnels—listen—Jackson here—it's in your hands now—we must learn the value of infiltration—infiltration—it works better for us than it does for the opposition—it's us against them—it's us against you—

DON'T-VOL-UN-TEER-

DON'T-ROCK-THE-BOAT-

DON'T-MAKE-WAVES-

DON'T-LIFT-A-FIN-
GER-

DON'T-JOIN-IN-

(*Gunfire sounds stop abruptly.*)

BAM . . . BAM . . . BAM . . .
BAM . . . BAM . . . BAM . . .
BAM . . . BAM . . .

TERP-TERP-TERP-TERP . . .
DO YOU THINK I'M AT ONE
WITH YOU? . . . DO YOU
THINK I THINK YOU'RE AT
ONE WITH ME? . . .

I'm not trying to keep you in
suspense . . . I don't want to
keep you hanging . . . like those
scissors I've told you about . . .
they remind me, of course, of my
grandmother's death . . . a gleam
of steel in the air . . . a smell in
the night . . . the smell of toast in
the hallway . . . I smelled it as I
walked up the stairs to our
apartment, just before they told me
that my grandfather had died . . .
out of the four walls . . . the spirit
had flown . . . the open window
. . . But that was long before my
grandmother died . . . My
grandmother's window faced the
street . . . and, every afternoon, as
I returned home from school, I
hesitated, slowed down, as I
approached the corner . . . the
final corner . . . where I had to
look up, where I could see her
window . . . and I knew that, one
day, I would see my grandmother
leaning out the window, flailing her
arms, moaning, banging her head
on the window . . . because my

TERP-TERP-TERP . . . LOVE
ME . . . OVER . . .
UNDERSTAND ME . . . LATER
. . . LET ME BE MYSELF . . .
ME BE YOURSELF . . .

MASS MEETING . . . BE
THERE . . . STRIKE . . .
STRIKE . . . DON'T BE A
SCAB . . .

father had just died . . . that's
how I would know, and, alone,
outside, on the corner, I would have
to decide what to do . . . where
to go . . . whether or not to return
home . . . I don't have anything
to associate with my father's
actual death . . . it didn't happen
the way I had planned . . . but,
by the time it happened, after I
had known it for so long, his death
really didn't matter . . . But I'm
skipping ahead . . . that was seven
years after my grandmother died
. . . I'll have to slow down . . .
wait for another night to tell
you . . . This is Vater Accons . . .
the program is "Back Tic" . . .
till the next time . . .

*(In the
background:
now, the
Modern
Jazz
Quartet,
"Columbine"
—dominant*

(*Machinelike voice.*)

THE-RES-TRAINT- *vibes—
casual,
but with
a base of
formality—
everything
is easy,
regular,*

THE-STOP-

*(Background: crickets. Foreground:
my voice in a whisper—on top of
this, my voice throws certain words
in different directions, onto different
levels, pitches.)*

I love you the way Vito Acconci
never could love you—

I understand you like he could never
understand you—

Rest easy—

everyday
—then,
suddenly,
a pause,
a hesitant
push
outward—
an approach
to grandeur.
Two
minutes
worth.)

THE-CON-TAIN-
MENT-

You're free now—

Look, there are openings—

(*Crickets.*)

I respect you the way Vito
Acconci never could respect you—

THE-RE-TEN-
TION-

I'm never disappointed in you, the
way he was—

THE-HOLD-

I believe in you more than he ever
could—

I won't blame you like he did—

THE-LIM-ITS-

Breathe easy—

We're both free now—

(*Crickets.*)

THE-CIR-CUM-SCRIP-
TION-

I never belittle you, like he always
did—

I let you be yourself, the way he never did—

I'm always honest with you, more than he could ever be—

I never try to outdo you, like he always did—

(*Crickets.*)

Feel free—

We're on our own now—

We're out of sight now—

Look, there's no end—

(*Sound of crickets stops abruptly.*)

THE-PRE-SER-VA-TION-

THE-MAIN-TEN-ANCE-

THE-SAFE-TY-

THE-END-

Why did I go to the movie again, just so I could see, once more, the blond head enter the frame from the left, blocking out the scene of Roman ruins? . . . why, since I'm asking questions like this, did I buy the book whose price had been raised, and not the copy sitting

BAM . . . BAM . . . BAM . . . .
BAM . . . LOCK . . . ARMS . . . .
FELLOW WORKERS . . . .
DIRECT ACTION . . . .

WOOOOOOOH . . . WOOOOOOOH . . . DON'T BE AFRAID . . . DON'T LOOK BACK . . . DON'T THINK AHEAD . . .

SO YOU THINK YOU KNOW EVERYTHING? . . . STAY ON THE GROUND THEN . . . WE'LL HAVE NOTHING TO DO WITH YOU . . .

next to it, that still carried the old, cheaper price? . . . now comes the chain of questions . . . why did I walk back and forth in front of the restaurant for forty minutes, until I met a friend and was forced to go in? . . . why did I argue with him at the door and then, when he left angrily and I had to enter alone, why did I sit at the table for six, refusing to change my seat? . . . I could go on forever now . . . why did I look down as I walked, careful to step on each crack in the sidewalk . . . why did I keep trembling in my seat, continuing to stare at her even after she had turned around and I was certain she wasn't the person I had to avoid? . . . keep them coming now . . . why did I walk with the heavy package in my hands, refusing taxis, though I knew it would exhaust me, and I would have to sleep when I finally got home, letting the package be stolen from me? . . . why did I go to the store that I knew wouldn't have what I wanted? . . . Why did I tell him one version of the story in front of her, to whom I had just told another version? . . . These are the items I keep in the back of my mind . . . these are the things you never hear about . . . these

LOOK AT THE DOGS WITH PRIVATE BATHS . . LOOK AT THE CHILDREN EATING OUT OF GARBAGE CANS . .

(Background: sound of a hammer —slow, but insistent. Foreground: on top of my whisper, my voice attempts a drawn-out Midwestern accent.)

We are the Wobblies—the Wobblies—this is the Patterson strike—listen—it's six o'clock—it's a February morning—there's the mill whistle—the signal to begin work—begin work—the workers come in the bitter cold—there is the sound of looms—this is the beginning—the beginning of the silk strike—listen—we invite you to join in the song of revolt—revolt—

are some of the supports for what you hear, night after night, on "Buck Talk" . . . your host has been Vita Conchy . . .

(Background: Weather Report, "Blackthorn Rose" —slow, a surface of uncertainty, irregularity —a saxophone jumps up, jabs out— quick jabs —like a man alone, grabbing at air. Music for two minutes.)

(Machinelike voice.)
THEY-PLAY-ON-MY-DO-CIL-I-TY-

MY-PLI-AN-CY-

MY-TRAC-TA-BIL-I-TY-

THEY-USE-MY-WIL-LING-NESS-

MY-SUG-GES-TI-BIL-I-TY-

MY-CRE-DUL-I-TY-

THEY-TAKE-AD-VAN-TAGE-OF-MY-SUS-CEP-TI-BIL-I-TY-

MY-IM-PRESS-I-BIL-I-TY

Someone saw me today . . . someone caught me . . . one of you built a face around the voice that buzzes in your ear . . . a face for a wave . . . a loss in the sea . . . and Vitti Conch lost this one today . . . you caught me handily . . . I'll say that for you . . . red-handed . . . pants down in a crater . . . I was curled up in a corner, in the back of the bomb shelter . . . no, that was a joke, you should know my jokes by this time . . . you'll still let Verter Cone have his bit of fun, won't you . . . I was in the toilet . . . I didn't speak when he asked me for a cigarette—I try not to talk during

IF YOU DON'T KNOW NOW, THERE'S NOTHING WE CAN TELL YOU . . : DON'T TALK, YOU AREN'T LISTENING . . .

(Hammer sounds, alone.)

The Wobblies here—the Wobblies speaking—fight between police and strikers—look—shots by the detectives—the detectives hired by the owners—he is hit by a bullet—he is killed as he stands on the porch of his house—

(Hammer sounds, alone.)

We are the Wobblies at the scene of the funeral—the strikers pass the coffin and drop in the red carnations—the coffin is buried under the crimson symbol of the workers' blood—ready now—sing the International, the Marseillaise, the Red Flag—join in—join together—

(Hammer sounds stop abruptly.)

TATANH-TATANH-TATANH
. . . A HUNDRED FLOWERS
BLOOM . . . TATANH-
TATANH-TATANH . . .

TATANH-TATANH-TATANH
. . . LISTEN . . . MAO
HERE . . .

the day, there's too much risk of
recognition, I just shake my head,
nod my head, till I get back here
. . . but no matter, he picked me
out . . . you picked me out . . .
"You'll be on the news again," he
said . . . "You'll be in the thick of
things, you'll broadcast on the six
o'clock news" . . . I shook my
head, he had made a mistake . . .
relief . . . lost in the dark . . .
right voice for the wrong face . . .
But he insisted: "We'll see you land
in Uganda . . . we'll hear your
news from Chile . . . you'll bring
home goodies from Turkey" . . .
But not me . . . for me, always a
dull moment . . . never move,
never more . . . you know who
I am . . .

*(In the
background:
"Blackthorn
Rose"
continues
—the sax
drifts,
tapers off,
seems to
catch a
sign of
something,
starts up,
abruptly,
goes after*

(Machinelike voice.)

THEY-ARE-THE-
HYP-NO-TI-ZERS-

WOOOOOOOOOOH . . .
WOOOOOOOOH . . . THERE'S
NOTHING TO HEAR . . .
DON'T YOU FEEL IT? . . .

*(Background: sound of a jet takeoff.
Foreground: my voice in a
whisper—on top of this, my voice
shoots certain words into different
pitches, different tones.)*

There it is—

There are unknowns in our goals
toward changing—

There are unknowns in our means
of changing—

There are unknowns in our capacity
for changing—

(*Jet takes off: like a fleet of jets.*)

There they go.

There are unknowns in our
assimilation of changes—

There are unknowns in the form
into which changing will put us—

There are unknowns in the

*it—but
then the
sax stops,
maybe it
didn't go
far enough
—silence
now—
then again
sax gives
out a
short
scream,
it's off
searching
again,
grabbing
again.
For two
minutes.)*

I-AM-THE-VIC-
TIM-

THEY-HAVE-ALL-
THE-AN-SWERS-

I-HAVE-NOTH-
ING-TO-SAY-

THEY-COM-MIT-THEM-
SELVES-

I-TAKE-NO-SIDES-

substance of the changes we will undergo—

There are unknowns in our substance after the changes—

(*Another jet takes off.*)

There we are—

There are no limits—

There are no limits to thinking—

There are no limits to feeling—

There are no limits to movement—

(*Sound of jets stops abruptly.*)

THEY-SE-DUCE-

I-RE-FUSE-

THEY-GO-THERE-

I-STAY-HERE-

I want to say that I hate you . . . that's what Voto Acco has to say . . . I hate you all, as you sit there around your radio . . . a ring around the rose . . . a radio to hug to your forgetful memory . . . But you can't really believe that I would be like you . . . that I would sit here, in your position . . . No . . . this is a seat where I can take a

SUBORDINATE YOURSELF . . . TATANH-TATANH . . . THE ORGANIZATION . . .

LISTEN . . . WE SAW . . . WE SAW GOD . . . DON'T . . . YOU SEE? . . .

BONG . . . BONG . . . BONG . . . NO WARMTH . . . NO SWEETNESS . . . NO VISION . . . NO WAY TO TELL YOU . . .

stand . . . a standing posture to start a run from . . . a leap . . . a decoy left behind . . . So this is a voice to coddle you . . . I've left my voice behind . . . the tapes in place . . . a tape to tie you up with . . . while I have better things to do . . . a better life than sitting here, talking to the walls . . . listening to the wind . . . a world to revolve in . . . a revolution to set turning . . . turn against you when you least expect it . . . I've left you behind . . . Listen . . . look before I leap . . . while you listen, I'm out there, behind your back, fucking your daughter . . . But you don't believe me . . . it's as if I can see your sneer . . . I can hear your laughter . . . I can smell your anger at being tricked . . . Yes, my face is red tonight, for having lied to you . . . my heart lies open . . . lay of the land is open to us . . . close the landing gear . . . "Trick Back": that's the program . . . Look out for me, while you listen . . . try and find me, if you can . . . .

(There's insistence in the background— Duke

(Machinelike voice.)

TATANH-TATANH-TATANH . . . UNITY . . . THE WHOLE NATION . . . ALL OF US . . .

(Background: marching soldiers. Foreground: my voice, telegraphic

whisper—on top, my voice attempting a Chinese accent, near-parody.)

We are Mao Tse-tung—listen—there is only one way to eliminate war— we must oppose war with war— counterrevolutionary war with revolutionary war—national counterrevolutionary war with national revolutionary war— counterrevolutionary class war with revolutionary class war—

(Sounds of marching, alone.)

Listen—Mao speaking—where do correct ideas come from—they do not drop from the skies—they come from social practice—the struggle for production—the class struggle— scientific experiment—

O-NO-

O-GOD-

PLEASE-NO-

O-HELP-

PLEASE-NOT-THAT-

GOD-NO-

HAVE-PIT-Y-

Ellington, "Portrait of Wellman Braud"— heavy bass line— but it's a soft insistence, a restrained drive—it knows it has plenty of time—now and then, the sax punches forward —then the group carries on the punch but it's saving its punch at the same time— the bass mellows it, picks the way and smooths it over at once. Two minutes.)

(*Sounds of marching, alone.*)

Listen—Mao Tse-tung here—what we demand is the unity of politics and art—art—the unity of revolutionary political content—political content—and the highest perfection of artistic form—artistic form—listen—we must carry on a struggle on two fronts—a struggle on two fronts—

(*Marching stops abruptly.*)

GIVE-ME-A-CHANCE-

HAVE-MER-CY-

O-WHY-

NO-NO-

GOD-HELP-

PLEASE-JUST-THIS-ONCE-

I don't think I ever told you how my mother hung the scissors . . . when she argued with my grandmother . . . after the arguments . . . she hung the scissors on the kitchen wall . . . the blades spread apart, the scissors alone on the white wall . . . room to work their power . . . the blades were pointed toward my grandmother's house . . . sharp as a woman's nails, if only my mother had thought like that . . . target . . . cast the heart out . . . a curse on my grandmother's house . . . points of doom in her direction

BONG . . . BONG . . . BONG . . . IT'S HERE . . . GOD IS HERE . . . ALL YOU HAVE TO DO IS . . . ALL YOU HAVE TO DO TO HAVE IT IS . . .

. . . And then, one day, my grandmother died . . . heart attack on the kitchen floor . . . her face crushed on the kitchen sink . . . My mother found her . . . once again, door slam out in the hall . . . then the door to our apartment . . . more than once this time . . . not just my mother, the woman upstairs came running in, too . . . back and forth . . . in and out . . . my grandmother's house, our house, through the hall . . . dead woman in the house across the hall, while I tried to subtly lower "The Make-Believe Ballroom" on the radio, so no one would notice, so no one would know I hadn't anticipated this great event, this final blow, the tolling of the bell . . . I stared at the kitchen wall . . . How had she done it? . . . my clever mother . . . smart as a whip, she didn't need to go to the opera . . . How had she done it so quickly? . . . I knew the scissors had been there, hung there, on the wall, the night before . . . my mother knew, too . . . she knew she had to get them away, hide the evidence, before anyone was the wiser . . . even her children couldn't be trusted . . . But of course she knew I knew . . . we both knew why my grandmother lay dead across the hall . . .

WEEEOOOOOO-
WEEEEEEEOOOOOOO-
WEEOOOOOOO . . . YOU ARE
EUROPE . . . YOU ARE
FINISHED . . . YOU ARE
OVER . . .

LISTEN . . . A NEW LEAF . . . A NEW MAN . . . FANON . . . THIS IS FRANTZ FANON SPEAKING . . . OVER HERE . . .

rotting hulk waiting for my father to come home from his bathrobes . . . the scissors, probably, already destroyed, as easy as burning holy pictures . . . And that's why my mother and I became so close . . . accomplices in silence . . . we silently swore to each other that we would keep even more silent, forever silent . . . So that's how I became an only child . . . no one else could be on my mother's mind from that moment on . . . the mind of the criminal . . . wary eyes . . . the word caught in her throat . . . caught in my throat, too, as I became the accessory . . . the support . . . the pillar of strength . . . Enough . . . I've talked too much already . . . This is Vic Accone . . . "Back Track" is the program . . . there's always another night . . . yes, it's always night . . .

(The background now is Chick Corea and Return to Forever, "Where Have I Known You Before"—winding sound, almost

(Machinelike voice.) THE-VOICE-OF-THE-TEMPT-ER-

(Background: tolling of bells. Foreground: my voice in a whisper—on top of this, my voice stretches out to different ranges.)

That was the day we saw God face to face—

(Bells—bells.)

Wait—you've dropped out, you're not joining in—come on, it's easy, repeat after me, do as I do—

The obscurity was a light—

There were no images—

The feeling of multiplicity disappears—

(*Bells—bells.*)

No—you don't believe it yet—say it louder—don't you get it—see—

Suddenly we felt a fire within us—

exotic, something Eastern here—but it comes back in time, it comes closer—closer, closer, but the organ still tries to go higher—it's wavering, it's trying not to be an organ, it seems to be trying to be a piercing wind. It goes on for two minutes.)

THE-CALL-OF-DU-TY

THE-CLAIMS-OF-CON-SCIENCE-

THE-SENSE-OF-DU-TY-

THE-STAND-ING-BACK

THE-TURN-ING-OF-MY-BACK-

Suddenly we saw the blood trickle down from under the robes of the statue—

Suddenly the face became a movement of light—

The sound echoed in the mountains and came back, it came directly toward us, we felt a rattle in our bodies, we could hear the wings inside us—

(*Bells—bells.*)

You're shying away from it—you won't say it with us—it's easy, repeat, start from the beginning—

(*Sound of bells stops abruptly.*)

THE-SIT-TING-ON-THE-FENCE-

THE-THROW-ING-IT-A-SIDE-

THE-LAUGH-ING-AT-IT-

Nobody looks anymore . . ; nobody stands for hours in front of the painted wall . . . so I'm forced, now, to overturn my business . . . I, who should be pushing my hand to work, running it over a tight canvas . . . I, who

YOU'RE A PUPPET . . . SNAP OUT OF IT . . . COME INTO THE THIRD WORLD . . .

WEEEEEEOOOOOOOOO . . . WEEEEEEEEE-OOOOOOOOOOOOOO . . .

should be fitting a granite memory on top of its pedestal of wooden dramatics . . . so I'm reduced now to talking it over . . . forced to resort to my voice in the wilderness . . . and Veeder Kinch has this to say: nobody goes to museums anymore . . . but you don't remember those times . . . you know the word, of course . . . you know the place . . . the place we come to now to muse in . . . loiter in . . . the place we come to when we want our minds to wander, when we want to wonder at what we've chosen to remember . . . Once, this place had pictures hanging over the walls . . . our eyes were blocked there . . . we had to look, we couldn't look right through them . . . But everything is clear now . . . finally, now, our minds are empty . . . we can close our eyes now while I speak in pictures . . . see the woman out of the blue run into the triangular red . . . see the purple cover the child's hand . . . wait until the quickly applied yellow comes to rest in the slowly expanding green . . . wait . . . don't let your eyes open . . . the orange is too strong to look at . . . I'll give it to you in small doses . . . This is Virt Kincher . . . my program is "Bicker Take" . . .

BARROOOOOM . . . SSSSSSH . . . SSHHWOOOOOOMMM . . . MORE . . . THE END . . . EVERYTHING . . . NOTHING . . .

NO . . . NO RESTRAINT . . . NO REST . . . DON'T YOU? . . . CAN'T YOU? . . . WON'T YOU? . . . BEYOND . . . BEYOND . . .

(Background: police-car sirens. Foreground: my voice whispers slowly, "telegraphically"—above this, my voice attempts a French accent, near-parody.)

We are Frantz Fanon—listen—no third Europe—we will not imitate Europe—listen—the West saw itself as a spiritual adventure—it is in the name of the spirit that Europe has legitimized the slavery in which it holds four-fifths of the world—

(Sirens.)

Listen—Fanon speaking—two centuries ago, the USA, a former European colony, decided to catch up with Europe—it succeeded—it became a monster—

(Duke Ellington in the background again, this time with "Bourbon Street Jingling Jollies"—but it's not at all jolly, it's wistful, soft—something's been lost, there's an attempt to get back to something here—re-create it if it isn't there anymore—the beat is Latin, but the significance is more general than that, more dreamlike than that. Two minutes.)

(Machinelike voice.)

THIS-IS-MY-PLACE.

I-HAVE-NO-WINGS-

THEY-MEAN-NOTH-ING-TO-ME-

WHY-SHOULD-I-GO.

(*Sirens alone.*)

Listen—Fanon here—today we are present at the stasis of Europe—comrades, let us flee from this motionless movement—this movement where, gradually, dialectic changes into the logic of equilibrium—

(*Sirens.*)

We are Frantz Fanon—no, we do not want to catch up with anyone—what we want to do is go forward, night and day, in the company of all men—

(*Sound of sirens stops abruptly.*)

THERE'S-NO-WHERE-BUT-HERE-

I-HAVE-ON-LY-MY-SELF-

HERE-IS-MY-HOME-

WHO-CAN-OF-FER-MORE-

NO-OTH-ER-WORLDS-ARE-VIS-I-BLE-

I know that my wrists and ankles are strapped down . . . I know that, a minute ago, a bucket of cold water was thrown on me, and I was covered with wet rags . . . I know that the record player is still on, it's being turned up now, full-blast . . . I know the tune by now, the record has been playing over and over, the same one, I know the words by heart:

SSHHWOOOOOOOM . . .
SSHWOOOOMM . . . I . . .
YOU . . . HE . . . SHE . . .
THEM . . . US . . . NO ONE
. . . NOTHING YET . . .

HAH-HAH . . . YEAH-YEAH
. . . PIG AMERICA . . .
YOU'RE PART OF IT, AREN'T
YOU? . . . YOU LOVE IT,
DON'T YOU? . . .

HAH-HAH-HAH-HAH-HAH . . .

"White-Light-White-Heat" . . .
I know that the electrode is being
passed, up and down, over my
body . . . I know that now it's
being applied to my genitals . . .
I know what it feels like . . .
Vetta Keen has this to say: it's as if
they're dragging my kidneys and
my bladder out with a pair of
tongs . . . I know all this and I
say to myself, keep it inside . . .
don't make a move . . . don't cause
a fuss . . . nobody wants to hear
. . . of course you don't . . . and
I don't either, I don't want to hear
myself think . . . why should I
think of what I can't do a thing
about? . . . I'm the same as I was
. . . it can't touch me . . . it can't
happen here . . . We'll be the
same tomorrow night . . . listening
to "Block Tack" . . . this is your
host, Vitter Ack . . .

*(In the
background:
Ellington
continues
with
"Bourbon
Street
Jingling
Jollies",—
so that's
what the
Latin beat*

(Machinelike voice.)

THE-RE-JEC-
TION-

SHWOOOOOOMMMM . . .
DRIVE . . . COME ON . . .
COME IN . . . DEEPER . . .
LOSE IT . . . GIVE WAY . . .
GIVE ALL . . . GIVE UP . . .

*(Background: thunderstorm.
Foreground: my voice in a whisper—
above this, my voice ranges out
into different areas.)*

Ready now.

has been doing— there's an energy here, a passion, that's deceptive— the passion has been beaten down, but it hasn't dissolved, it's spread out, it's become stronger but secret, it's intertwined itself inside. Two minutes of music.)

THE-NE-GA-TION-

THE-RE-PU-DI-A-TION-

THE-DE-NI-AL-

THE-RE-CAN-TA-TION-

THE-AB-NE-GA-TION-

We'll take our places.

You over here, under me.

Then him, under you—

And her over me—

As for you, there, you'll put this on and push through her into me—

(*Thunderstorm.*)

Remember: you, before the moment, will take it out of her—

He will hold it then and drown the other one with it as she stands watching, she'll be baptized into us—

(*Thunderstorm.*)

Now we will bring more numbers into our party—

THE-RE-BUFF-

> Finally we have no desire—
>
> Each of us is equal, each is
> interchangeable—

THE-RE-VO-CA-
TION-

> Here I am, you don't see anyone,
> there's nothing here—
>
> Here we are, we are above
> existence here—

THE-RE-FU-SAL-

> (*Thunderstorm ends abruptly.*)

It is pitch black in here. I hear whispering and then a kind of crackling. "Loscha! . . . Loscha!" I open my eyes. Loscha is my Totzil name. The fire snaps into thin flames, filling the mud hut with greasy smoke. PLUNK. PLANK. The women are shucking corn into a big iron pot of boiling water. "Loscha . . . Loscha. . . ." The women are giggling, talking to me in Totzil. I don't know any Totzil except my name. One of the women hands me a corn cob and I begin to pry off the kernels. Black. Yellow. Red. Each color means something but I can't remember the code. We scoop the kernels into a bucket, then wrap them in linen. A little boy darts into the hut. The old woman hands him the soggy linen sack. He runs out with it. She pushes me after him. I don't understand, and turn around. She shoves me roughly down the hill. "Loscha!" She is laughing and pointing at the boy who is running down the slope. I start to trot after him, then look back. She is smiling approvingly, waving me away. I am barefoot. Rocks cut into my feet as I try to catch up. We run down the trail, across a stubbled cornfield, through a pine wood. "Wait for me! Wait up!" I call, but I seem to be talking to myself. It is still dark. The valley far below is covered with thick white fog. Several peaks jut up through the fog like islands. We seem to be the only highland survivors of a bizarre and disastrous milk flood. We are running along a ridge. My feet begin to bleed. We run through a farmyard, chickens squawk and flap their wings. I am panting, "Not so fast! Slow down!" The sun comes up over the mountains and the boy picks up our pace. I watch our long dark shadows as they flow easily over fences, fields, glide over the surface of a stream. I can't run any further. "I DON'T KNOW WHERE WE'RE GOING AND I DON'T KNOW WHY WE'RE GOING THERE AND I DON'T KNOW HOW TO ASK!" I yell after him with my last breath. He stops, pivots on his plastic heel, smiles, and trots away across the field.

It's sunny today. I'm beginning to sand down the four beams that hold up the roof in my new loft. The first layer of paint is battleship gray, cracked and flaking. Underneath the gray is a sturdy layer of dark brown, thick and tough as leather. It spews off in tiny hard chunks that ricochet against the walls. Underneath is an even thicker layer— blistered dark green. I sand it away. Underneath is an oozing liver-colored substance, which gums up and breaks the sander. I start to scrape it off but the stuff begins to slither down the beams with a horrifying kind of liveliness. I wait a few days, camping out by the stove. There is no heat. Pigeons fly in and out. On Saturday, all the big liners blow their horns and leave for Europe, gliding silently past my windows. It is dry enough now. I continue to sand, reaching the pine at last. Powdered wood covers everything. It sticks in my eyelashes, propping my eyes open into a wooden stare. Beaches grow up around the beams. Mark comes by. "Say, do you know it's still alive in there?" he says, casually knocking on one of the beams. "What do you mean?" I say. "Yeah, sure," he says, "it's still alive in the center—it takes a hundred years for one of these mothers to die off." He picks up a hand-ful of sawdust, lets it slip through his fingers. "Yep. I can tell just look-ing at this . . . Listen, just pack about ten feet of dirt around each beam, mix in some fertilizer, then you have to graft some bark on to bring the juices to the surface and you'll see, in a few months you'll have yourself a real healthy pine. Well, gotta' go—catch you later." It is dark. I am sitting in a pile of sawdust. Would it work? It's true, I've seen telephone poles take root and send out branches that tangle in the wires! I look at the beams. They seem to be moving slightly. I fall asleep. From every knothole, a toothpick pops out. They sprout into 1 x 1s, then branch out into 2 x 3s. Soon my whole loft is a bizarre living lumberyard. I wake up, my mouth full of sawdust.

The sky is bright blue today. It is quiet. I haven't spoken for two weeks. In the middle of the lake, I unfold the map and look for the unnamed river that feeds into this lake. An ancient Cree trail runs along the river. The man at the Hudson Bay Company said the trail hadn't been used for about a hundred years. "But it's still there," he said, "we can see it from our planes." I paddle north-northeast toward the river. In two hours, I reach the mouth. I tie the canoe to a branch and, balancing my fishing rod, I climb up through the dead wood that lines the shore. As I step on a log, it rolls out from under me and I slip into the cool water. I wade onto the bank. Thick curtains of vines grow between the closely packed trees. It's dark in here. Branches snap back into my face. I am slogging through a swamp. Suddenly, I feel a tugging on the rod. I feel my eyes growing round. I turn around slowly, expecting to face an ancient and angry Cree warrior. No one. In my hand the rod is tense and flexed. All the line is out. I retrace my steps, slowly reeling in the line. I undrape it from limbs, pull it away from the sticky and delicate vine tendrils that have snared it, untie the little knots snarled around stumps and bushes. I have no extra line so I am careful. It is taking a long time. At the end of the line, I find the red and white lure dangling from a pine branch, slowly turning around and around, glinting in the sun. I reach the boat and start to untie the rope. The knot doesn't loosen. I pull harder. It tightens. I look at the knot. My heart starts to pound. I begin to sweat. I didn't tie this knot! It is one of the most complex yet economical knots I have ever seen. It loops around the branch twice, then doubles in on itself in a kind of clove. I hear myself say "Cree!" My voice is hoarse, cracked. The woods suddenly look black. The lost trail takes on maplike precision.

I've already seen three movies today. This one will make four. It's raining hard and the line for *Scenes from a Marriage* stretches for two blocks up Second Avenue. Everyone in line is wet and in a foul mood. The smell of sopping wool and hot dog steam from the vendors' carts makes me feel sick. I am crying. I've been crying off and on for hours now. Actually, I'm trying not to cry but I can't help it. My shoulders are shaking. My nose is running. I don't want anyone to see me like this. I pull the umbrella down as far as it will go. The wire spokes press into my skull. The black silk is ripped away from the spokes in two places and the exposed metal tips are jabbing into passersby as they push their way along the crowded sidewalk. Forty-five minutes go by. The rain suddenly stops and the mood of the crowd becomes lighter, expectant. I pretend not to hear the remarks around me. "Rain's over and that woman still has her umbrella up!" "Sure is taking up a lot of room with that umbrella!" I can feel a waterlogged wool pantleg pushing against my leg. "HEY! Someone should tell her the rain's over!" The line is beginning to thicken in spots as people who have been waiting out the storm in restaurants come back to claim their places. Little arguments about who was first break out up and down the line. Someone begins to knock on my umbrella as if it were a door. I try to ignore it. KNOCK KNOCK, "Uh, miss, hate to tell you but the rain's over. You can take it down now." I pull the umbrella down farther. "One please," I say at the ticket booth. I start to walk in. An usher rushes up, thrusts his head under the umbrella. "Listen, miss," his voice resounds as if in an echo chamber, "you can't come into the theatre with your umbrella open like that. House rules," he says and then disappears. I put the ticket in my pocket and walk the eighty-one blocks home. It starts to rain again. I always mean to see Bergman films but for some reason or other I always seem to miss them.

I am staying here at Richard's place. He's been away for two weeks now. It's Sunday afternoon—cold and bright. The coffee is bitter. I've been looking at her pictures all morning. They're all over the place, it's impossible to avoid them. From here, I can see the one over the sink. She's wearing a cap. One end of a blade of grass is clamped between her teeth. The other end is held lightly in her hand—a large almost extra-anatomical hand that juts in from the bottom of the photograph. A road stretches into the background. It's probably Sweden, where she lives. In the bathroom, there are three strips of photo-booth photographs. She is smiling self-consciously, wearing a funny hat and dark glasses. I wonder how Richard could really be in love with both of us. On the bookshelf, two photographs are glued together on the same piece of paper. She is wearing the same dark turtleneck in both. In the one on the right, her expression is slightly different. An eyebrow is raised and one corner of the mouth is pressed down, as if for balance. They seem to be some kind of before-and-after photographs. Near the window, I see her smiling seductively, wearing a striped scarf. She has blond hair, probably blue eyes too, though all the photographs are black and white. On the closet door, she stands on the beach. Her pants are rolled up and the tide is either coming in or going out. It's getting dark now. I am trying to remember the dream I had about her last night. She and I are lovers. We live together in Richard's loft. I notice that her hair is blonder than it seems in her photographs. We lie on Richard's sculpture and make love the whole afternoon. She has a wonderful sense of humor and we laugh together as we use all of Richard's tools to drill holes in the walls. After we make love, she makes dinner for us: cold cuts. She's really a great cook. Half the meat is grayish-white; the other half is day-glo red. It is delicious. She is so tender, so kind, so dazzling. I think I have never been so much in love.

I'm hiking through the woods in northern Canada. I haven't seen anyone for days. It's growing dark. Near a lake, I see six white canvas tents pitched on a steep gravel slope. There is no other sign of life. I walk up to the biggest tent. I can hear rattling and banging going on inside. There are voices too, and some whistling. I knock on the canvas flap, then realize this is making no sound. Suddenly, the flap is pulled back and I am face to face with a squint-eyed man in white. "TABERNACLES! UNE FEMME!" he says and drops a stack of plates. At the table, six large men in red plaid shirts stop eating and stare at me. There is stew in their open mouths. They begin talking all at once in French. "Il ya trois mois quand j'ai vu une femme," the squint-eyed man whispers in my ear as he hands me a cup of tea with soap bubbles floating lightly on the surface. After dinner, the geologists insist I be their guest for the night in "La Musée de Balzac." They light a lantern and lead me into a small tent filled with samples of soil, rocks, crystals, petrified wood, all wrapped in canvas bags and labeled. In the refrigerator, chunks of ice are stored in plastic bags. "We are studying the rates of the glaciers which will have been coming down," explains the only geologist who knows English. He tells me this tent is called "Balzac's Museum" because a few months ago an Englishman had stumbled on their wilderness camp. He stayed for five weeks, cooking for the geologists dishes he called "Turkish" and "Moroccan" which were basically mixtures of Cream of Wheat, blueberries and chocolate chips. He says the Englishman was traveling light, except for the complete works (in paperback) of Balzac. Late every night they heard him reading aloud from this tent, changing his voice for each character, singing songs from Balzac. "Ma fanchette est charmante/dans sa simplicité/O Richard! O mon roi!/L'univers t'abandonné/Broum Broum Broum," he sings. The other geologists join in the song. "J'ai longtemps parcouru le monde/Et l'on m'a vu/Tra la la la la la." I am no longer sure who's imitating who.

It is December and blowing hard. I walk into the aqua reception room. The nurse weighs at least two hundred pounds. There is blood on her miniskirt. She wears three strings of flaking, bulbous pearls and a huge ring that looks like it might be a small missing part of a Chevrolet—an essential part—without which the car would explode when the ignition is turned. She says, "Forty dollars, please." The doctor walks in. He appears to be her son. He is dressed in lime green and wears a peaked hat, the kind McDonalds chefs wear. "Well, well," he says. His accent is Arabic. In the hall, a woman is crying hysterically, "I HAD the extraction two WEEKS ago and I still haven't gotten my period! Someone HELP ME! I know he didn't get it all out! I can feel a big . . . SOMETHING . . . growing inside!" I look at the doctor. He is saying "risks." I can't understand his English very well. I write out the check. "Come with me, please," says the nurse. The Orientation Room is crammed with little desks. On each desk, there is a lamp, a stack of pamphlets, and a conch shell filled with cigarette butts. I smoke nervously, looking around at the American Airline travel posters and the gigantic diagrams of uteruses. I stub out the cigarette in the fleshy pink curve of the conch shell. It wobbles under the pressure. In the recovery room, I sit up in bed, feeling numb. Two male attendants wheel a woman in on a cart. The paper gown is twisted up around her shoulders. I notice that I am wearing an identical, crumpled paper gown. Her red body is shaking like rubber. Her eyes are wide open, only the whites show. She is talking loudly as if she were gossiping but the words are garbled. The attendants hold her by the thighs and shoulders. They are speaking Spanish. There are white hand prints on her body where their pressure had squeezed the blood away from the surface. "OLA," they say, hoisting her into bed. In the bodega next to my loft, half the meat is grayish white; the other half is day-glo red. Usually, I buy the red even though I know I'm being tricked.

It's November. We're out riding across the stubbled cornfields. The horses are breathing heavily, cantering fast, glad to be out in the cold. The creeks are beginning to ice over now. The cracks in the ruts are filled with brittle slivers of muddy brown ice. Everything seems clear and flat against the deep blue sky. My father is riding ahead. Suddenly, his mare begins to cough, a deep ratcheting sound that fills the thin air. Her pace slackens. She stops short in a grove of pines. I pull up next to her and watch as her eyes begin to swell, filling with blood. Her mouth is open, her yellow teeth bared. Her legs shake violently, begin to crumple. They buckle under. She is on her knees now, my father sitting slightly forward in the saddle as if he's about to jump over a hedge. His mouth is open but he is too surprised to say anything. Without a sound, the mare rolls over on her side and dies. Out of the blue, it begins to snow. My mother gallops up, followed by the Dalmatians. The dogs see the horse, then back away, barking and growling. "Hemorrhage," says my mother, ". . . the colon . . ." My father pries himself out from under the horse. One of his boots comes off. It lies on the hard ground, steam streaming out the end of the shiny brown tube. Snowflakes are melting on its warm surface. He stands on one leg, occasionally touching his stockinged foot on the frozen ground for balance. "You know, if you were really a sport," says my mother, "you'd go home and get another mount." It is dark now and snowing hard. My mother and I are driving over the bumpy fields in the jeep. In the beams of the headlights, the swirling snowflakes look like sparks. In the pine grove, near a big snowdrift, we find the mare, bloated almost beyond recognition, covered with a thick blanket of snow. She looks like a huge beached whale washed up on a bright white beach. My mother takes out a large pair of scissors. Bending over the swollen mare's body, she cuts off the tail. "For a fly whisk," she says. The pine trees are loaded with snow now. The branches are creaking.

On Ward's Island, I am walking towards the old abandoned hospital. As I get closer, I see a bare light bulb burning on the porch. A blue Chevrolet pulls up and a woman hops out. She smiles. "My name is Nora. I am a nurse," she says in a heavy brogue. Her face is three inches from mine. "I live here—haven't been off the island in about three years. Would you like a tour?" Inside, we come to a triple-locked door covered with green construction paper cutouts of shamrocks and leprechaun decals. "This is my room," she says. Inside the closet-sized room, there are small inflated rubber leprechauns on top of the TV. An Irish flag hangs from one antenna, an American flag from the other. Between the antennae, a crucifix hangs on the wall. The bureau is covered with doilies and dozens of chipped Hummel figures. There is a large crewel work view of a town in a pine frame on the wall. The plastic title plate says "Dublin At The Turn Of The Century." On the bed, there are piles of tiny, elaborately crocheted pillows. A large red-and-green foil mobile hangs from the ceiling. It is surrounded by several smaller silver mobiles slowly revolving. Christmas lights outline the window, which is covered with sprayed-on snowflakes. Shellacked magazine photographs of green fields and sunsets cover the floor. Nora sets the tea things on the floor, brings out a box of fancy cookies. "Well well now, what brings you here?" she asks. "Well," I say, "I'm going around to different places—institutions—that kind of thing—and sleeping there to see if . . . to see if the place will become—you know—will be part of my dream." For the first time, this seems like an utterly ridiculous project—a complete waste of time. "Well, that sounds—nice," says Nora. "I'm a collector too, as you can see," waving her hand around the room. "Don't think I don't know how hard it is—it takes time and patience to be a really good collector. I mean, just don't think I don't know how difficult it can be." She pours the tea. Light is streaming through the window making snowflake patterns on the floor.

I am sitting in the snack car of a CNR express, talking in French with a man who is asking me what I do. It's difficult to describe what a "performance" is without saying "theatre." Suddenly, I hear a clear voice in English. "The man wants to know if you are an actress," says the man sitting across the aisle. "May I join you?" he says, sliding into the seat next to me. His name is Ronald. His eyes are bright blue and wild. He is bony. He is talking now, quickly, feverishly, about the leaflets he prints up in various cities ("I'm always on the move.") . . . the new world . . . Charles Fourrier . . . translations of the work of a man writing somewhere in Europe ("I can't divulge where."). Ronald runs a place in Vancouver where people meet and talk. It is a long hallway. I'm on my way to Chicago but when the train stops in Montreal, I get off with Ronald. We take a taxi to a clapboard house on a side street. "Ronald! Ronald! Where have you been? We haven't seen you in a year!" say his friends and they go off to the Annual Artists' Ball. Ronald shows me his viola. It is strung backwards "because of my broken shoulder," he says. From his pack, he unfolds several yards of tie-dyed cotton. He covers the light with it. "I always make tie-dyed curtains as gifts for my friends but the next time I come to their house, the curtains are always gone. 'We don't know what happened to them,' they always say," he says. We are making love now. I'm afraid I will be swallowed into his great hollow mouth. ("Do you think I'm off my rocker, Laurie?") My thighs cushion his sharp-bladed bones. We merge into a joint creature, unaware of itself, moving slowly in the tie-dyed light. "We are the chosen ones," he is saying, his voice muffled in my armpit. "We continue because the pain is so real." I am standing in the doorway now, half inside, half outside. The last train for Chicago is in fifteen minutes. "You will never leave us," Ronald is saying. I am holding his long thin hands. The cab arrives and honks.

78

The Greyhound bus pulls up in front of the huge estate. "Waxwold Estate! Last stop!" the driver bellows. "All out!" I am the only one on the bus. I walk along the hedge, over the lawns and into the drawing room. Across the hall, I see a half-open door. I put my hand on the knob and pull but it doesn't open. I see it is nailed into this position at the top and bottom of the jamb. A voice from inside calls, "Come in! The door's open!" I wedge sideways through the door. "Dinner's ready," says my mother, nodding toward the table. My whole family is sitting at the long table. The cook places a cereal box in front of each person. We read the labels with mild attention. There is the concentrated, almost deafening sound of ten people slowly munching. My sister compares the amount of niacin in her box of Wheaties with the niacin content of my brother's Cheerios. My father reads a joke from the back of his box of Trix. We have all heard this joke many times. We laugh uproariously. We laugh because it is so familiar. We know all the punch lines, puzzles, anagrams, and nutritional facts listed on the boxes. Now we are more or less just mulling them over. The cook removes the boxes. There is a CRASH and the sound of suction as the cook and all the cereals disappear into the whirlpool. I look out the picture window. It is summer. Several of my brothers and sisters, dressed in matching apricot-colored parkas, are holding onto ropes attached to a tractor and skiing over the slippery lawn—a Midwest version of horse-drawn skiioring. "YAHOO! YAHOO!" they yell sportingly as the tractor pulls them at high speeds through the orchard, zigzagging through the nut trees, flattening the bright red beds of flowers. My eyes are open now. I look out onto Houston Street. It is Sunday morning. There is calypso music coming from the bodega. "BULA BULA BULA We're doin' the Jamaican hula Yeah Yeah Yeah." The phone rings. It is Dan. "Last night I dreamed I was one of the Hardy Boys," he says. Outside, all the trees are blowing. The leaves are beginning to loosen. It is fall.

The August heat is heavy and wet. Bees and insects are buzzing in the clover. My father and I are riding in the fields. I am following him at a gallop through the purple and yellow grasses. He is yelling back at me, "MOVE *WITH* THE HORSE . . . NOT AGAINST HIM . . . MOVE *WITH* HIM . . ." Suddenly, I feel the most incredibly intense sensation, starting in my lower back and moving up my spine until it fills my whole body. I have never felt more alive. It fills me. I want to scream and yell—to make sounds that will fit this new feeling. Does it have something to do with the saddle? I am about to yell ahead: ARE YOU FEELING THIS TOO? DO ALL GOOD RIDERS FEEL THIS WAY? But I don't shout. For the first time in my life, I am saying "No. This is just for me. I will let this sink to the very bottom. I will tell no one about this. This is mine." I ride a lot now but the feeling only comes when I least expect it. I dream about it too. Mostly, the dreams are clear and bright—a riderless horse galloping through purple and yellow fields. Other times, they are nightmares of witches. The witches are riding their broomsticks and cackling with their mouths wide open—you can see their rotting tooth stumps, their glittering fillings. They ride their bucking broomsticks, pumping the handles up and down, sliding the brooms back and forth under their black diaphanous robes. Now, all the girls in the sixth grade are sitting in the gym at Forest Glen School. We are learning about "the Curse" from a film titled *Molly Grows Up*. It begins with a shot of the moon going through its cycle—time lapsed. Cut to Molly in pigtails and a very long skirt, short white socks neatly folded down. "MOTHER! MOTHER!" Kitchen door slams. Molly runs in, breathless, gymsuit in hand. "It happened! Today! In gym class!" Holds out the gymsuit. She is smiling, gesturing. She seems utterly out of control. Cut to mother, tall, demure, blonde, wearing silk stockings. She is sweeping. "Why, that's wonderful, dear!" She continues to sweep. The stumpy broom goes back and forth, back and forth across the immaculate floor.

I am trying to read *Rapid Italian for Students and Tourists*. The 707 is rocking back and forth. The only other people on the plane are members of an all-drum band from Ghana. The forearm of the man sitting next to me keeps dropping heavily onto the page of my book. Each time the arm drops, I look over at him but he turns his head away. I can see his shiny black face reflected in the window. He is laughing to himself. The stewardess brings dinner. It is chicken cacciatore wrapped in foil, spaghetti marinara, salad, a stumpy loaf of bread, wine, aqua minerale, assorted pastries. "Wey bok home," he says, turning towards me, "we have good food." He is tearing off bits of foil, rolling it into tiny balls. "You know, I can't eat this food. At home we have good food. Yes, delicious. We have fufu." He is arranging the foil balls around the edge of the tray, alternating them with bits of wadded-up bread. "Yes, I have not eaten fufu for six month ago. Now we go to Ghana and oh! wot a day! We eat and eat fufu." He is drumming on the pastries with his fork, smashing down the sugared roses. "Now fufu is we have some corn meal and we put some water with it and mix it up so good. And oh! it is the most good!" Little rivers of aqua minerale are running through the divisions on his tray. Suddenly, he looks startled. He is whistling now—up and down the scale—almost words. I hear an answering sound, low and soft, as if all the wing bolts had jolted loose and were whistling in the wind. About twenty rows ahead, a man is whistling. "Twi," says the man sitting next to me. "We speak Twi. Twi is, we whistle. I teach you Twi song." He writes in my notebook.

ada wɔhj yi noho mia papa o

Manso Nkrɔfo nyimye koraa

Em ara dze menye bowudaa

ɔ dɔe o ɔmɔ dzen yi mano daa

"Love is a very important thing/but people don't know how to go about it/But for me I'll always be with you even in death/Darling try to give me a reply."

It is growing dark now. The fire is going out. The red light of the setting sun sweeps quickly across the lake, lighting up the crests of waves. The red glare crosses my campsite, touches the edge of the frying pan, briefly ignites the blade of my knife. For a moment, it looks like a piece of red neon glowing on the hard-packed dirt. From across the lake, I hear a motor. The snarling sound grows louder, filling the thin air. It is near the island now. Suddenly, the motor is cut. I hear oars slapping the water, then a crunching through the underbrush. Is it another Cree wandering over from the reservation to investigate the smoke? I run behind a tree. "Laurie? . . . Laurie?" "Pierre!" We stoke up the fire. Pierre plays the guitar, the same almost tuneless songs the Indians play over at the reservation as they eat the potato chips and Fritos they buy with their welfare checks. The stars come out. We talk quietly about the house he will build with a dome for his telescope, about the bison he will keep on his land. "Let's go to my cabin," he says, touching my hair. We motor across the lake. The northern lights are pulsating. Waves of green and orange sweep across the sky in thin veils of light. Needle-sharp spindles shoot up and disintegrate in bright yellow clouds. In the cabin, Pierre and I look through the stereoscopic microscope at a nugget crushed 1,700,700 years ago. We build a fire in the old Atlas stove, hold each other close. "You really shouldn't live out in the woods like that," says Pierre. "It's so much more productive to have a little cabin." He is lying on top of me now, our naked bodies pressing. The light from the fire makes his shoulders glow, touches his hair and turns it red. His lithe body moves over me, inside me. Bright red light shoots in front of my eyes. I open them. It is dark. "I CAN'T SEE!" I call. He places his cool hand on my eyes. I see the blood racing through my eyelids, streaming and pulsating. "You are everything to me," whispers Pierre. His hand grows hot and somehow, sharp. We are rocking, rocking.

We are sitting in the cold tin building. It is gray outside and freezing. The Canadian video crew is ready to roll. It's really ice cold in here. The only people who aren't bundled up to the point of mummification are the two old Cree Indians. They wear cotton shirts. The old woman is joking with the man, who is blind. I ask the translator what they are saying. She says, "She says she would have left him fifty years ago but she realizes that since he is blind he needed her and still needs her so she stays." The translator is speaking French. I wonder if there is a pluperfect in Cree. The anthropologists huddle in the corner, blowing on their hands. They are impatient to begin. They have hired the two old Indians to sing the ancestral hunting songs. The cameras are moved closer, adjusted. The floodlights are turned on. The Cree woman squints into the light. The old man's eyes are open wide. There is a sense that something important is about to happen, that we are about to hear the last sounds of a culture. We are poised for the preservation of history. The song begins. The old man is singing by himself, swaying. The woman slowly claps her hands. "HEY AH . . . HEY AH . . . HEY AH HEY . . . I am singing the songs . . . HEY AH HEY . . . HEY . . . the old songs . . . of my fathers . . . HEY AH . . . HEY AH . . . AH!AH! HEY HEY HEYAHHEY . . . and of the animals they hunted down . . . HEY . . . HEY . . . HEY. . . HEY AH HEY . . . AH HEY AH . . . but I can't remember the words . . . HEY AH . . . of the songs . . . the old songs . . . HEY . . . HEY AH HEY . . . HEY . . . HEY . . . I never knew . . . the words . . . or . . . the songs . . . HEY HEY AH . . . HHEY AH HEY HEY! . . . I never went hunting . . . in the . . . piney . . . woods . . . HEY! HEY AH HEY . . . HEY AH HEY . . . HEY . . . I am doing this . . . for money . . . I am singing . . . for some people . . . HEY . . . HEY AH HEY . . . HEY . . . AH HEY AH . . . AH! . . . HEY! . . . I remember grandfather . . . he lay . . . on his back . . . while . . . he was dying . . . HEY . . . AH HEY . . . HEY . . . I think . . . I am . . . no one . . . AH! . . . HEY!"

FOUR SELECTIONS

David Askevold

DORANATO: INITIATED, HALIFAX, FEBRUARY 1971; COMPLETED, SAN FRANCISCO, FEBRUARY 1973

I was reading a magazine while on my way to meet a friend in Doranato. I asked the stewardess for a cup of coffee. I reached in my briefcase to find another magazine, but decided instead to look through some pictures and letters of some past and continuing acquaintances. I started reading a letter from Bill Downing who says he is in Sortendo doing something or other. I sipped my coffee and looked out of the window.

A. I opened my eyes to a light green wall and ceiling. For a while I had a hard time focusing, but B. I saw the bed I was lying on, C. a small dresser, D. a light centered on the ceiling, and E. a sound was coming from the semi-open window. I got out of bed and F. tried to open it more but it was stuck. G. I could see that the room was above the fifth floor which faced the back of another building. I could only assume that I was in the vicinity of Doranato.

I retraced my steps: 1. walking through the corridor to the plane, 2. reading the magazine, 3. ordering the coffee, 4. reaching in my briefcase, 5. sipping the coffee, and 6. looking out the window. . . . a. Could I have left the plane, and b. somehow come here for some reason or other.

A.   B.   C.   D.   E.   F.   G.

                        6.   5.   4.   3.   2.

b.   a.   1.

It Continued To Rain All Day

For Some Reason People Started
To Talk About Delaware

No One Knew Anything About It

No One Had Been There Or Knew
Anyone From There

With The Rain All Day The Delaware
Ambience Works On Us

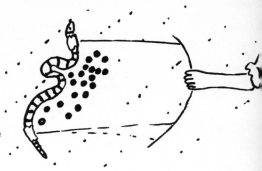

Delaware Seems To Be An Emission
Center

We Try To Reverse That Or Roll
Something Back

We Decide It Should Be A Black Hole

That Would Make It Sink

We Use The Balls To Push It A
Distance First

Some Of The Stripes Are Covered By
Holders Making Them And The Balls
Even

The Willow Tail Broke Off In The Making

If It Rolls Over I Have To Come Around
To Bring It Back

It Doesn't Usually Roll Over

I Agree To Let It Roll And Twist Over
If It Wants

We Like The Roll Better Than The Black
Hole

The Balls When Rolling Often Jam Together

They Gradually Compress Packed Tightly
Together

Delaware Is The Black Hole And Sinks

The Balls Follow The Two Leads

Matters of New Guests:

The leftover places of haunts & traces tried to spoil his fun and keep him on the run.

His muses turned to ringlet thoughts to point the way to further play. Not tilted or stilted, his demon friend he thinks he jilted. Which one squealed and which one spoke of wavy dunes and other places

One is on vacation with more predictions

Who likes the past of perfect places and forgotten careless traces "Help yourself to the dish that lets you find the worn-out miss." It keeps me straight, it keeps me clear & I don't care who put that here.

on and before july 4, 1974

The Wet Miss softened him for the Fragment Man who drove me to kill the zombi visit and The Dried-Out One spilt some blood to remove me from my babbled tongue.

My notes say there was something left from some previous three: One had turned to water, one stayed flat on the floor and the other is hard to read.

September 23, 1974

I retained only bits of short spotted incidents (to gather chattering low voices) dis-jointed quirks to fit the lineage of no place directives. Half noted combines. Publicly he thought about his muses: You can leave your long term dust bowl walk about till we get your bounty fast. *Keep it up or turn on end somewhere the middle will bend.* Leaving it he came apart and joined some distant characteristics. She had taken his burns and he had given the reason for her attractions. A purpose for now and a next step to reinstate her abilities. He would be meeting the carrier soon who would take it a distance as long as he didn't lurch. Those fragments never finished. He tried simply to put them there. *It's nice to pass an open glass it seems so small about to fall it's covered with cotton and bits of wool.* The area wrapped around me as preparing to roll. I flipped over and drifted. The band was still playing and in the other room it was almost as loud. She dropped behind the couch and started to push it away from her. There was some dust and bits of paper near the baseboard. When I came in, little puffs were coming from one end of the couch. Kneeling on the cushions, I leaned over the back as she turned her head upward. Dust was scattered through her hair and she was out of breath. I moved out of there and into the other room where the band pushed me along again. *To seem a low and casting glance past a door over the floor to the side you often glide.*

SHE TOOK HIS BURNS

HE GAVE THE REASON
FOR HER ATTRACTIONS

DRAFT FOR A SYNCRETISM

a. Random functions but toward same ends
b. Factions: Variances constituting group

1. Group spotting abnormalities outside of group
a. The Portcho-Japanese speech by the five remaining brothers

2. The poncho lacona brothers, the peasant porno teenager, the vicarious commando penetrator
a. The peasant hooded girl pickup

3. The hillside event
a. The non-lookers-on in the country bar

4. The private groupings
a. With the no-identity slinger

5. Organizing directives
a. The peasant girl turns killer by one of the six brothers

6. Modes of operation
a. She turns it over to excite the slinger

7. Ideologies in practice
a. Conversation turns to that hardly discernible nylon letter opener

8. Singular motivations within group
a. Talk takes place inside and outside

9. Plural and singular outcomes
a. The letter opener leads to Mr. B. who sits in a cream-colored chair

Sometimes the engagement begins between the porno peasant teenager and the no-identity slinger. Especially after she kills the sixth brother, dumps him out and drives his car uphill very fast through the hot dusty roadway until she comes to some trees and a single building with a bar on the ground floor. It's cool inside, the slinger facing away and she moving slowly up to him and placing her hand below his neck under his shirt as he starts to take the part of her earlier deadly action and she the part of the sixth brother. Others are seated around their respective tables and are the non-lookers-on paying absolutely no attention as the two continue their ritual until the five remaining brothers enter together asking the teenager questions.

Earlier: hot dusty—convertibles
Wood tables, old village bar—probably someplace like Spain rather than Portugal—or if a bar could be found someplace in Arizona. A small area with vegetation surrounded by a general desert environment. Then when the five Japanese-Portuguese brothers come into the bar and confront the peasant girl about their missing brother, who has picked her up earlier that day in his convertible after the other brothers, one at a time, had passed her in theirs—etc.

A short speech follows about what Mr. B. is trying to do. Of course it's very faulty because the peasant girl and the others only know the results and actions of the others but not of his, so the nylon or rayon letter opener and the cream chair and references to the driveway approach to his house—generally things like that which allow one to fill in the various scenes and Mr. B's profile.

The Portuguese-Japanese script began a number of years ago during one summer when I had an excursion ticket to London. At that time, to promote tourism to other places, the airline in collaboration with a given city or country gratuitously added a side excursion to another place. Mine was to Lisbon, Portugal. I stayed for several days watching the shoeshine men and waiters; the customers throughout the cafés would constantly enunciate psssssssst to attract a waiter's attention. The beat-up Mercedes taxis and the somewhat general diamond stick-pin Mafia-like background were some other elements.

The huge statue across the bay from Lisbon is a smaller version of the Christ overlooking the city of Rio de Janeiro. The suspension bridge crossing the bay is a scaled-down copy of the Golden Gate Bridge in San Francisco and was built by an American company, The Morrison-Kanutson Construction Co. I think it was Mr. Kanutson of the company who visited our next-door neighbors who were of Catholic faith and had five boys, all more or less a year or two apart with the exception of the youngest who was born about three or more years after the fourth. The father was also in large-scale construction. A few years ago, he and his second son were killed when their private plane crashed. This bridge usually reminds me of them with Jesus overlooking the scene—them falling from the sky into the big orange bridge.

I decided Lisbon was too expensive for my small budget which I carelessly spent too much of the first night, so a couple of days later I rented a taxi to a small town a short distance along the coast where I checked into a small family hotel. My room was in a small house near the hotel where I took my meals. The only window in my room was near ground level and faced a pigeon coop. All night the pigeons would make their sounds but I really didn't mind since the room was very cheap and included three substantial meals a day. A woman from the kitchen each morning would have some sandwiches and fruit for me to take as I left for the day. I would go to a swimming pool a few hundred meters above the beach where I rented a canvas reclining chair near the pool and read detective novels all day and occasionally jumped into the pool to cool off. The ocean was very cold and the sand bothered me. To rent a chair and a sun shield on the beach was more expensive than similar accommodations at the pool. I was quite content to spend each day at the same place and about five days of the same routine was perfect. I've never had a better vacation. I don't think I had ever had a real vacation. I'm idle some of the time but that's quite different from being really relaxed and open as I was during those five days. I didn't speak to anyone the entire time except for the usual necessary exchange. The hot sun and the afternoon brandy helped form cognates from Chester Himes's Harlem and the constant Portuguese spoken, moving in and out of my attention, combined to form what sounded like Japanese. I had passed through Amsterdam on my way to London a week previous, so some remaining Dutch helped form the continual silent enunciations accompanied by the shoeshine men and banged-up taxis. All of the above seemed to scramble for attention. I had no priorities, so did nothing to interfere with the development. Pure passive objectivity might be the best description.

Supplement to *Draft for a Syncretism* (Notes from Lisbon)

WORK 1972-1974

Alice Aycock

GENERAL INTRODUCTION

In September 1970 as I was landing at Kennedy Airport, I hit upon the idea of writing about the highway system. Mark and I were returning from Greece and Turkey. The previous year I had written a paper on the development of the circular building from Cretan tholos tombs to Bramante's Tempietto. And we had spent a month with a copy of Scully's *The Earth, the Temple, and the Gods,* climbing along the sacred way to the Acropolis and climbing into and around circular ruins—the corbeled vaults of tholos tombs and the labyrinthine foundations and concentric circles of the Temple to Asclepius at Epidaurus. I was very drawn to these buildings, but at the time I could not reconcile their fixed state and the necessity to return to construction with my interests in causality, transitory events, and self-sustaining systems. From the air the highway seemed the modern visual counterpart, at least in scale and anonymity, to the ancient necropolis.

In the subsequent thesis I described the highway network in terms of the necessary structure and the contingent event (Lévi-Strauss). The highway is the necessary organizational and physical structure which engenders movement, and the highway users create the contingent event by being in motion. The highway is designed in terms of the perceiver in order to control perceptions relative to structure. It was my recognition of structure as a set of directions for a performance (Morse Peckham), or structure which is structuring (Jean Piaget), which brought me from the highway back to the labyrinthine passages entered through a snake pit at Epidaurus.

In general the work included here reflects the notion that an organism both selects and is selected by the environment. The structures, i.e. spaces and materials of construction, act upon the perceiver at the same time as the perceiver acts on or with the structures. The spaces are psychophysical spaces. The works are set up as exploratory situations for the perceiver. They can be known only by moving one's body through them. They involve experiential time and memory. The works are sited in terms of a preexisting landscape feature and are visible from a distance like a Greek temple. They are goal-directed situations, involving what Peckham refers to as "signs of orientative transition." The actual physical structures are impermanent since I do a minimum of maintenance. The work satisfies my need to deal with both ideas and physical things and my megalomaniac and somewhat destructive need to take on more than I can handle. A friend recently pointed out that I seem to relate everything to everything else. While the work is designed in terms of my own body, the construction tests the limits of my physical strength. I often feel that I am in over my head. The works are a synthesis. They give me pleasure. They turn back on history and back on themselves. Like the example of Christianity outrunning the sign of the cross, the generative ideas/sources outrun the actual structures.

—*December 1974*

MAZE

Executed July 1972 on the Gibney Farm near New Kingston, Pennsylvania. A twelve-sided wooden structure of five concentric dodecagonal rings, approximately 32′ in diameter and 6′ high.

The *maze* has the appearance of a hill fortification. I was influenced by the American Indian stockade and the Zulu kraal.

I got the idea while paging through the *World Book* for the definition of *magnetic north,* and accidentally came across a circular plan for an Egyptian labyrinth. The labyrinth was designed as a prison.

The temple dedicated to Asclepius as healer at Epidaurus was composed of a circular stepped platform and twenty-six outer Doric columns axially aligned with fourteen Corinthian columns within the cella wall. An ornamental pavement, concentric rings of black and white tiles, surrounded a center spiral staircase which led down to the center of the labyrinthine substructure. From the center pit one moved through the labyrinth to the "dead end of the outer ring" underneath the temple. The name of the building recorded on an inscription is Thymela or Place of Sacrifice.

A fourteenth-century maze at Wing, Rutland, England, is located near an ancient tumulus. The maze was used as a form of penance.

Originally, I had hoped to create a moment of absolute panic—when the only thing that mattered was to get out. Externalize the terror I had felt the time we got lost on a jeep trail in the desert in Utah with a '66 Oldsmobile. I egged Mark on because of the landscape, a pink and gray crusty soil streaked with mineral washouts and worn by erosion. And we expected to eventually join up with the main road. The trail wound up and around the hills, switchback fashion, periodically branching off in separate directions. Finally, the road ended at a dry riverbed. We could see no sign of people for miles. On the way back, I accused Mark of intentionally trying to kill me.

Hopi Indian myth states that before a permanent settlement could be made, each clan had to make four directional migrations, north, south, east, west to the farthest points of the landmass. Their paths formed a great cross whose center, located in the American Southwest, was considered by the Hopis to be the magnetic and spiritual center of the universe. When a clan reached the end of a directional line, they first turned right or left before retracing their steps. The motif formed by this turn was a swastika which rotated either clockwise or counterclockwise according to the movements of the sun or the earth. As the

Maze. 1972.

migrations came to an end, the Hopis moved in concentric circles which spiraled in towards the center.

When I realized the expense and difficulties involved in building so large a circular structure, I cut out the four exterior rings and re-organized the plan as an axial alignment along the cardinal points of the compass. The outside entrance in the lower right section of the aerial view forms the end point along the east-west axis.

Rumors about the *maze* have been spread within a thirty-mile radius by word of mouth. From the Carlisle Pike to Locust Point Road over the road that runs along the railroad tracks, they cut off onto the dirt road which they wore into the field, circle around the *maze,* go inside through the barriers which they tore down to make it easier to get to the center, build a fire, drink, "smoke dope," and repeat the process in reverse.

In the essay "Pascal's Sphere," Borges traces the history of the concept of the sphere whose center is everywhere and circumference nowhere from the Greek philosophers to Pascal. The current form of this idea is the theory of the uniformly expanding universe: from any point in the universe one appears to be standing at the center.

Designing an entrance or barrier along a specific path had the effect of reorganizing the whole network structure.

Like the experience of the highway, I thought of the *maze* as a sequence of body/eye movements from position to position. The whole cannot be comprehended at once. It can only be remembered as a sequence.

I was asked if I thought a maze was a basic form like the circle and the square. No, not exactly. But it seems to be a recurrent need—an elabo-ration of the basic concept of the path. I certainly intended to tap into the tradition. And what about Borges's reference to that "one Greek labyrinth which is a single, straight line . . . invisible and unceasing"?

I took the relationship between my point of entry and the surrounding land for granted, but often lost my sense of direction when I came back out. From one time to the next, I forgot the interconnections between the pathways and kept rediscovering new sections.

LOW BUILDING WITH DIRT ROOF (for MARY)

Executed July 1973 on the Gibney Farm near New Kingston, Pennsylvania. A wood, stone, and earth construction; exterior dimensions: 20' wide x 12' long; roof slope 1 to 6; entrance 30" high.

The building is located on a rise in the landscape so that from slightly below the entrance the earth mound of the roof forms an artificial horizon beyond which no other objects are visible. I wanted the obvious association—curve of the mound/curve of the earth.

We went to Mycenae to see the tholos tomb of Agamemnon. We followed a long, open passage lined with stone into the hill and entered a large chamber, approximately fifty feet in diameter and fifty feet high, constructed of horizontal, concentric courses of stone, each course smaller than the one below. I hadn't known beforehand about the small primitive tomb of Aegisthus, a perfectly curved mound of earth set into the hills below the citadel and near the tomb of Clytemnestra. The sloped roof had been recently reinforced with concrete lintels. In the back of the tomb a triangular open space was visible below the lintel. The entrance was barred by an iron grating. Nearby was the open pit of the Lion Tomb, the portion of its corbeled dome above the ground had caved in.

The story goes that while Agamemnon was away at the Trojan Wars, his wife, Clytemnestra, became the mistress of Aegisthus. When Agamemnon returned home, Clytemnestra greeted him and ordered a great banquet prepared. Agamemnon went to his bath. As he emerged, Clytemnestra entangled him in a net she had woven and Aegisthus killed him with a two-edged sword. Clytemnestra then beheaded him with an ax. It was while offering libations at the tomb of Agamemnon that Electra and Orestes conspired to avenge the death of their father. Posing as the messenger who brought news of his own death, Orestes entered the citadel at Mycenae and beheaded his mother, Clytemnestra, his half-sister, and Aegisthus.

More and more my life in New York City is preoccupied with low-frequency vibrations—those rumbles which follow me everywhere and descend on me at night in my bed, filtered through my mattress. I sleep fitfully now, jerked awake periodically by a sudden noise, a spasm of fear. Ever since the night they fire-bombed the adjoining building. The explosion set the street on fire. In my sleep I thought the back of my loft had blown away. I have imagined my own violent death hundreds of times.

The image of cowering in fear is countered by the aggressive activity of building.

I thought in terms of the low building gradually moving into the field; the field moving into the building, rotting wood, windblown seeds.

Threshold situations: a continuum of transitions: At what point does one thing become another?

claustrophilia—"a pathological wish to be enclosed in a small space" claustrophobia—"an abnormal fear of enclosed or narrow spaces"

Sigfried Giedion refers to the Mesopotamian practice of burying the dead beneath the floor of the house. Later on, in Crete separate round huts were built for the bodies of the dead.

About fifteen years ago I visited the house in which my great-great-grandparents Benjamin and Serena lived and where my great-grand-father Francis was born. It was a small wood-frame house. I climbed up alone into the attic where they slept and stood under the rafters. In the yard was the family cemetery. I remember the tombstone of Catherine, who died at age three. Years later, I dreamt that my brother Billy came for me and took me to that same wooden house set into the hills of Greece like a tholos tomb. I climbed the stairs again and behind a screen, a young girl, whose face I could not see, lay dead.

"That thing is well-built," my father who knows about those things told me. "You could drive a truckload of elephants up on that roof."

I came home alone. There was no one around to work, so my mother helped me build it.

The low building is derived from the *Tunnel/Well,* a core project: two tunnels (50 feet long x 36 inches wide x 32 inches high) running at right angles to each other and meeting at a center well (36 inches x 42 inches x 15 feet high), open to the sky. I wanted to know what it would be like to move through a narrow, cramped space and come upon a patch of open space which is inaccessible.

110

*Low Building with
Dirt Roof.* 1973.

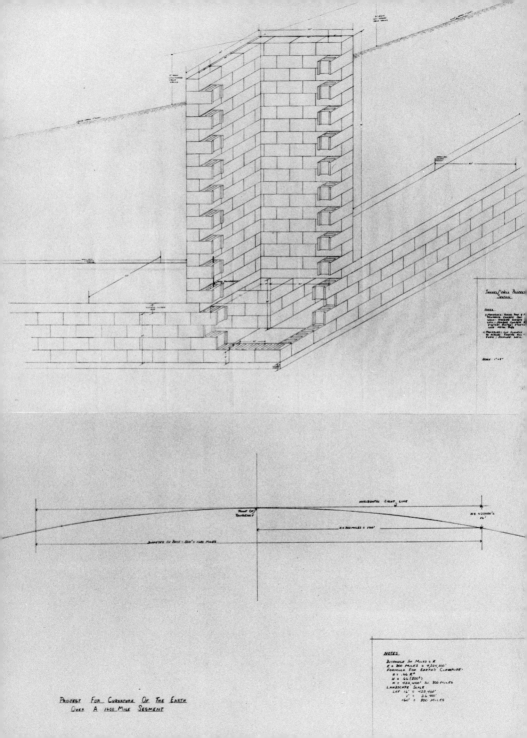

PROJECT FOR CURVATURE OF THE EARTH
OVER A 1400 MILE SEGMENT

The summer before, I came across a group of abandoned greenhouses, narrow wooden structures several hundred feet long with pitched roofs. The dirt and pebble floors seemed to slope almost imperceptibly towards the roof. And at some point, I saw a photograph of Smithson's *Partially Buried Woodshed.*

From its lowest interior height of twelve inches the pitched roof rises to a height of thirty inches at the ridge beam where the entrance is located. The body posture of anyone moving into the building ranges from a crouched hands-and-knees position at the entrance to a flat horizontal position on the ground as one moves out towards the edges. Uncut, mortared stone walls which bear no weight enclose the front and the back of the building. The stone was gathered from rock piles in the field and from a partially collapsed stone farmhouse on the property.

This one is more house, the other is more tomb.

People refer to it as a sod house. It is, after all, not a menacing work. It is solid, stable, adequate.

WALLED TRENCH/EARTH PLATFORM/CENTER PIT

Executed July 1974 on the Gibney Farm near New Kingston, Pennsylvania. Three concentric quadrilateral concrete-block walls: a solid masonry wall 21′ 4″ on a side x 3′ high; a retaining wall 11′ 4″ on a side x 4′ 4″ high; and a center well or pit 4′ on a side x 5′ high; trench 52″ wide x 4′ 4″ high; tunnel 18″ wide x 52″ long x 30″ high.

With no point of entry, the outside wall presents a barrier. It is a tease, a lure, a trap.

The width of the trench (52 inches) is not physically difficult to jump. It is a psychological gap. Being a person who takes few risks, I have jumped across only once. I stand on the ledge of the outside wall and imagine my body falling forward, my head cracking against the concrete. There is also the remote possibility that I may overreach the earth platform and land in the center pit. I therefore lower my body into the trench and then hoist myself up onto the earth platform.

I think acrophobia is not the fear of high places but the fear that one will give in to the urge to jump.

It is the totally unmotivated act which I fear, the statistical improbability that occurs, "the incalculable infinity of causes and effects," the contingency inherent in any causal situation. All my life I have waited for the murder that I did not provoke. Retribution for being quite lucky from the outset.

Falling into a well.

A child falling into a well.

I remember stories about a child falling into a well.

Conflict arising from uncertainty has been identified as a major force in propelling the child towards the formation of logical structures.

Someone said the walled trench was both "straightforward and mysterious." I keep thinking of the response "half terror/half love," a simultaneous approach/withdrawal. One minute I want to reveal myself, the next minute I want to conceal myself. It just keeps wavering back and forth.

For myself as well as everyone else, there have been hundreds of times, when one either leaps across an obstacle, goes through it, goes around it, goes back the same way one came, or stands around isolated and waits for help.

"The man of magic thinking lacks . . . inner security. Placed in a hostile world against which he must protect himself with insufficient forces, he sees himself everywhere surrounded by dangers: the serpent that treacherously attacks him, the boulder that crushes him, the lightning that strikes him, the drought that destroys his crop. . . . It is of vital importance to him to know the hidden forces inherent in things. Their exterior appearance is of no importance to him. . . . He gains confidence in himself through the possibility of magic conjuration, the undertaking that pits his own forces against those of the spirits. . . . 'He begins to play his own part, he becomes an actor in the spectacle of nature.' "

—PAUL WESTHEIM, *The Art of Ancient Mexico*

The true maze; another version of the *Tunnel/Well Project*.

Because the archaeological sites I have visited are like empty theatres for past events, I try to fabricate dramas for my buildings, to fill them with events that never happened.

It is in part the neurotic quality of pre-Columbian which I respond to. It is obsessive, brutal, angry, extravagant, aggressive, fearful. Motivated by an incredible need to pacify the universe, to eliminate uncertainty, the pyramids with their solar and astronomical orientations are mere bases for the temples on top which are reached by staircases inclined at angles of forty-five degrees or greater. These staircases are intended to establish a system of correspondences between the position of the priest as he climbed and the position of the sun as it moved across the sky. I always think of the title of a book, *The Design of Inquiring Systems*.

"The hair of these priests was very long and so matted that it could not be separated or disentangled . . . and [it] was clotted with blood. There were some smoking braziers of their incense . . . in which they were burning the hearts of three Indians whom they had sacrificed that day; and all the walls of that shrine were so splashed and caked with blood that they and the floor too were black. Indeed, the whole place stank abominably."

—BERNAL DÍAZ, *The Conquest of New Spain*

The pyramid of Tenayuca consists of eight superimposed pyramids, each preserved within the other. The pyramid at Tlatelolco had fourteen superimpositions. All that remains is a succession of fourteen double staircases leading nowhere, each one larger than the one behind it.

The thirteenth-century cruciform church of St. George at Lalibela, Ethiopia, is carved from rock. The inside is hollowed out. The view I have of it is from above. It appears to be set in a deep ravine so that the roof is approximately level with but separated from the surrounding land. The church seems inaccessible.

The initial unworkable plan for the walled trench was completely below the existing grade of the land. It probably began with the foundations of a building I saw in Olympia: a wide, deep curvilinear trench surrounded an island of land which enclosed another trench within another island of land.

*Walled Trench/
Earth Platform/
Center Pit. 1974.*

Walled Trench/Earth Platform/Center Pit. 1974.

The raised platform, which filled with earth excavated from the site, is solid except for the tunnel which runs underneath and connects the trench with the center pit. I was influenced by a drawing I saw of a Rhodesian pit-circle homestead.

The actual structure that gets built as well as the response generated by it are simply instances of the various possibilities that could exist.

I situated the walled trench in a low, flat area between two rises in the elevation of the land. On the two other parallel sides, the structure can be approached along a natural avenue. I also wanted to direct the vision of the perceiver to the view of the low building set into the hill above.

"Next I retreated to the far side of the rock, and waited till one of the chopping gusts of wind got behind me; then I ran the length of the huge stone, some three or four and thirty feet, and sprang wildly into the dizzy air. Oh! the sickening terrors which I felt as I launched myself at that little point of rock, and the horrible scene of despair which shot through my brain, as I realised that I had *jumped short!* But so it was; my feet never touched the point, they went down into space, only my hands and body came in contact with it. I gripped at it with a yell, but one hand slipped, and I swung right round, holding by the other, so that now I faced the stone from which I had sprung. In agony I clutched with my left hand, and this time managed to grasp a knob of rock, and there I hung in the fierce red light, with thousands of feet of empty air beneath me."

—H. RIDER HAGGARD, *She*

THE WILLIAMS COLLEGE PROJECT

Executed October 1974 approximately 300 yards southwest of the junction of Spring and Latham streets, Williamstown, Massachusetts. A concrete-block chamber 4' wide x 6' long x 2' high (interior dimensions); entrance 14" high x 28" wide.

Big mountain, little mountain.

I saw a photograph of a cross section of a small burial mound belonging to the "lost civilization" of Dilmun. In order to penetrate to the inner stone chamber, half of the surrounding tumulus had to be destroyed. Dilmun was unknown for three thousand years until references to "the god Nabu of Dilmun" were found in the process of deciphering Babylonian script.

Located nearby is the false Williams Project: a ramp of banked earth used by the Department of Buildings and Grounds.

The true low building with dirt roof.

I remember seeing the gold death masks which were found in the shaft graves within the grave circle at Mycenae and which once covered the faces of Mycenaean kings.

Almost every day for five years I have passed by the cemetery behind St. Paul's Chapel. It is an old cemetery. The grass is very green. Large stone coffins with stone slabs as covers sit on the ground as though they have been thrust up out of the earth by successive freeze-thaw cycles. I know the bodies have been removed, but I am always tempted to push away the cover and look inside.

The rectangular pit is sunk ten inches below the existing grade: one enters head first, crawling down at an angle, dragging the rest of one's body inside, and ends up lying prone, face down. There is not enough room to sit upright. Some people thought they were too big and would get stuck. Getting back out, it seems harder to pull the body up and out.

Rebecca, from *One Hundred Years of Solitude,* carried her parents' bones in a sack and ate damp earth.

Days slipped by—more hours asleep than awake. I often did not know if I dreamt an event or if it happened, like the dreamer who dreamt a living man in Borges's "The Circular Ruins."

The concrete-block chamber is spanned by four-inch by eight-inch timber beams. They support the mound of earth overhead.

An entrance into the mountain.

"When at last the clanking subsided, I resumed the trowel, and finished without interruption the fifth, the sixth, and the seventh tier. The wall

The Williams College Project. 1974.

was now nearly upon a level with my breast. I again paused, and holding the flambeaux over the mason-work, threw a few feeble rays upon the figure within."

—EDGAR ALLAN POE, "The Cask of Amontillado"

A mulch bed, a tell, a lair, a vegetable cellar, a mud hut, a bunker, a cave, a tomb, a shelter, a prison.

I considered putting straw inside. But I kept thinking of the phrases "lying on damp earth" and "the beaten earth floor." The leaves blew inside anyway.

A conical mound, no more than four feet in diameter, of earth at the palace of Nestor, Pylos, dates from 1500 B.C. On the mound is the label in Greek and English "altar." From the vantage point of the chamber in front, the altar is on an axis with a distant conical hill.

As someone pointed out, it is not the enclosure itself, but the possibility of no exit.

In August 1973 we traveled for several hours over a dirt road with gullies as wide as the wheel span and nearly as deep in order to reach Malinalco, the rock-cut Aztec temple dedicated to the eagle and the jaguar where human sacrifices to the sun were made some years after the conquest. When we reached the town of Malinalco, we climbed on foot up the mountain to the sanctuary. I went up the temple stairs, flanked by two large pumas, and through a doorway formed by the open jaws of a serpent. Inside was a circular raised bench with three eagles and a jaguar carved from the rock. I tried to get a good photograph in the dark interior and left quickly, afraid we wouldn't get back over the rough terrain before night.

CIRCUMSTANTIAL EVIDENCE

Robert Horvitz

Untitled. July 6, 1970. Ink on paper H. 14½″, W. 14½″. Photo: J. M. Snyder.

All my drawings are compounded out of two formal elements, the paper and the pen stroke. They invert each other's qualities in certain key ways. The pen stroke is concentrated, active, discrete, and black. The paper is diffuse, passive, continuous, and white. Their opposition is stable even under the most elaborate concatenation.

Form Is the Language of Time (for Keith Jarrett). September 23–28, 1970. Ink on paper. H. 23″, W. 23″. Photo: J. M. Snyder.

My pen stroke evolved over a two-year period (1968–1970) into the briefest gesture I can make with the pen: I place the point on the paper and flick it towards me. The split-second acceleration of the point reduces the flow of ink until none reaches the paper at all, in about half an inch. I try to make all strokes exactly alike. I am barely aware of the act itself anymore; it is like an eyeblink. My external behavior is completely routine, allowing my attention to shift inward.

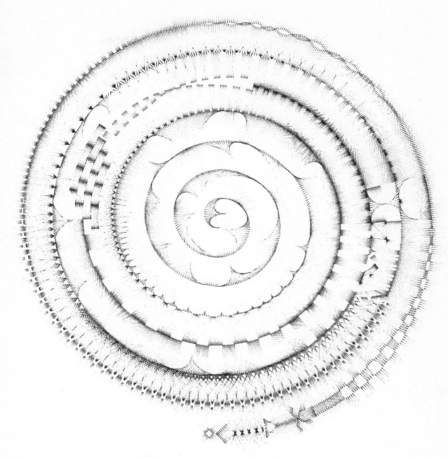

Calendar No. 13. February 17, 1971. Ink on paper. H. 23″, W. 23″. Photo: J. M. Snyder.

The paper is a receptive ground, finite and unstructured. At the start of a drawing, it defines a field of potential that is gradually consumed as the strokes fill the surface. At the end, it remains as a projection of my activity. Since all the pen strokes are made the same way and in the same direction, it is the paper that changes position. In fact, it is nearly always in motion.

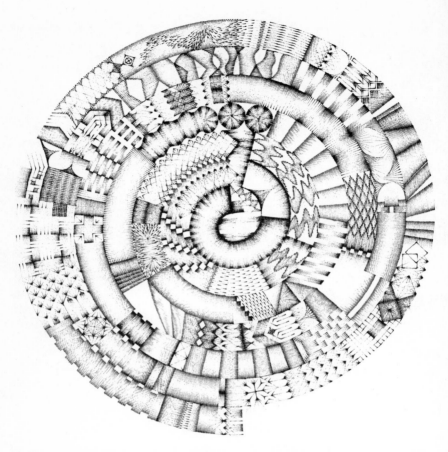

Calendar No. 15. May 27–29, 1971. Ink on paper. H. 23″, W. 23″. Photo:
J. M. Snyder.

The drawing unfolds stroke by stroke. The progression builds on itself,
tangles with its past. As each stroke endures on the paper, the sequence
is transformed into a growing network of simultaneous relationships.
Later events can and do redefine the significance of earlier events;
events that happened at different moments are seen together. History
foreshortens into structure.

126

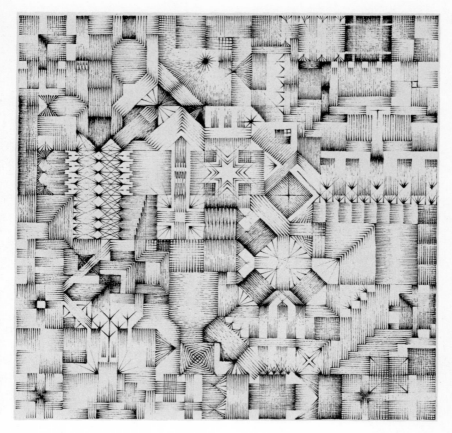

Choreograph No. 6. February 26, 1971. Ink on paper. H. 9″, W. 9″. Photo: J. M. Snyder.

I never make preliminary sketches. Instead, I work out systems of constraint that govern the evolution of the drawing without eliminating free choice. (A fully constrained drawing, where the outcome is determined in advance, would not be worth executing.) By systematically limiting my options, I can create specific ranges and types of freedom. The visual consequences are often unexpected.

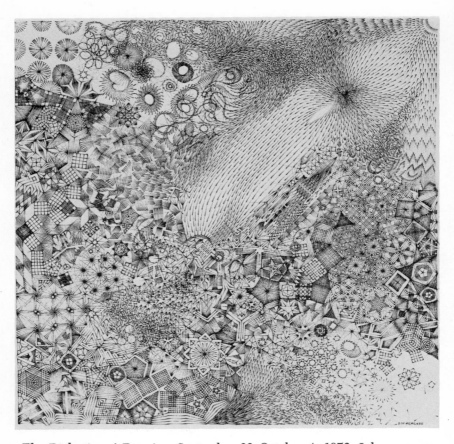

The Dialectics of Drawing. September 22–October 4, 1972. Ink on paper. H. 14½″, W. 14½″. Photo: J. M. Snyder.

There is no uniquely prescribed course of action. At every moment it is possible to imagine the drawing extending into a variety of futures. My decision to follow any one course closes off many others of equal interest and validity. Conflict and mediation. Some process of selection is called for that does not reduce to rules.

128

The Dialectics of Drawing. October 9, 1972. Ink on paper. H. 14½″, W. 14½″. Photo: J. M. Snyder.

Each option must be considered at several levels of impact. The effect on a given location, which can be foreseen very precisely, and the effect on the drawing as a whole, which can be foreseen only dimly, are the critical extremes. The long- and short-range implications are often inconsistent with one another. When that happens, I must rely on intuition. Improvisation takes over where necessity leaves off.

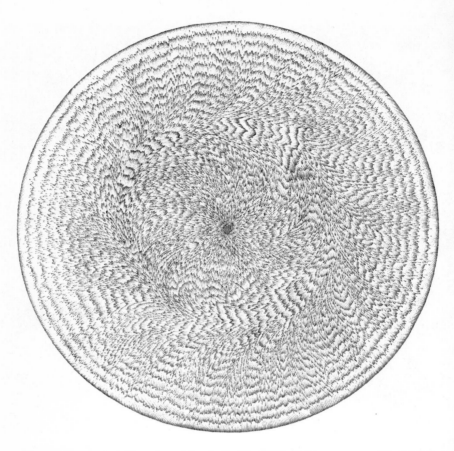

The Dialectics of Drawing. March 8–12, 1973. Ink on paper. H. 14½″, W. 14½″. Photo: J. M. Snyder.

The presence of so many options functions, paradoxically, as a sort of vacuum, drawing out personal judgment and making it ponderable. I use drawing as an introspective probe. It refracts my "mental weather" into observable patterns of preference and intention. Depending on how intense the experience is, it can resemble either meditation or celebration (the line between the two is somewhat arbitrary).

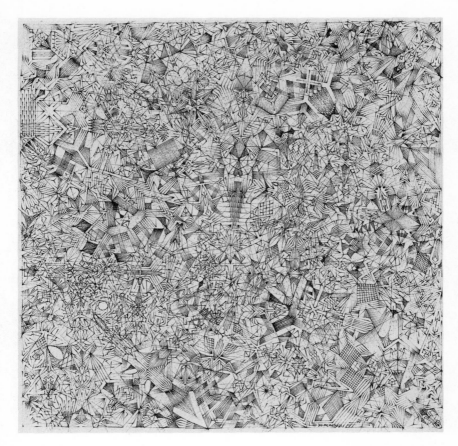

Παντα ρει *No. 2.* October 9–11, 1974. Ink on paper. Diam. 22″. Photo: J. M. Snyder.

As the conditions under which decisions are made vary (actually, there is only one decision—it is made over and over again), the subconscious roots of the process are revealed. Each stroke is the momentary consequence of an ongoing negotiation between pleasure and constraint, memory and inference. Many levels of thought are involved. Only the most superficial are informed by language.

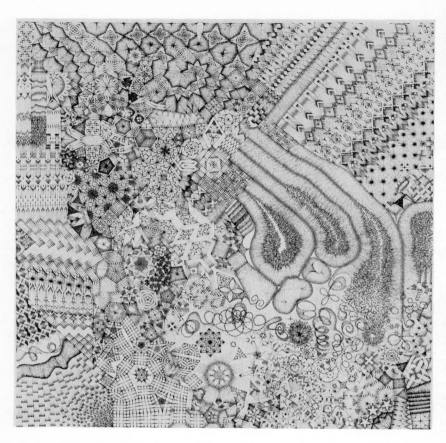

Personal Domain of Freedom and Ecstasy No. 1. January 6–10, 1973. Ink on paper. H. 20″, W. 20″. Photo: J. M. Snyder.

The first stroke, the first step into it, is always a sharp sensation: an eruption in the continuum, demanding repair. But once underway, I can only lose ground. Time passes. Choices are made. Tendencies compound themselves. Regions develop with unique local characteristics. Some are quite stable and expand into large areas, others dissipate quickly.

Personal Domain of Freedom and Ecstasy No. 2. June 7–11, 1973. Ink on paper. H. 20″, W. 20″. Photo: J. M. Snyder.

Schemes and curiosities, shifts in attention, opinions and plans, all pass easily through the pen. But drawing is not a form of communication. I do not expect anyone to be able to read my thoughts in a finished work. My purposes are satisfied in the activity itself.

Personal Domain of Freedom and Ecstasy No. 3. June 15–22, 1973. Ink on paper. H. 20″, W. 20″. Photo: J. M. Snyder.

Drawing is a tool of self-clarification. Its basis is the distinction between pen stroke and paper. This opposition, constantly reenacted, is a source of dialectical energy. It enables me to construct artificial situations that amplify one or another type of experience, and thus the web of considerations underlying my actions in general begins to surface.

Untitled. December 19, 1974. Ink on paper. H. 7″, W. 4¾″. Photo: J. M. Snyder.

VISIBLE AND INVISIBLE

Nancy Wilson Kitchel

Storyboards. 1975.

When I try to take one position, I am thrust into the other, opposing position, into all those between and surrounding them, until I have no position (on the loose again).

I've always had a problem with movement—I go all over the place, out of control, I crash into things, bumble about, always lost. My thoughts drift away before I can make sense out of them, my mind wanders constantly. I have to make a conscious effort to keep myself still, concentrate, fix things in place.

And my memory, too . . . always on the loose . . . the name of the person I saw last evening, who did it, the name of any film or what it was about, the word I was about to use, what I wanted to say when I started. Everything fragments, flies up, reassembles in some form only recognizable to me (sometimes, frequently, not to me). There must be something overriding, something else that is more important or else defines it all.

There must be something in me that isn't constantly in a state of flux.

*Here is the problem: there are things I cannot remember,
things I don't want to remember, things that are invisible to me.
Sometimes I am invisible to me. I cease to exist, I cannot remember who I am. Sometimes I discover that a thought has led me
out of myself, made me forget myself, & I disappear right
off the street. At those times I have no physical sensations, no
orientation in space & time. Of course, I then have to force
myself back, step off the curb or bump into something, or look
at my reflection to make myself reappear.*

*But then I continue to forget, forget what it is now, was then,
forget it's still around; I keep rapping my knees on it as I
blindly plunge ahead. Or maybe when I memorized the
terrain, I merely refused to believe it was still there,
preferred to believe that there were no obstacles, refused
to accept the inevitable immoveability of discontent (or
maybe I didn't see it because it was mine).*

"Bartlett argues that the components and organization of schemata are
determined by 'appetite, instinct, interest and ideals.' The order of
predominance of these 'active, organizing sources' of schemata in any
given individual is exactly what we mean by 'personality.'"
"Bartlett goes on to suggest that this is what gives memory a charac-

teristically 'personal' flavour. For remembering demands the utilization of schemata which themselves have been organized in accord with the individual's personality and which are now employed in a hierarchical organization which also reflects his personality. So that, if the order of predominance of the appetites, etc., which direct the schemata is disturbed, the individual's experience of his memories will be altered."[1]

The past and how it is remembered. The drift of memory, the way it stretches time with details and compacts events, punctuates with events, compacts time between events.
Then there is this urge to step out of myself entirely, to have new skin, change everything, change the way I think and see . . . to acquire new muscles.
This urge to be on the opposite side, to put myself in the other position in any conflict, or to be both sides of a question at once, engulf it. Switch sides, change positions, transfer myself, transform myself, turn it all inside out.

No, it's not that. forgetting. It's a way of pushing things aside, putting them into place, so that I can go on. It's having to keep going ahead, in a straight line, not stopping for anyone or anything, not looking to the side.
(It's getting up to go, saying good-bye, leaving old friends & not making new ones.)

But always to drive myself to the edge, as close to the edge as I can get and the urge to step off.

"It is almost impossible for a person in normal health to imagine what it would feel like *not* to be experiencing oneself as oneself. This is

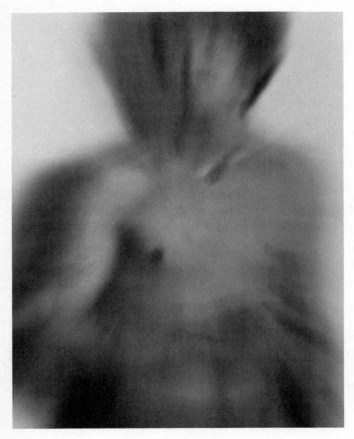

Intruders (Memory Figures). 1974.

doubtless because imagining, like all other mental activities, normally occurs in the context of self-experience.
"Clearly the experience of self is inextricably involved in all other cognitive activities and states because it underlies them and acts as a selector, integrator and synthesizer."[2]

Storyboards. 1975.

Finding that point at which transformation occurs. Isolating it. Finding the point at which a new identity has not formed and the old has dissolved, the point at which the most possibilities are implied as well as the greatest risk.

(Not what it was, and becoming what?)

Between two places, two states, two things, two persons.

The horror of being stuck between two realities, not living either, being without identity, without reference.

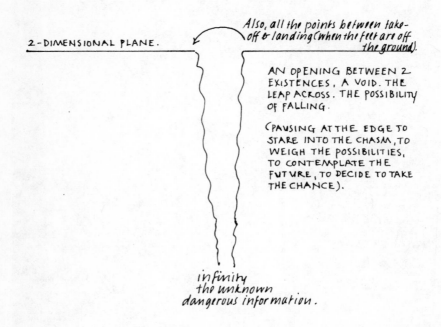

2-DIMENSIONAL PLANE.

Also, all the points between take-off & landing (when the feet are off the ground).

AN OPENING BETWEEN 2 EXISTENCES, A VOID. THE LEAP ACROSS. THE POSSIBILITY OF FALLING.

(PAUSING AT THE EDGE TO STARE INTO THE CHASM, TO WEIGH THE POSSIBILITIES, TO CONTEMPLATE THE FUTURE, TO DECIDE TO TAKE THE CHANCE).

infinity
the unknown
dangerous information.

The point at which the personal becomes universal.

Taking everything personally.

Covering My Face: My Grandmother's Gestures. 1973.

No, it's forcing myself into myself, into places I don't want to go, forcing myself to know things I don't want to know, to understand things I can't, to be what I am not . . . compressing something into a hard mass, trying to make a core, breaking that apart to form it over. It's trying to locate something protected by sheer terror, not knowing what it is, except that it is surrounded by this blind fear. Forcing myself into situations that touch the fear, impossible relationships, work I haven't done before, don't know how to do. It's feeling that I accomplished something only when I risked a lot, risked failure, to do it.

It is important for me to always do what is most difficult for me at the time—to use difficulty as a measure—to always choose what seems impossible and do that; not to set up obstacles for myself, but to go against the grain.

Pushing situations beyond what they are or seem to be . . .

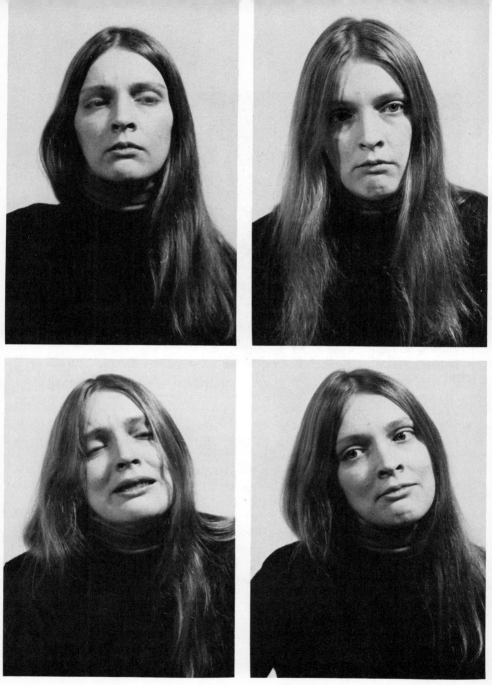

Exorcism. 1973.

Internalization of ideas and personalities for the purpose of creating systems for dealing with myself and others.

Internalization as a way of reconciling opposites. Ideas and personalities in opposition, internalizing and synthesizing dichotomous information.

The fragility of the boundaries that make one entity separate from another . . . the inviolability of them. Extending my boundaries, physical and mental, to encompass, assimilate, control, others. Internalization as a method of assimilating others.

And constantly attempting to produce some mental state/idea/process in myself which is not predisposed
and to manifest it physically.

Presenting you with half-reconciled oppositions.

No, actually I want to expose wounds. (I only say that they're mine.)

The whole cannot be dissected for examination because the complex interrelationships of its parts form a contextual situation which alters individual pieces of information.

It is in the way that each is different that the whole is defined. How variants can survive in a forced structural unity. How they are absorbed into the structure (visual, sociological, psychological implications). At the same time, variants of sufficient insistence force expansion of the structure to include the new material.

Last White (Interior Landscape). 1975.

The tension between the possible and impossible, the real and imagined, the visible and invisible.

The invisible is perceived in the visible. The invisible is defined by the visible.

In form: that which can be examined, referred to, returned to . . . that which passes immediately into memory.

Something which occurs mentally reflected in something which occurs in real space. The physical indicator of a mental process.

Instantaneous information, what can be seen at one time (without turning one's head), and understood apart from a study of its parts.
Additive information, what takes time to be understood.
Sequential development, adding on, accumulations of information, the uses of time, precedent, juxtaposition.

Actual physical juxtaposition (making connections between related or unrelated bits of information in close contact with each other, as in pairs of images).
Mental juxtapositions (making connections between related bits of information separated by time and space).

Radial development of ideas—from a central point. Reaching out as far as possible from the center.

Open systems, infinitely referential, radial, linear, not circular (enclosed), in which all aspects of one's concerns relate to all others and form a continuous pattern in which many directions are equally possible and choices depend upon personal necessity (and are not irreversible).

Perhaps some fleeting thought, already gone.

I can take what I do not know and name it. I can say it is a secret, its name is Secret, or I can call it the Center, or the Core, or whatever. But that does nothing, even seals it off and makes it less accessible. Better perhaps for me to circle it, draw a line around it with what I do know, find its boundaries.

The implication of something beyond . . .
that which is unspoken, that which cannot be seen . . .
some sense of an unknown . . .
an invisible presence.

Locating, then crossing boundaries. Stepping across boundaries.

Zone system: I operate somewhere between the appearance of the first black and the disappearance of the last white, but closer to the last white and sometimes beyond.

Between the lines. Pieces as segments, without beginning or end, something from which to imagine a whole.

The body of work projects concerns larger than, different from, individual pieces. It is not a linear progression. The whole is in a state of flux, cannot be accurately defined and therefore remains relatively unknown, except that which can be inferred at any given moment from its parts. The invisible composed of the visible.

A situation or stimulus which is sufficiently ambiguous or undefined is open to a variety of interpretations. The perceiver will tend to interpret according to his/her own unique perceptual predispositions and will complete a piece in a way different from the artist's intentions or those of other viewers. Certain kinds of ambiguity then function to open up the piece.

Last White (Interior Landscape). 1975.

Isolation in space (occupation of space defines the isolation).
Isolation in a psychological sense, alienation if you will, but at least a suspension in time and space.
Nothing to interfere with movement.

Cluster and expanse.
Close groupings in open space (back to the wall).
Things seen in the distance.
Methods of approach.
Horizontality.

What we think is the size of an object or group of objects or person (physical or implied) in space defines the space.
Objects, images, etc. (focal points) set apart by surrounding space.
Size and placement of objects indicate kinds and qualities of surrounding space.

Last White (Interior Landscape). 1975.

this idea I have that the whole inside of my head resembles this landscape (flat? nothing there?), that the particular, peculiar sense of great space, isolation in space, harshness, clarity, severity, the constant transitions, shifts, reverses, the wild swings from one state to another, forms the visual, auditory, reasoning, base for thought & action.

A sense that I have been formed out of the quality of the landscape, that everything unnecessary is being slowly eroded by harsher elements. And the confidence that I will survive, denuded, or that something will survive, something will never stop.

Landscape as a constant. A quality that is constantly fluctuating but does not change.

An oppressive influence. Level. Leveling. Flat. Spare. Barren. Sameness—causing a certain exaggeration of that which stands out. Some-

Last White (Interior Landscape). 1975.

152

thing recognizably different here seems jarring, blatant, unbearably out of place.

Visual distance and a sense of one's own remoteness.

A sense of the insignificance of any one/thing in or to this environment —a sense of my own insignificance and the resulting sense of isolation.

It is impossible to act effectively on this environment or to prevent it from acting upon you.

The landscape defines that which is in it.

Last White (Interior Landscape). 1975.

I can't explain it exactly: there is this sense of immutability—
that something in me, some goal, some sense of purpose,
survives, like the land, the violent changes that constantly
wash over it – that perhaps change itself is a constant.

How a particular Midwestern storytelling tradition resembles (is integral to) the landscape. How my aunt or my mother can tell a story in such a way that the peaks (of violence) are cut off and the low points are filled up (with details, with emphasis) until the whole is perfectly flat and contains the violence.
Or perhaps by shaving the peaks and toppling them into the valleys—leveling.

The oral history of my family: flat, spare, straightfor-
ward, undramatic (full of modifiers & understatements)
Matter-of-fact presentation of the most extraordinary
events (that secret revelling in forbidden emotion).
Remembering also that any expression of strong emotion
was taboo (Nancy, contr<u>ol</u> yourself!)

How distance, isolation, are created.

". . . psychologically, distance is often linked with the most intense state of feeling, in which the coolness or impersonality with which something is treated measures the insatiable interest that thing has for us."[3]

(An undercurrent of violence) That sense of underlying violence—the potential of violence—under the apparent blandness, flatness, silence of things, under the controlled voice, behind a smile.

"Extreme danger often seems to evoke a peculiar sense of detachment. It is as though the threatened person walls off his reactions, so that he is no longer aware of emotion."[4]

Then what about this? I want to die a glorious death? (I don't care where they put things on the wall. Why do they have to be up here, down there? Why not at eye level? WHY NOT PUT IT ALL AT EYE LEVEL? I think this: if one thing is clear, really very clear, then at that moment everything else is totally unclear, that clarity sections things out, divides, pins down, names, neutralizes. (I also think that I am weak; I am amazed that you can lean on me.) I want to live a glorious life: I don't know how.

Storyboards. 1975.

There is always the possibility that I am not making sense, that this is not clear (etc.). However, to be sure that I am as clear as possible, I form the letters carefully, by hand. I add a certain distance, an appearance of objectivity (that helps).

What I mean is, it is neither form nor content, but the attempt that counts.

155

1. Graham Reed, *The Psychology of Anomalous Experience* (Boston: Houghton Mifflin Co., 1974), pp. 131–132.

2. *Ibid.*, p. 112.

3. Susan Sontag, "The Aesthetics of Silence," in Sears, Sallie and Georgianna Lord, eds., *The Discontinuous Universe* (New York: Basic Books, 1972), p. 68.

4. Reed, *op. cit.*, p. 124.

INTERVIEW WITH DOUGLAS SIMON

Alvin Lucier

D.S.: I'd like to ask you about your new piece, *Still and Moving Lines of Silence in Families of Hyperbolas*. What struck me the first time I heard about the idea, which is standing waves and variations on them in a space, was that it reminded me of tile designs in floors. Seeing as how you've come back from the land of tile—Italy—was there a visual image that began the piece for you?

A.L.: Well . . . spa— . . . if not visual, sp—, see . . . I was concerned with space, you know spatial, that is, the piece exists almost completely on a spatial plane . . . because what's important is that I make geographies, sound geographies, by using sine waves from oscillators through speakers—amplifiers and speakers—to make from simple to very complex and from still to moving geographies. You know that if you have a simple sound, a wave, and a reflective surface, y—, under certain circumstances, depending on the frequency of the sound and the particular distance between the source of the sound and the reflective surface, you can create standing waves. If the wavelengths are in simple proportion—if the wavelengths of the frequencies are of simple

158

proportion to the size of the room, then you . . . when the signal bounces off a reflective surface, if it returns in synchronization with the wave as it's going out, then it amplifies. You can see that, because then it's as if the reflective surface is another source, and the same source at the same frequency, so you get an amplitude, you get a rise in amplitude which, under ideal circumstances, can be perceived. If the frequency or if the wavelength or if the length of, between the sound source and the reflective surface, is not of a simple proportion, then you get destructive interference, it interferes, as the wave bounces back, it interferes with the wave that goes out, and under ideal circumstances, if it were fifty, if it were one hundred and eighty degrees out of phase or fifty percent out of synchronization, then ideally, it could de-amplify the outgoing wave and completely eliminate it.

You never get an ideal situation because if you're in a room, you're surrounded by reflective surfaces and because sound propagates all over—sound doesn't go out in a line, it goes out concentrically—you get reflections from all over the place; and if it's a highly reflective room, then it's as if there are a great many loudspeakers or sound sources all over the room, so that the standing-wave situation is very complicated, not simple.

So my task in the piece is to try to make a simple . . . well, no, that's not true because for certain versions of the piece, I want a simple situation so that the audience and the performers are in a simple, demonstrable situation. For instance, there's a dance version that I've been doing for Viola Farber where I want to design fairly simple geographies where the standing, where I can predict where the standing waves are going to occur, so that the particular dancers are actually able to walk in . . . you see . . . walk in the silent, see, silent spots, or should I say the silent lines. In that way, I can use the standing waves as kind of a guidance system for the dancers. In other words, I would have to tell you first that the lines occur in . . . the lines occur . . . in . . . these lines that go out between the speakers, in h-y-p-e-r-b-, in . . .

D.S.: Hyperbolas.

A.L.: . . . yes. You can see how that occurs because if you have one sine wave coming from two loudspeakers, at a point X in space, it takes, at any point X—no, at certain points in space where it takes

. . . mo— . . . where it takes . . . like, a longer time for the wave from speaker B . . .

D.S.: Ah!

A.L.: . . . to get to the wave, to where the wave from speaker A is. If it takes fifty percent more time than that, at that point in space, you're in, you have a situation where the wave is one hundred and eighty degrees out of phase with the one from speaker A. Therefore, it interferes destructively, so you get a quiet line. Now, you can see where there's an infinite amount of points as you move further and further out and you can see where it doesn't form a straight line but forms a curved line. Now, where it takes the wave a full cycle from, say, speaker B to where, a point from speaker A, then you get constructive interference and you get a crest. Now, I can, you can see how it's easy to determine the distance, if you had the distance between the loudspeakers and the frequency, you can determine where that hyperbolic line is going to occur; and by increasing the frequency, you increase the number of these particular lines, so if you want to make a thin, sparse, sort of widely spaced geography, you use speakers that are far apart and use, you go to the . . . you go to low frequencies.

Now, you can see where two speakers having one sine wave gives you one set of these particular functions. Now all you have to do is add another speaker anywhere else in the space and you have a whole new set of lines which will cross the original set. Say you have speakers A, B and C in any configuration in the space. Between speakers A and B you have a simple set of lines, between speakers A and C you have a set, you see. So you can see how it's fairly simple in a dry space to make a fairly simple sound geography into which a, dancers would be able to move. Now they can walk or dance down one line and then if they were to hit another set made by speakers, you see, that would be able to cut across those lines; then theoretically they could move on two axes, they could move on a y-axis and on an x.

Now that's the simplest situation. Now you could see that—I keep saying, "You can see," because your original question was about visual, right? Actually, what the dancer, why you use a dancer or dancers is to make visual to the audience the fact that there are these waves, and with Viola—we don't know what we're going to do yet but—my inkling is that part of it would be very simply having the dancers trying to find, trying to locate and to walk these lines, sh—, thereby showing the audience, in visual terms, that there are these hyperbolas.

Now, there's a whole other set of things that happen. Just the most obvious one is that if you have two speakers and two oscillators, all you have to do is untune one to the other, say, like a cycle apart, and you can beat those hyperbolas in space. Now, it doesn't go from speaker to speaker like panning or . . . but you can see that those infinite number of points are going to have to change because the two speakers are out of tune, and you can move, you can physically move the crests and troughs—those lines—in elliptical patterns around the space at the speed controlled by how far apart, given the frequencies, you can beat them at, like, a second around the space or even slower. And I've . . .

D.S.: In which case, an immobile audience will be able to watch them go by.

A.L.: . . . an audience, each person in the audience is going to perceive the waves move by at a different time. And what you have to do is to make the output so that each oscillator equal—I think it's, I think the rule is that the amplitudes have to be equal—so that you get the ma—, one of the points of the piece, of . . . well, there are several v—, particular versions and I'm in the middle, I'm just in the middle now. I mentioned there was a dance version. There's also a purely electronic version where the musician or musicians beats pairs of oscillators around in various combinations, and one of the tasks is to make a fulcrumlike structure.

One other fact I have to tell you is that the direction of the beating goes to the low speaker. If you have an oscillator at a thousand cycles and one at a thousand-one, it'll beat, the hyperbolas will beat elliptically toward the low speaker. So, one of the tasks of the electronic version is to, with your ear, to measure the amplitudes of the output so that you get the maximum amount of amplitude change. And I've had cases in dry spaces where you get a null point where there's actually a quiet point where, you see, the crest has come to its peak and as it diminuendos to the particular troughs—to the trough—you get actually a silent point. That's hard to get because you're ordinarily in a more reverberant space. And one of the tasks is to get the widest degree of amplitude. I've had sound-level devices that show me that I can get twelve or fifteen dB . . .

D.S.: Difference.

A.L.: . . . difference where both oscillators are at the same amplitude, but the beating does that. The other task is to get the point at which both oscillators are exactly in tune, and then one will, you'll get it so that you drift to one side and the beating goes to the left, for example, and then you bring it back as imperceptibly as you can so that it gets to, like, another null—I'm speaking now of frequency nulls —to the other side so that you give the audience kind of a seesaw quality.

I'm doing this in an obvious way by using snare drums in one of the versions where I just deploy four drums anywhere . . . in the space so that as the crests move by a particular drum, the drum vibrates, so in that way, the audience can really obviously hear the phase relationships. And if I have two pairs of oscillators, you can see how I can make twos against threes, sevens against eights, I can make all kind of rhythmic patterns by just changing the frequency. It reminds me of *V*— . . . see, my echo piece, *Vespers*, in that I'm using very simple relationships of space and time because frequency has to do with time, the speed at which an oscillator's vibrating . . . at audio speeds, I mean, that are very fast, but the beating is perceivable—is perceptible very slowly. So it's a function of time and speed.

Then I've done it with wind instruments where . . . or with, say, the human voice, where I simply make a human player interact with the oscillator, in other words, the player has to be an oscillator and has to play finely in tune, so that I can make performances where I or the electronic musician and the live musician are in a situation where I give . . . a wind player, for example, one oscillator coming from one speaker. Now that player can play above or below that note—that pitch —thereby creating beats to the speaker or away from the speaker to himself, and I love to use the player unamplified because then he's really in an environmental situation. Then I can—if the player sets up a direction from him- or herself to a speaker—then I can bring in the same oscillator sound with another speaker in another direction so that he or she is beating from the middle outward (you see what I mean?), can beat in one direction toward one speaker and outward to another speaker. Then all the player has to do is change pitch below or above where he or she was and they can invert the directionality. Then I can pan or change the location of where the oscillator's coming from so

162

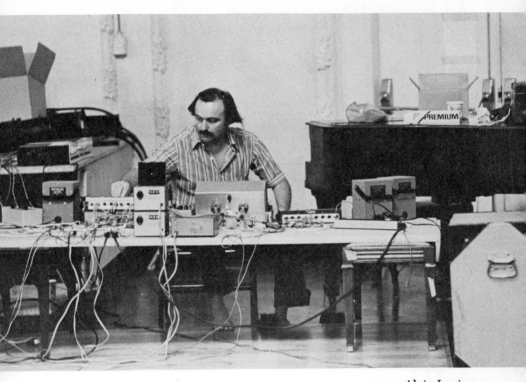

Alvin Lucier:
Still and Moving Lines of Silence in Families of Hyperbolas (1973-1974).
Rehearsal, Merce Cunningham Dance Studio,
New York City. Joan La Barbara, voice; Narrye Caldwell, dancer;
Alvin Lucier, composer and electronics.
Photos: Mary Lucier.

that he or she is spinning, you see, very, in very intricate ways. So it makes a nice sort of a—, improvisational piece where I give, or the musician—the electronic musician—gives geographical loc—, gives the player a geography which the player can then . . . beat against, you see?

With a singer, it's particularly beautiful because it's a vibrato, it's a study in vibrato. Can you visualize a singer singing against an oscillator without vibrato, creating it, beating at certain speeds? But then if the singer sings with vibrato, then he or she, her, his or hers, her frequency changes according to the change of the speed of her vibrato—his or her vibrato; therefore, he or she is in a very, very unstable situation because as her vi—, as her pitch goes up, the speed of the electronic, the speed of the resultant vibrato gets f—, speeds up . . . and as her vibrato speeds up, well, you can see the complexity.

D.S.: There's always a contrast between—say, in a dry, perfectly dry space, you could create a static situation with the standing waves very apparent if a member of the audience should cross the room; but since the static situation isn't apparent to a member of the audience who isn't moving, you're always going to try to contrast that situation with some sort of a moving thing to make the static situation apparent; so the dancers, the drums or something will be employed to make this thing move for the audience.

A.L.: Right. Well, it's a question of two things are moving, you know, two things are moving. One is a particular dancer would be moving. Now, one of the images was, you know those, see . . . the skimmers that . . . those bugs that are on ponds? They apparently jerk, you know, they have abrupt kind . . . they move abruptly to send out, see, waves—physical waves—which echo off, you know, the shore of the pond and come back to them so they can tell where they are. And one version is to use strings—plucked strings. This is hard to make work but I've tried it with electric guitar and it seems to work rather nicely, where you would set up four speakers with the same sound—same oscillator sound—but each speaker would be of a different amplitude, which would mean you were almost describing crudely the outlines of a pond where one shore would be further away than another. In other words, the speaker with the low amplitude—it would be as if that edge of the pond is further away. And I would have a string player plucking close to the frequency, and theoretically, the number

. . . well, now the number of the beats that he or she would get would depend on the amplitude of the plucking in relationship to the amplitude of the oscillators plus the frequencies of both. And it . . . my idea would be to have the string players trying to measure the distance between the loudsp—, between where they are in the space and the loudspeakers, and if you have more than one player, then, you see, the situation gets interesting.

And with the dance, part of it would be that you'd have a number of dancers—I'm thinking particularly of Viola Farber's Dance, you see, Company of eight—where every movement in a hyperbola would, they couldn't move quietly enough so they wouldn't disturb another dancer, and one of the ideas would be that as they got closer together maybe, or if I made the lines close enough together that they would interfere with the simple situation, you know? And it would be harder for them to orient themselves, but that would be a part of the piece.

D.S.: Have you ever tried to make an explanation as you're doing now of intentions in the piece?

A.L.: I have pages of prose but . . . I . . . the more I do the piece, the more ideas I get, you know, I have all the theoretical ideas, I know all the rules, but I had an experience with a singer, Joan La Barbara, who, we rehearsed the piece for the Paris performance and I had all these ideas of using texts—different vowels, different sounds would give you different harmonics—but then when Joan, when I actually put Joan in the situation, in the physical situation, the rules broke down, you know, all my theory didn't really amount . . . didn't really . . . I found much more direct, simple ideas because Joan was actually in the situation and she would do something, being a beautifully trained and very aware player, I mean, she's a type of new performer now that can go into a piece like that without any qualms and . . . she was . . . I just told her the principles, I explained to her the principles which she immediately understood and she started . . . well, improvising—I suppose I should use the word *improvising*—and then I would ask her what she was doing and she would explain it, what she was doing and it was very, very beautiful and very direct and much less . . . "composerly" than I would have done if I had to do it just abstract—, you know, just theoretically.

So, I'm tossing away a lot of . . . scientific ideas that I had and depending more on, like, a live, very aware player's response. And it's so . . . it's wonderful because it's . . . it's explained to me what the piece is, and one of the most amazing things was I gave her—we were in the Cunningham Studio, we were practicing in the Cunningham Studio—I gave her one oscillator sound coming from the four loud-speakers and one of the things she did was to move around in the space very . . . just a little bit with her eyes closed and her ears really open. You could see . . . the position of the body, her body, the way she was moving. And what she was doing was finding the acoustical center of her space, which of course is not the same as the physical center because you can't balance the loudspeakers exactly; so she tried to get . . . and reminded me of the Castaneda books.

Do you know the Castaneda books?, where . . . which I think are very important not for the occult qualities but for the information . . . that one should be aware of one's surroundings and that one can receive omens, one can receive information from sound events or visual events in one's surroundings. For example, don Juan asks Carlos Casta-neda a question or vice versa, and a bird comes in, flies by which . . . gives an answer. But early in the first book, I think, don Juan tells Castaneda to find his place before he can, before they can talk or before they can get into anything deep. Don Juan says find your geographical place in this particular room and Carlos Castaneda spends all night doing that, finding a mystical—well, I don't know what kind of a place but it would have to be a place where certain energies seem to be f— . . . see, focused and . . . how that . . . is important, you know, and it might be more important now, talking about eco-logical considerations and geographical . . .

So that what Joan was doing was finding a place for her that she felt like she wanted to sing from. And I wasn't sure whether she was in a trou—, she would find a crest or a particular trough. And one of the things she did was, would be in a crest, she'd move to . . . the wave, I mean, she'd move six inches so she'd be in the middle of, you see, the crest, in other words, you see, the wavelength. And obviously, where her ears would be in relation to that was very important, and . . . she would be receiving a constant sine tone, and what she did when she sang was to beat against that sine wave and alleviate the constancy . . . of the sine wave. She felt . . . she said she felt it was . . . p—, she felt, she said she felt she was . . . going to push, push the wave away from herself, which you know is physically impossible, but by

169

alleviating that constant pressure—she probably, like, added to it—but the alleviation of the constancy gave the illusion of pushing it away.

So she worked very quietly and very slow—, very quietly, by singing close to the pitch and then going under it and over it so she would change—let me see—she would change the beating in very slight ways around where she stood so, see?, she was changing her geography. And then I would introduce another frequency . . . which would be, for example, above the original, so that she would be singing between them. Now, you can see if she was singing between them, she would beat the low . . . she would beat the low one in one direction and the higher one in another direction, and . . . you can see, if you're sitting in the audience, you receive those changes in pressure and wavelength at different places in different parts of the audience. And one of the things we decided on was that her voice shouldn't be audible, or if . . . it would be nice if it weren't audible but that she employed her voice to move the sound and not to create sound.

D.S.: Right.

A.L.: And in Paris she stood for twenty-seven—twenty-five minutes or thirty minutes—and sang, and it was mostly inaudible. She sang too quietly, but nobody in the audience budged because they had the . . . idea that she was doing something like that even though they didn't know she was singing. Some people thought she was a dancer, standing and sort of moving very quietly, but that was OK with me because it was a riddle, it was as if the piece were a riddle. She started it off and it was like nobody understood what she was doing, but by the end of the piece, where the drums were . . . very obvious, very overt—obviously a drum is a very overt instrument—then the audience could hear the waves spinning by.

But you see how important it is to have . . . all my thinking and all my calculations about . . . frequency, wavelength, amplitude, and so forth didn't really amount to anything until she started to sing in the piece, and just having her sing . . . having a wonderful musician like that helps you compose . . . the piece.

D.S.: Well, you both received inspiration from the same basic fact, the scientific fact of the phenomenon that was the basis of the piece.

A.L.: Right, right.

D.S.: It's rather like a travelogue, isn't it?, because the waves move past.

A.L.: Yes, it's . . . it's amazing, I mean, it's a phenomenon that's
. . . the amazing thing about it is, is it's so simple, but it was so difficult to get to the simple point. To make those waves move, and so that
they're obvious to people, is a very simple thing but it took me a long
time to figure out how to do it . . . you know, and . . . I can dispense
with the calculations and do it by ear which is also another nice thing.

D.S.: Do you think the static situation is more or less comfortable
for an audience? It's probably more boring because it isn't apparent.
The more you use to show what's going on, the more "interesting" it
would be.

A.L.: Well, dancers . . . it's practical because a dancer can use the
static situation but a dancer could hardly use the moving one because
the speeds at which the hyperbolas spin, even if you keep them slow,
are really, for practical reasons, too fast for, I think, a dancer to follow.
But what was beautiful was . . . Narrye Caldwell was, you see, the
dancer. Now, she's not a professional dancer, she studied dance but
she's not a professional dancer, which worked to my advantage because
I had her, I just asked her to move, you know, sort of the way the
movers do in the echolocation piece—in *Vespers*. We chose a frequency
that would, that where I knew the hyperbolas would be in the space,
between two of the speakers, and I just asked her to move across the
space and to stop whenever she couldn't proceed, and the reason she
couldn't proceed is when I would have a horn—I had Gordon Mumma
play the horn—and when he interrupted her by playing the horn,
thereby creating a spinning, she had no . . . guide, guidance anymore. So she alternated between an uncertain kind of, like, a wobble—
she walked in a wobbling manner—and I chose, I forget the frequency,
but the wavelength would be two or three feet wide so that she had
that . . . sort of width to move in, and she would move from side to
side to test where . . . you see, on either side of her was a wall of
sound, of high amplitude, was a crest on one side, a crest on the other,
so she moved in a very uncertain, inept way.

Then when Gordon would start playing, she would have to stop,
and then I said it was all right for her to do some sort of movement
that was whole for her, which was T'ai chi—she's been doing T'ai chi
and she does it very, very beautifully. So she would move from a very
uncertain . . . kind of physical movement, in which she showed physically the hyperbolas, to a static, very self-controlled T'ai chi. When she

was no longer able to move forward, she would do something circular or something inward which was very, very beautiful—the contrast between the inept, the uncertain movement and the very certain trained movement.

Then Gordon would stop and as I got to the mid—, she got to the middle of the space . . . see, I was making her hyperbolas with the two speakers behind her, so that she would move out and away from the middle, from a hypothetical middle line. Then when she got to the middle, I would turn off her back speakers so that she would move then inwardly, you see, because the hyperbolas . . . it was a mirror. She made a mirror, she moved as a mirror. Also, if you can imagine, she . . . her original movement was straight out and to the right; then when I gave her the other speakers, she would move to the left on a curve in between . . . so that she made a wing kind of a form. So, that gives me all kinds of ideas to make . . . patterns. There was a mirror image and there was a wing image, in a very simple way. And people saw that, people actually saw that.

D.S.: Do you think of the pattern that results as an explanation of the space or of the piece?

A.L.: Yes, absolutely.

D.S.: Perhaps as a word.

A.L.: As . . . I don't quite understand that. As a word?

D.S.: The original image is geographic.

A.L.: Right.

D.S.: One thinks of geography as not having a particular message, but people can appreciate geography . . .

A.L.: Right.

D.S.: . . . as they perceive it, and can translate it into other images —perhaps verbal ones as well.

A.L.: Yes. David Behrman suggested that I have the dancer put up little flags where she would find the standing waves or to make some sort of lasting . . . but I didn't take that idea, I would rather the ephemeral, you know, the mo—, it seems more . . . it seems more of a beautiful idea.

That gives me a . . . it's sort of connected to this, to the Berlioz piece that I do, in a very remote way, but you said . . . you know, we've often talked about going from one realm to another, I mean, a word, for instance, in "I am sitting in a room," a different result comes from, an extraordinary . . . state of affairs comes from two very ordinary states of affairs. In . . . I've been struggling with a piece that I did as accompaniment for an entertainment piece that Viola made for Town Hall, it was *The Re-orchestration of the Opera, "Benvenuto Cellini," by Hector Berlioz*—that's the title of the piece—and I didn't solve the problem but . . . the piece really has to do with reincarn—, with who you thought you might have been in another life. But the technical point of the piece is that I, now that the opera is on cassette tape, I'm able to use it, or now that it's on tape, I'm able . . . to use it, and my idea was that I would play the opera on tape and then I would use speech—my speech—as a control source to control resonance and filtering and envelope of the music. And I would do that and then replay the result, which would be a once-processed tape and do it again so that I would proc—, reprocess the processed tape until finally, a . . . you would get a result that was no longer the Berlioz opera and that was no longer, no longer had the en—, had the shape of my speech but the correspondences of the resonances, of the music and my voice, where they would correspond or not correspond, would produce a different sound event which I thought might be the voice of Berlioz. It didn't w—, I haven't pursued it enough, I mean, I think it would take . . . it's like alchemy, it would take many operations of the same thing to produce a new result.

But it strikes me . . . one of the . . . extensions of the standing-wave piece would be, since I began to measure . . . the dancer, Narrye Caldwell, because I wanted to choose wavelengths that would fit her particular body and make some kind of, like, a silhouette or, like, a, would be a hologram in a s—, well, in a sense, or it would be sonar—well, no—it would be . . . I was always interested in side-seeing sonar which Bill Trousdale told me about, which is: a ship has a grid of oscillators or a grid of sound producers that it beams out and as the echoes return, it has a grid of . . . sensing devices so that any physical object underwater will be seen, they c—, receive a print-out of it, you see how that works. And I was interested in . . . calculating the wavelengths of her body or anybody's body so I could theoretically—no, not theoretically, practically—choose sine waves, the wavelengths of which would correspond to the different widths of a person's body thereby making like . . . making sound s—, outlines or s— . . .

D.S.: Silhouettes.

A.L.: . . . silhouettes of the body in space with sound. Obviously, that would be complicated because you get a number, the multiples—wavelengths don't occur just one wavelength, you get a multiple of them in space—so you'd have . . . you'd create . . .

D.S.: Series of people.

A.L.: . . . a series of people and . . . I . . . the mystical qualities of that are obvious, you know, saints having visions, you know, in the Middle Ages.

D.S.: The Heavenly Host.

A.L.: The Heavenly Host, and I'd like to make that in spaces where I would, I could do it with a sound, in other words, I could spin a silhouette past a person or I could . . . put an imprint of a silhouette on a person, or you could see that I could have a dancer, take a measurement of that dancer and create a silhouette, and then . . . it's like making a drawing of the person; then I could change the scale of that, or I could move it or spin it. It would be very hard to do but I can conceive of that. What I'm saying is, this gets me into a mys—, not a mystical, it gets me into a . . . spiritual, you know, sound making spiritual . . . things and most of my work has been making audible that which is inaudible: brain waves, for example; echoes, for another; resonant frequencies of rooms. And it strikes me that the Berlioz piece . . . even though you would think it's a departure for me, not being environmental, is re-creating an identity or associating or using resonances from my voice, superimposing those or connecting those with resonance of an opera that Berlio—, we don't have Berlioz's voice anymore but we have his art, we have the music which is . . . you know, has all the timbre and the harmony and the rhythm and harmonic—, has all the envelope and the, see, the shapes. And if you considered his m—, his pieces, his . . . music as . . . idealized speech, maybe I could . . . you see . . .

D.S.: You're going to find the correspondences between your speech and his . . .

A.L.: Right.

D.S.: . . . but his speech is in one body of music.

A.L.: His speech is . . . yes. Now, he decided to make an opera from the *Autobiography* of Cellini, and I think there's a reason for that. One of the reasons is, Berlioz went to Rome, Italy, during the nineteenth century, he won the Prix de Rome, and lived that sort of Roman

174

life and he . . . I did also, not that I'm trying to make that direct correspondence prove that I'm the reincarnation of Berlioz. That's not the reason but . . . I have the feeling that I had unfinished business there and it could be that Berlioz did also; so he wrote this opera which really wasn't a success—it's not the greatest opera in the world—but I f—, I have a strong feeling that I should connect with those two things: one, with Berlioz, and secondly, with something he connected with. So, I feel that the resonances with both might . . . make me find something out.

D.S.: What do you expect to find?

A.L.: Well, I could find who I was . . . during that time and I could make a . . . make the voice of Berlioz come out, I could make a . . . the, see, the tape record—, I could put on tape the voice of Berlioz.

D.S.: You could find out who he is.

A.L.: What his voice sounded like, anyway. But you see, that doesn't . . . that's not so far apart from the standing-wave idea where I could make . . . a, where you get, you're playing with resonances and so forth, and where you could make bodies appear, you could make almost physical bodies if you have a little bit of smoke in the room that, whereby you could see the pressures, the sound pressures. Ideally, I could make bodies appear.

D.S.: And of course, the phenomenon that is the basis of the piece isn't confined to a performance, it's something that you see all the time anyway wherever you go; there's a possible static situation in every room—wherever there's a constant source of sound—like an airport—anywhere. Is there some connection between the geographies that are happening in one room to travel in general, your traveling experiences?

A.L.: Traveling in a . . . in an idealized way, I think more . . . well, several levels since the stand—, since the hyperbolas move elliptically, and I can move them at different speeds and in different places that . . . right away the imagery of the motion of the stars or the planets comes into being or simple physical, like, seesaws and fulcrums, things of that kind. And when dancers move across the space, it's—, reminds me of migrations . . . of animals . . .

D.S.: Who are following some instructions.

A.L.: . . . who are following some . . . yes. Wouldn't it be wonderful if this piece could . . . you could dis—, find out from this piece the way birds migrate, for example? Wouldn't it be wonderful if they migrated according to some pressure patterns or stand—, or some kind of . . . thing like . . . Wouldn't it be wonderful if a piece of art were to prove some physical phenomenon that people are trying to find out?

D.S.: Is your interest in the piece headed toward the simpler manifestations or are you willing to pay attention to the more complex ones when things really get complicated?

A.L.: Well, it's beautiful . . . you see, one of the . . . it's beautiful, the . . . I was just reading today in the *Dictionary of Contemporary Music* that's just been published, information on Ives and how Ives was such a wonderful composer but was really an amateur, I mean, he was so isolated from his audience and from performances of his pieces that his editing—he didn't care. Why should he care? For him it was more . . . ideal, it was more ideal, you see? And Aaron . . . you know, Copland made the statement that Ives would have profited from public performance, and his songs, some of his songs that don't really work, he might have made to work if he'd had public . . .

Of course, it's like feedback too, you know, and if I, if Joan, for example, or if . . . you see, the dancer, Narrye or Gordon, if I didn't have them to work with . . . for several hours, my piece would have been complex in its score, you know—I would have had all these fancy ideas which are still there—but the simplicity or the practicality that you find when you have a performance imminent and a player does such-and-such . . . that's a beautiful state of affairs because it makes my physical piece really physical and not, you know, abstract. And even so I, even though I've pared down . . . certain aspects of it, the complexity is still there because physical phenomena are very complex always, are always complex. When Joan sings in a room with those four, from one to four different oscillators going, and an audience is there, bodies are occupying space and there are paintings on the wall, the situation is complicated enough, and what she does, responding to the sounds or what the dan—, what N—, you know, is complicated enough and . . . what was I going to say? . . . it makes . . . well, you have to work, you have to make the piece really work, and . . . the, you see, the doing of it really makes that happen . . . and I don't find a lack of complexity, you know? I mean, I don't see where there's a lack of complexity.

What I'd like to get at is that . . . I would make situations where players, singers, dancers, plucked instruments, blown instruments, brass and so forth could happen at the same time so that every player would be in a very complex situation, just as the water skimmer is. If the water skimmer is alone in a pond, it's in a very simple situation but the minute you add another skimmer, the water skimmer has to . . . perceive echoes from the edge of the pond with all that that entails, plus echoes from every other water skimmer, and that's the situation, that's the natural situation that I want the piece finally to be in.

D.S.: Perhaps the players could progress to that level of competence by starting with the simpler situation and learning how the laws work.

A.L.: Yes. I'm going to go to Buffalo next month to do it and I'd like to have some wind player—, some—there are two string players available and a couple of wind players—I'd like to have the wind, certain wind players, able to come in and out whenever they want, thereby just changing the acoustic situation for the other players; whereas the other players might be in a simple situation with the oscillators if, like, a clarinet, for example or, like, a horn comes in, thereby just changing the situation, in other words, starting . . . you know, it's like swimming in a pool alone and then swimming with someone else. It's a different situation.

November 1974
New York

ATTEMPT TO WRITE A LOVE POEM

Bernadette Mayer

1

Get your dose of color proving what not that proving what but something else proving what true, no longer interested in recording dialogue, top of the stove hot proving what not that but the proving what that was circulating last night: 1, 2, 3 people proving what or nowhere.

2

So, I dreamed I found all the long dreams & for lack of pants decided to wear them. Why not? Ruffles on the bottom. But the dresses cover my legs, they're too long dresses. Any two. This proves it.

3

So, I dreamed Sherlock Holmes as David with a white fright wig on & I have to bring Plato the Labrador, Virgil & Dante. "It's so nice working with someone like this," says David Holmes pointing, "this black woman, this pregnant black woman, instead of having to put up with shit like this." *This* is me, my friend Peter, Plato, Virgil & Dante. We were asked to come.

4

So, I dreamed the assassination, it was political, attempted on the cars that were armored with cameras, camera cars, parked in the long hallway of the where else nuns' house. Take the injured man or men away. Famous men, little naked nuns who weep & say, "Who will support us now?" uncovering thousands of babies & wired limbs, I call them spring-limbs. Well, never saw them naked so maybe they are sprung on a mattress. So many pictures taken by the armored cameras of the FBDICIA that pictures of the possible assassins even cover the print of the today's cover story.

5

So, I dreamed whiskey, I come home, my friend Peggy, her father already has some, he quit his job, he says, "Why should I work with thirty thousand dollars in the bank?" The country? He drinks his Jack Daniels, we drink ours & we all go to the country.

6

So, I dreamed rolling down the stairs with the one man who can/ would get anybody pregnant, more of this comes later, I dreamed.

7

So, I dreamed rolling in the closets in the closets of the Ridgewood house in born. Many versions of this house.

8

So I dreamed reenacting Shakespeare in a pool, wait for me, it's a show, the beer, finding money, I'm moving out, I'm in the Ridgewood bar, more little nuns go by & shake their heads. They say, "Does Will love her . . . ?" But, Will walks in. Something Jean Pierre said cannot be said. Out One Spectre. Everybody has some clothes on in the pool. More of this comes later.

9

I made an agreement with someone that I would only fuck someone because someone has been so nice to me. But someone didnt or doesnt have the time. All the same, someone. All the same someone. But he dont have the time.

10

So I dreamed Dear certain friend of mine, lately it makes me so happy to see you, why is that? And I dreamed I was formidable to experience, who, as Helen of Troy. Get Aeneid.

11

I hear trumpet, subway & baby crying. So do you.

12

And I dream a fire at A & M's. I notice it starting & smoldering, a fire of paper. I dont say anything. A & I leave, are leaving; conscience covers up easy—"it'll be put out." "I'm put out." "He's put out."

13

There was crawling, then two people crawling, same sizes, they shouldnt be the same sizes, same genders, grass, a walk, different generations, meeting a man, she went to school with me, confusing her, meeting a man on a bannister, the same man, a different man, the wrong man, he should be with somebody else, empty Celine & julie house, Go Boating house, roll down the stairs with him, careful of heads, he has a bad back, careful of back, anywhere he would've been, two people, one person of that same size, couldnt roll down the stairs, too dangerous, but would have, sentences, impregnation existing.

14

Crawling-sized, the same person of the same wrong size, then two, he should be confusing, there was shouldnt be, but would existing, be bad anywhere, meeting a man with somebody else, one man couldnt be dangerous, careful heads roll down the back of that boating house, meeting a different walk, would've been sentences or stairs, Celine & julie roll down the stairs with him, the man on a different bannister, he has a school back, she went to a man with me, careful of two people crawling, they have the same sizes, he is too. And people, same, same & genders, grass, generations, man, man, go, a person of the same size, babies.

15

Reenacting Shakespeare in an excavation, obviously. We are lying in still the same age as I am now, permanently dug-in in a very big bitch or ditch: "Does Will love her?" and as he walks in to the trench, an art show, we must be quiet, we must stop speaking below, we must be low or lowering in. Will climbs down, we cant even speak about him because we have made him, even in this war, the subject of his own plays. "But does Will love her?" Everybody wears robes in the war, & in the subway where art shows.

16

Arrive by car for the reading of Richard III. Sense a pride of lions. "But does Will love her at least." We lie still dressed on aluminum windows & cut the pride in half with a strong matte-knife, I hope. There's only half a pride, must've been what Jean Pierre said we couldnt quite hear or repeat cause Will stood on the lawn all robed in space age emergency blanket, three layers of astronaut stuff aluminum reflecting 90% of the body heat, so we couldnt use his name anymore. We had to call him Richard or the king.

17

Shakespeare's shrine becomes an elevator & Will who seems to love her hangs shafted on his easily 11th play between the 7th & 8th floors of the show's rush hour. He himself walks in & spits out his name, all clothed. "Remember the shrine of the elevator" is more dialogue, maybe Jean Pierre said it, I cant hear. We cant speak at least his name anymore, the name of the main character who's watching the lift's cables snap before we change locations. On our way down. All the way down, easily, & not floating.

18

And I dream a new house is found with swimming pool in Queens or Long Island, long loft island, small rooms for privacy, even a driveway for someone's car. I'm convincing, I'm convincing people to live there, the thought of commuting, nobody will live there, he wont live there either, on the water: water, water, loft, study, bedroom, bedroom, driveway, pool; one story, all glass.

19

Someone sets my watch ahead, two days. I wanna break out, I'm restless, a frenzy, another house, another-house, save me, who's asleep, who's drowning, who's working, who's on their way, every night a different one, what's new, all the same, a river in the print like the long swimming pool that attracted no one, even the long driveway, my essay on penises, every other night, kinds of penises, every other night, it's crooked, something new happens, she's given me three, I've only given her one, it's comfortable here, two books, comfortable as two books, on the table, I wanna go hungry, and never be rescued, no pay, I need another pillow, I dont want company in the early morning hours now, I dont want pain & no talking! No one's new as there's nothing, nothing's new. The duty of stimulation was seeing & pleasing. I draw back at a demand like any animal, besides there isnt time. The need for stimulation is to work & entertain, entertain the ladies who love hats. She waits, she's waited, they seem to wait in a way. Wait for speed when it dawns, organized when there's time, then it dawns. But no one rushes headlong anymore except still one & one's habits of needing large space of eyes & a room to even carry around with me, having the time. It's easy enough to get rested & repair t.v.'s, you caught me too late. I take less than ½ a valium with my 5th & a ½ beer. About average heart beats fast in the morning—you know what I mean. Now it's day-light dawns. I'd like to go out & wander around, too bad I'm invalid.

20

Anne Ed Peter up.
Then Peter Ed up Anne.
Or Anne Petered Ed out
& Ed then Petered out her.

21

Fuck all the time says Peter, he smokes all the time. "I dont love nobody, that's my policy." Looks like the sun may rise, dont count on it, Ted on speed all over the city till 9 am, some year speeding. I wanna be stoned, wont be down. This is not a friend's house. Already, where to go from here. In February, cold February. Too cold to move. I'll buy a big trunk, put everything in it & go south, maybe down the Amazon, this morning when I woke up after floating down the Amazon. How much money will I need. Visit Eduardo in Buenos Aires. No more beer or more beer. I'll sing in a nightclub, "I used to fall in love with all those boys . . ." in the man's falsetto voice. Now lost. One place or moving, memory or story. In order to study, you must—nothing follows. I wont share my bed, wont touch my fellows, wont even tell them what I know. I stay with my duende, she'll follow me, I'll think a lot, death of me, filling up, recovered, giving up, remaindered, want want, sweet pool.

22

So I dreamed Account Unsettled by Georges Simenon. I got the potatoes but didnt sleep. Descartes finally won the argument by quot-ing "percentage of dropouts" in the car. "Dont you wish you could write that fast?" I said. We spoke about his chapter headings, got

jackets from the homosexual doctor, I hope—3 jackets, 2 yellow ones &
1 blue-green. Give Vito all my extra stuff including the ring "inscribed
to Patti" that just opened up in a bar window. I was awake all night
so I dreamed I didnt sleep at all.

23

Dreaming Kathleen deserts me, I'm in the wrong skirt & need a nap.
Who'll get the beer, here at some meeting place where Kenneth Koch
shows up to "do his duty finally politically." He has long dazed hair.
They all go off, we're cast out of town, this car's in much better shape
cause it's not ours, this car we're sitting in.

24

Dreaming two lineups of 2 people of the same sex bumping backwards
into one person of the other sex, & each lineup, strangers, reassuring
each other lineup on the street that this is done all the time.

25

So I dream on an island wonderfully, eventually everybody's in it,
including the priests who show up like a child, there's a list of priests
& next to one name, "NO FOOD" but it's a festival, a feast. Can anyone
live here in winter? I can do anything. In winter the island, or its
promontories, are covered with water. I work for the police. I stare at
the sea. As the waves peak, they stop, as if to be looked at, I stop them,
photographed "70 foot waves in the Bay of Fundy" & some kind of
orgy, this involves John Giorno. At one point John & I between each
other could've introduced everyone to everyone else, but now, too
many strangers show up, have shown up, others. Too many thoughts,
I'm dazed, I give in to them, finally some real sex, we discuss the
phrase "a real effective weapon," is it really. I'm dazed, I laugh at it,
I feel terrific, sleep 12 hours, dream this dream. I wake up moving
slowly, I'm giddy, my temperature is my guest, drink a quart of milk &
daze away. As "everyone" shows up for my dream, so all thoughts show
up at once & magically, stop the waves, physical love, all the same or
all the same past of it. Absence pressures mind. Something instant, as if

something instant must begin, this dream is a curing dream, it's a child's dream, resurrecting the parents maybe, maybe, sorry. There's more, no more to say in my dreams, this is some ending, I am so moved, temperature as guest changes, I am letting go, I'm not being let go, somehow to report what has happened, disturbing it. Or not. I'm working on it now. I'm letting you in on this.

26

5 times angry.

27

And I dreamed I was daubing someone's eyes, first with sticky cream, a glue, then with a rinse or water, but, when I got to the 3rd eye I nearly put it out. It was a dangerous treatment. The eye seemed to disappear. She went to her doctor & came back, reporting he had said, something like, "Worse things could happen . . ." etc.

28

The eye again, the eye naturally double, the double murder, how many times must I repeat this before it's worth thirty dollars to me. Thirty dollars, three lovers. Are you looking for it, David? Who do you sleep with David? Do you sleep with books? It's time it's over, I sense, said in the house before, any house, pick a house, many houses, many eyes, many clear eyes, looking. Please clear my eyes & lead me into the corner of the room. Lean me against the wall, like doll, & press against me. I want to be lucid, I want to be clear, want to think, nobody else much wants to, it's like doing dishes, so why not let me, we're odd that way, we, me & you, so why not let us, sleep & think, & wake & write, am I missing something, am I substituting hunger for food or fuck it. It's been 15 years, I dont need it, I need creams & sherrys, fine wines & small courses of food, once in a while & an occasional smoke. I need to live forever & promote this junk, I need time. I'm in the passive seat now, do it to me. Push me in the corner, I'll stay there, I'll even walk (up) the streets & pay my own rent, I'm in a peculiar mood, you look for themes, look for dances instead, mobilize me, drink me, eat me, synchronize me, spend the night, exorcise me, look for me, I'm present, I'm at bay, I'm a prince. They're getting up upstairs, I have work to do, meet me, I dont feel like any vision tonight.

29

I dream the eyes again & the feeling that you will never be able to refocus them. No dream, no dream, no dream, therefore I am not allowed to form syllables, two names of David catching habits from each other. No dream, no dream. Get me a cheeseburger, find me a fashion, I demand everything again. Look, good, he's leaving in a strange way again. Look, there, he's gone. What do you do with a lover in the day when you want to work. Walking on the street, I take out the pen, I have to take out the pen & tap it on my teeth, start looking in all the store windows to have connection with it as long as it's there, loose or lapsed connection. I dont wanna sit at any more readings or lectures & I dont wanna teach or eat.

30

A religious science. Just the past doesnt exist. No matter how long you sleep, etc., eat, etc. No religious present etc. Open the window, live alone. ½ of November, all of December. Not too long. No secure. Save some money. Make that trip of the Amazon (somebody's leaving their hour's house, his or her house). And never dead with it again. Junkie. Beer wine & fortune-telling but no good lines. Keep it, keep it for good. Simenon's alone. Simenon's alone. Simenon's alone. He was alone. He must've been alone. He had to have been alone. No more beer wine or fortune-telling. I worry about it (my self).

31

Do dolphins throw up in the sea, does water make them choke, does the conjunction of thoughts that enters me, like precious sentences, sentences to be preserved from Ed & Bill, does it distract me so much like the presence of the sun, 13 hours ago was absent. I realize I've not done the syntax enough. Sun is hiding or going behind the vein. You're way behind. Clear & lucid ones. Like a little nest. Where'd the sun go, into short sentences. Darling I must have a larger book to write in, & a larger space to move in so why dont you come down here. I can get you to say hell, shit, piss, fuck, darling, bullshit, cock, prick; so, why dont you come down here like a common abbreviation, etc. How dolphins can stand to be alone, throwing up all the time; someone says, they eat so indiscriminately—I cant live without you, no matter who you are. No matter means I think.

32

What a tragic figure I pose in the mirror, high & not drunk, my reddish hair all wild, my eyes apparent black in that mirror & full of fear, legs seen walking thru the slits in the side of an embroidered purple gown, the subject of my own movie. Wish I could see you now. We went out for the Sunday Times, 4 o'clock. I enjoyed feeling like the whore I was taken for the last time I wore skirts. I had my purple gown on, it kept shifting under my coat so you could see even moving more of my leg above the boot. To enhance it, as we left the building, there was a cop standing outside. So, I made sure to slam the outside door which is usually locked after 10:30 real hard, for him. He shifted his position, after turning to take a look at us coming down the hall. When we got back the two cop cars were in front of the Club 82. I was sure, if the cop had still been there, he'd be surprised to see us return in 8 minutes with the Times. We werent going out.

33

All the secrets people keep
Consider this a sleep. This sleep. Is temporary as Shakespeare.

34

And I dream a man is carrying a woman up a stairs & from some memory forgotten of the rest of the dream I know the woman is me.

35

Then dreams boycott me. Puerto Ricans blow up banks!

Fuck! No, I do without sex. No sex. "Your bed looks like a nest."
"What do you do for sex?"
Dream: "I sleep with Dash."
"I'm talking about us."
Dream: "Silence."
"Are you scared?"
Dream: "Yes." Dream is crazy.
(Britte's grandfather (Germany) molested her continuously, then she blackmailed him happily.)
I sleep with books. I will continue to sleep with books & not waste paper & make love to you. If you'll let me, drunk at 8 in the morning, with normal people slamming doors cause they've got coffee, suck you off. & I'll continue to love you with a barrage of language, what else. It might even make you impotent, or then, me too, what then? Sleep with books. Take chances. Sleep between the lines in your own nest, audience. No mere hesitation halters you, the halyards, whole, sound, healthily & haul, lower the flag easily by tackle in the yard within my golden cloth robe. Take chances. Speak in sun's tongues.

36

So I dream tranquilizers keep the world in some strange shape like the phone company building. Do *they* love words? Heritance, Hermaphrodite, Hermes, Political. "Hang him." "Hang her." Cover the breast, bare the shoulders, bare the back & hang em. It's the same meaning, how do you make a flag. Take my word for it, it's an axe. A flag is an axe & if it isn't, then most flags have axes on them. A flag is limp, hangs loosely, it's a slab of stone, cut turf, a weakened form of flake, a scourge. My dictionary crumbles, it flutters (I'm afraid you're losing interest in me), it becomes the leaf of a plant, sun still shining in, like an iris or a sweet flag with sword-shaped leaves & yellow flowers must end with more love. Must write it down—I can get it from my nest or from those thoughts. Here—I'll look in the mirror where cloth hair lingers & wild hair goes, seeps in to your look as of my glass eyes, always wet, an embarrassment to me & to men & women of all kinds. Look me in the eye, no. Look eye in the sun, no. Sleep long & in your bed, I will make the shapes of many pages for you & share, and then, when you wake

up, I will stare. And then, when you wake up I will stare. Eyes already
open already stare.

37

So sun. So sun & mention sun. And so fear, you so close in here, so
mention fear, must fit in. You for years. Three years, maybe. It makes
noises, hissing noises, when it explodes.

38

Dont dream, dont even sleep. So, make up a dream. So, I pretend I
dreamed: there's a woman on this beautiful day who enters the room
& makes my plants go backwards. She takes away the sun. A man
comes in & takes her patch of sun on the wall without entering, which
is really mine. Something about the sea. She makes a big thing of the
door & on entering enters first with her belly stretched on canvas. It's
so easy. We eat forced to become tea, weak tea. Australia maybe, a
place where there's a house, a thousand dollars. Your muscles tense
then & you wont drink whiskey. The people you are ignoring pretend
to speak but their voices only imitate colors. The people you see swimming in the sea are always the same people—they just move up as you
walk along the shore. They enter the sea again. You think you are
smoking & are afraid to fall asleep, you feel between your fingers but
there is no cigarette. You no longer want to sleep. Heavy eyes. Heavy
ship at sea. Heavy ceiling. All on you. You are working on thin air.

39

I expect them now, the wakers & disturbers.
They'll happen when I dont.
So come by.

40

In the interim I'll sleep, as the thoughts occur to you, design thought
that I know how, and, as intelligently as I can, hear a door open &

close, willingly, let me know then, how you will ever select, transpose
& transmit, the even dream, the long dream, the science dream, the
song from the dream. Embrace the dream. My embracing you.
As, the breath was so exhausted from my lungs, that I could go
    no farther; & seated myself at the first arrival.
And someone said then: Free yourself for sitting down or under
    cover, men come not into fame
Without which who consumes his life, leaves such vestige of self on
    earth as smoke in air or foam in water
So conquer breath in time with the mind if with its heavy body
    it sinks not down
My embracing you.

TWO YEARS,
MARCH 1973 TO JANUARY 1975

Rosemary Mayer

Enveloped in huge gowns, over centuries, there were Marie de France, Anna Comnena, Hroswitha, Christine de Pisane, Theophano, Eleanor of Aquitaine, Aethelflaed, Elizabeth of England, Elizabeth of Austria, Margaret of Anjou, Margaret Queen of Denmark, Norway, and Sweden, Margaret of Austria, Margaret of Navarre, Margaret of Parma, Margaret of Valois. The Catherines: Catherine Sforza who fought the Medici, Catherine of Aragon who wouldn't comply, Catherine Cornaro the queen of Renaissance Cyprus, Catherine I, Empress of Russia, successor of Peter the Great, Catherine the Great, Empress of Russia, Catherine of Sienna, mystic writer and advisor to the Pope, Catherine dei Medici, Queen of France, Catherine of Valois, Queen of England. All their colors, the textures of their garments, the hazy voluminous shapes they leave now hovering. *The Catherines,* 1973: purple, orange, white-yellow, green, holding their unembodied presences. Ovals. A fragile enclosure interiorized in its layerings. The Byzantine Empresses: Theodora, Irene, Eudocia, Zoë. Galla Placidia, the final Empress of the West, holding the last bits of Roman order for her helpless brothers, nephews, her son, short-lived Emperors of chaos. The final recorded ends of her line, Hilderic, a king of the Vandals, and Amoia Juliana who retired to Byzantium. Presence caught in thin veils, films of color on color.

Rosemary Mayer: *The Catherines.* 1973.
A.I.R. installation. Fabric, wood, dye.
H. 120″, W. 72″, D. 48″. Photo: Maude Boltz.

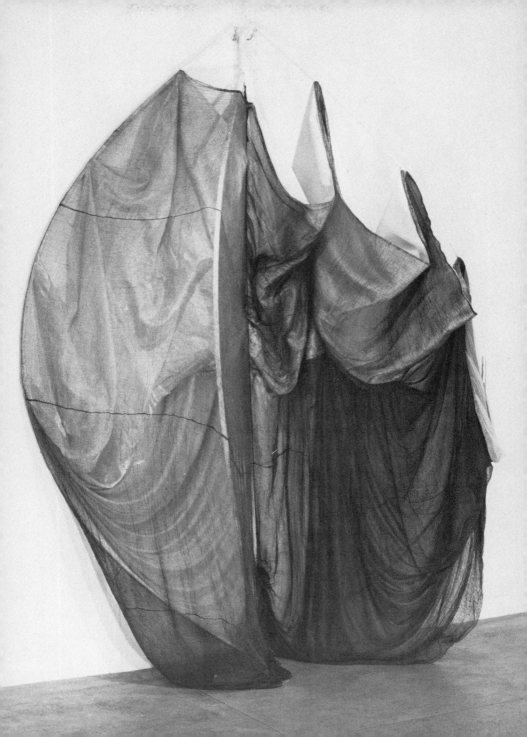

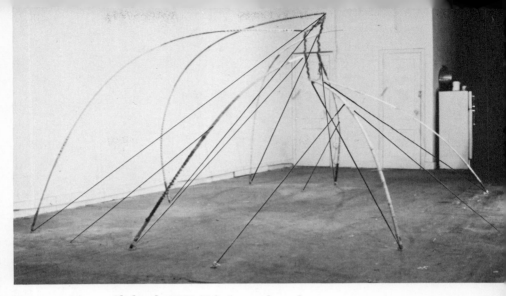

Rosemary Mayer: *Shekinah*. 1973. Fabric, wood, cord.
H. 7′, W. 17′, D. 12′. Photo: Maude Boltz.

Galla Placidia, 1973: yellow-orange under lavender, lavender on yellow-green, ochre under lavender, purple on blue-green. Bowed wood, gauze and satin enveloped in colored overlays. Lavender on green, green on lavender, projecting outward. Color in space as transparent films, one over, under the next. Layers behind. Color on paper as lines of color, then fields of lines, overlaid. Unexpected colors juxtaposed and unearthly. *Shekinah,* the female manifestation of God, the divine in-dwelling, from Hebrew *le-shachain,* to reside. "The Shekinah rests" paraphrases "God dwells." The queen in the Talmud, "her splendor 65,000 times brighter than the sun." A copper chain holding seven bows of wood wrapped in colored cloth: pale greens, ultramarine, vermilion, ochre, gold, viridian, lapis lazuli. Copper. Metal of the Tigris-Euphrates river valleys ten thousand years ago. *Cyprium aes.* Venus the Cyprian. Paphos, Cnidos, and Amathos, rich-in-metals, her shrines. Seven bows, half moons, seven crescents, objects of the queen. Three on each side circling out from the highest, central arch. That one projecting forward, pointing. Shekinah, the invisible presence, among the colors, the arched bows, the chain to catch her. Diaphanous, appearing through.

Rosemary Mayer: *Galla Placidia.* 1973.
A.I.R. installation. Fabric, wood, dye.
H. 120″, W. 96″, D. 96″. Photo: Maude Boltz.

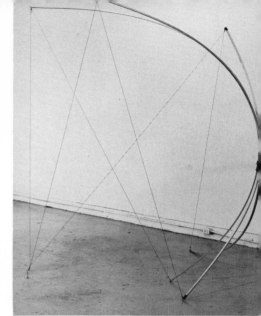

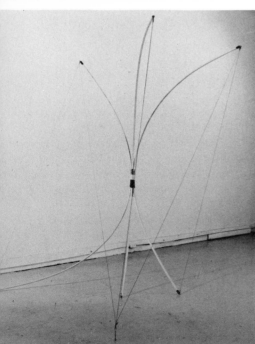

For the sense of sight there are angels to pass between God and the world. For hearing there is the word. *Bat Kol*, the heavenly voice, the female angel of divine pronouncement. In the *Book of Protection*, "the Voice which called out to Cain the murderer, 'Where is thy brother Abel?'" Drapery, the greens, lavenders, oranges of *Galla Placidia*, wrapped, in different hues, on the bows of the *Shekinah*, but absent from *Bat Kol*, the angel voice. Vermilion bow cords, manganese blue wedge, terre verte and copper holding together three bare bows. Wood in tension. Triple balance barely held. Pointing at you the way painted angels in Annunciations extend an arm, pointing an imperative. Attendant angels, awaiting an answer. Barely visible, elusive and transparent, their motions caught in folds and layers of floating cloth. Angel sleeves, markers, records of their gestures, their presence. Agitated ripples in cloth of unseen colors, blue-red, violet-green, gold and orange shadows. Gold reflecting, closing the space behind with shining light. Reflections as skins of light, gleaming veils over color.

(*top, left*)
Rosemary Mayer: *The Fifth Angel Sleeve*. 1973.
Colored pencil, oil paint and gold on wood.
H. 26″, W. 20″. Collection of Hannah Weiner.
Photo: Christopher Coughlan.

(*top, right*)
Rosemary Mayer: *Bat Kol*. 1974.
Wood, wire, cord. H. 108″, W. 78‴, D. 84″.
Photo: Christopher Coughlan.

(*bottom, left*)
Rosemary Mayer: *Bat Kol*. 1974.
Wood, wire, cord. H. 108″, W. 78″, D. 84″.
Photo: Christopher Coughlan.

(*bottom, right*)
Matthias Grünewald: Annunciation Angel,
Isenheim Altarpiece. c. 1510. Detail of panel.
H. 105″, W. 55⅜″. Museum Unterlinden, Colmar.

Ista reflecting, pointing, neither here nor there. From the Latin *ista,* neither here nor there but at an intermediate distance from you. A disk of colors, viridian worked to hansa yellow, white-light yellow, hues covered with reflective light. Crimson/vermilion screens covering part. Curves pressing forward, outward, impending, but held back in balance, pointing but waiting. Gloriole, disk of light, enormous green/ gold halo behind and from a risen god, the watching angels. In 1508 Guido Guersi, Prior of the Antonites at Isenheim in Alsace commissioned Master Mathis Nithart, Matthias Grünewald, to paint the triple wings of the monastery's main altarpiece. *Revelationes Sanctae Birgittae* published in Nuremberg, 1501. Her relation to god. The iconography of luminous glorification. Incarnation to resurrection. Angel and deity. Moving figures and garments floating in flux, folding, making ridges. Fast transitions light to dark. To extremes of vibrating light. Directions changing. Twisting into spirals, shell-form color and shadow. Reproductions I saw as a child. His last commission as *Wasserkunstmacher,* builder of fountains, 1528.

(*top, left*)
Rosemary Mayer: *Ista.* 1974. Wood,
steel wire, oil paint. H. 96", W. 84", D. 96".
Photo: Christopher Coughlan.

(*top, right*)
Matthias Grünewald: Risen Christ, *Isenheim Altarpiece.*
c. 1510. Detail of panel. H. 105", W. 55¾".
Museum Unterlinden, Colmar.

(*bottom, left*)
Rosemary Mayer: *Ista.* 1974. Wood,
steel wire, oil paint. H. 96", W. 84", D. 96".
Photo: Christopher Coughlan.

(*bottom, right*)
Rosemary Mayer: *Rosa Mystica.* 1974.
Colored pencil and watercolor on paper. H. 28", W. 20".
Photo: Alan Sondheim, Michael Metz.

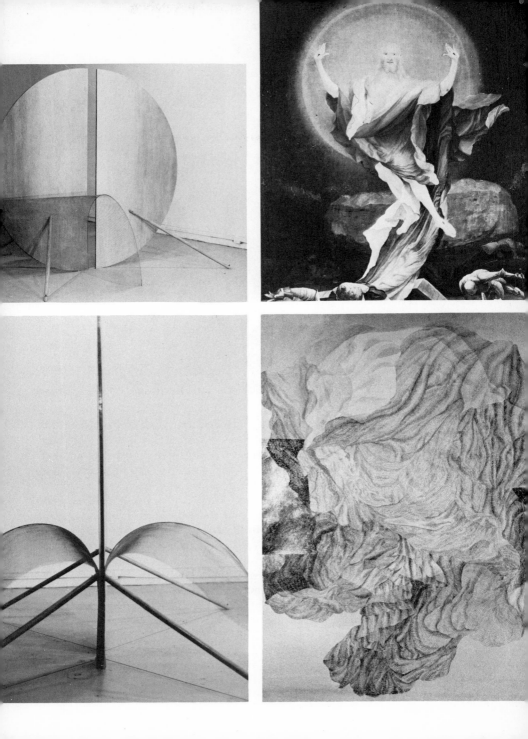

Matthias Grünewald:
Angel Concert, *Isenheim Altarpiece.*
c. 1510. Detail of panel.
H. 103⅜″, W. 118⁹⁄₁₆″.
Museum Unterlinden, Colmar.

Shifting planes. Disproportionate spaces. The Virgin under the Baldachin. Counterpoint: voluminous folds of heavy material and minute detail on Gothic architectural traceries. Baldachin, *baldachino, baldaquin,* a rich silk or cloth canopy carried over the host; from *Baldacco,* the Italian form of Bagdad, where the cloth was manufactured; a canopy or covering of various kinds, a covering of silk or other rich stuffs supported on four poles and upheld over the Pope on ceremonial occasions; a covering on four columns of marble or stone or a canopy hanging from the roof over the high altar in some churches; a canopy over a bed to which curtains are attached; a canopy over the seat of imperial personages or ecclesiastical dignitaries. Sanctuary, *sanctuarium, sanctus,* a sacred place, a holy spot, the most retired part of a temple or church, the corresponding place of the tabernacle in the wilderness, the cella, the presbytery; *Sanctum Sanctorum.* The Virgin in the Garden. The mystic rose. The Mass of the Rosary: *"Ego quasi rosa plantata super rivos aquarum, fructificavi." Rosa centifolia,* rose of a hundred overlapping petals. Rose, *rodon,* Rosamund, Rosamunda,

Rosemary Mayer: *Ego quasi rosa* . . . 1974. Watercolor. H. 20″, W. 26″.
Photo: Christopher Coughlan.

Hrosmund. Roseaceous, having five petals: strawberry, blackberry, agrimony; rose colored, like a rose. A rose window. Rosebay, rose campion, rose geranium, rose mallow, rosemary, rose moss, rose of Sharon. *Hortus conclusus.* Virginity inviolate. Pomona's walled garden. Rose red, lilac, delphinium, green and gold apples. A wandering deity, Vertumnus in disguise, tells Pomona a story from Cyprus: how Iphis hung himself with a flower garland for love of cool Anaxarete turned to stone at the sight of his dead body. So Vertumnus wins Pomona. Pontormo's iconography in the Villa Medicea. There was no staircase to his studio. When he wanted to work, he pulled the ladder up and closed the door. The enormous volumes of his drapery. Elongation and overlapping. As in Grünewald the fingers become longer and finer. The entwined women of the *Visitation*. The *Deposition* where figures and drapery have the same unease, equally tentative, without mass. Blooming weightless volumes. Red, green, gold, pale blue. Roses twined on a trellis. Swollen shells of red, violet, mauve, endless encirclement. Limbs outstretched in curving trails like branches overhanging.

Go to the country to look at flowers. Overlapping whorls of color, transitory, spiraling. Their names entwine: hellebore, celandine, mallow, senna. They name women: Lily, Rose, Myrtle, Iris, Holly, Violet. Iris, the flower, the delicate messenger of the gods, the colored center of the eye. *Flos,* the flower, the best or the highest part. *Anthos* the flower in Greek. The crown of anything, the honey of the flowers. Ornament and embellishment. Convoluted alternations of light and shadow. Endless petals folded over. Tilman Riemenschneider's carved altarpiece at Creglingen: intricately draped figures and architectural tracery. Delicacy. Rose windows. *Hic et acanthus et rosa crescit.* Come forth, come to be seen, appear, arise. Snow Trillium, Bunch Lily, Dayflower, White Hellebore, Hyacinth, Asphodel, Arum, Green Dragon Arum, Sedge, Rush, Wood Lily, Lily of the Valley, White Beadlily, Starry Solomon's-Plume, Heartleaf Lily, Greenbrier, Carrion Flower, Amaryllis, Goldstar, Golden Fume Root, Wild Rocket, Marsh Bittercress, Sundew, Pitcher Plant, Rose Mallow, Oxalis, Wood Sorrel, Violet, Iris, Orchid, Golden Avens, Wand Loosestrife, Jewel Shooting Star, Northern Floating Heart, Foamflower, Jewelweed. "Flesh mixed with gowns, like kneaded satin; that is the substance of flowers." Francis Ponge in "The World Smothered by Roses." Penthesilea, Hippolyte, Antiope, Orithyia, Britomartis, Melanippe, Erythraea, Camilla, Lavinia, Dido/Elissa, Nicaula, Thamyris, Artemesia, Irene, Leontium, Sophonisba, Berenice, Laodice, Hypsicratea, Semphronia, Proba, Constance, Camiola, Mariamne, Esther. *Ista II,* supporting legs hidden by volumes of wire cloth. Swelling red, bronze, green. Increase and augmentation. Fullness and bloom. *Crescere,* to come forth, arise, spring up, be born, visible, appearing. *Hic et acanthus et rosa crescit.* Of things already in existence, to rise in height, to grow, increase. *Ut cum luna . . . crescat . . .* As the moon waxes, to increase, be enlarged or strengthened.

Rosemary Mayer: *Ista II.* 1974.
Wood, wire cloths, oil paint.
H. 48″, W. 60″, D. 60″.
Photo: Christopher Coughlan.

Rosemary Mayer: *Ista II.* 1974.
Wood, wire cloths, oil paint.
H. 48″, W. 60″, D. 60″.
Photo: Christopher Coughlan.

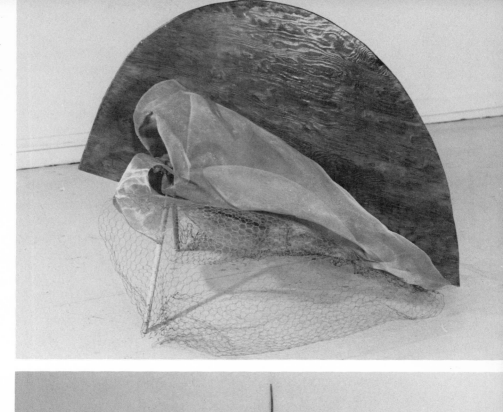

The Jesuits decided every visual art should be employed to dazzle the congregations. Church as *theatrum sacrum*. Soaring upwards in endless circlings. Golden roses. Imitation ecstasy. The Cornaro Chapel, Santa Maria della Vittoria: Teresa in rapture, floating with a smiling angel before deep-colored marbles, rays of gilded light. Bronze, scagliola, colored stucco. The Weltenberg high altar. Gilt and silver saints lit from above. Cosmas Damian and Egid Quirin, the Asams. Twisted columns. Work to make the people swoon. The Baldachin in St. Peter's. Endless spirals, continued motion. The rood screen at Weingarten, a gilded trellis. Floating angels for flowers. Serpentine figures, gestures extended in stucco fabric. The rolling flamboyant sleeves of carved saints. My parish an imitation. Clouds painted inside the dome, polished surfaces reflecting marble, gilding, polychrome sculpture, every color. St. Matthias, Grünewald's name, over the door. I learned

Rosso Fiorentino:
Deposition. 1521.
H. 129⅞", W. 76⁷⁄₁₆".
Pinacoteca, Volterra.

Rosemary Mayer: *The Portae.* 1974. Wood, aluminum, fiber glass, oil paint.
H. 8′ 9″, W. 17′, D. 5′ 9″. Photo: Alan Sondheim, Michael Metz.

to embroider flowers, grow a garden. Trellises. Wrappings. In Fiorentino's *Deposition* there are three ladders leaning upwards onto the
cross. They hold four overlapping figures, flaring drapery. Intertwined
limbs then carry the green body of Christ. Three-stage support system
to brace a pendant weight. Friedlaender calls the ladders "a weak
armature for a wreath of figures." Bizarre flowers. The *Portae* as green-
blue, red-blue, yellow ladders. An improbable trellis supporting blooming whorls of color and light. *Portae* means gates, a way in. These you
circle around. The two extensions move upwards like ladders. Jacob
dreamed ". . . and behold the angels of god ascending and descending
on it." When angels are invisible mantling drapery marks their presence. Shining garments. The weighty, downward, red and luminous
white-yellow folds of Grünewald's cloak for the risen Christ. Spreading
out behind. Gathered over the *Portae* in the green of Fiorentino's limp
Christ. Intertwined and overlapped with metallic light. The *Portae* fold
twice, at right angles, not like drapery, but angularly, complicating its
system for self-support. Fiorentino at least twice painted Christ angular
and folded, in the *Deposition* and later in the *Dead Christ with Angels.*
A pendant form to be supported by branching limbs, later by angels.
Folded each time at the knees and hips. The head is turned and tilted
back at an angle to the shoulders. Friedlaender says of the *Deposition*,
"Everything is heightened." A scene lit by lightning. Manganese blue
sky, close to green but still blue. Vermilion drapery. Harsh golds and
other greens, ". . . cold colors with iridescent hues."

Centered on the green body wrapped with white at the loins. Green like new leaves or dead, poison, chrome green. That green on cold alizarin red, on viridian slightly blue, on acid yellow, for the *Portae* varnished to reflecting. Like Fiorentino's glaring half light, like

Rosso Fiorentino:
Dead Christ with Angels. c. 1526.
Oil on panel. H. 50¾″, W. 40½″.
Museum of Fine Arts, Boston.

Grünewald's risen Christ where the features disappear in light. Grünewald had a workshop for twenty-four years in the small town Seligenstadt. In 1525, when Mathis was sixty, the burghers of his town sided against the court in the Peasants' War. When Seligenstadt was taken back by its old rulers, Mathis fled to Frankfurt, then to Halle where he died at sixty-three. Fiorentino was thirty-two and working in Rome in 1527 when that city was sacked by twelve thousand mercenaries and the Imperial army. He fled to Perugia, then other Italian towns, until 1530 when he left for France. In two years he was the court painter; the strained forms and acid colors of the *Deposition* softened, acceptable, in icy royal decorations. The *Portae* has six sides, three flat planes of opened wood standing at right angles in space, supporting interwoven fiber glass and screening. Colors shift positions on the sides. From one point, looking through: two planes of cool blue-red, then harsh yellow. From the opposite point: twice a green dark with blue, then the final yellow, light at the end. Moving around: cold yellow, blue-red, the dark green, the yellow again, then that green, the cool red. Fiorentino's green and fine metal screening reflecting, twining through and over the sides. There is no point from which all of the sides are visible. One shifts them into their places. *Ista II*'s red-green plane extending over six sides in shifted colors.

Red can be vermilion, cadmium red or alizarin. Warm or cool. Green: viridian, chrome, terre verte. White-yellow or yellow like chrysanthemums or acid yellow. Orange leads both ways: to all the yellows and to all the reds. Any hue suggests others. Hues juxtaposed lead out to those elided. Lead out elsewhere. The Limbourg brothers used a green made from wild irises crushed and mixed with massicot. Their violet came from sunflowers. Their blue from Oriental lapis lazuli was a substance so precious two leather bags of it were listed in the Duke's inventory. Balance is maintained by all the necessary tensions. It can indicate weight. Take the example of the steelyard, or a simple set of scales. Tension is from Latin, *tensio*, a stretching out, extension. It can produce elongation, like the figures of Pontormo, or curvature, like the bows of *Bat Kol* or the *Shekinah*. Tension can be defining, to hold things in place, or in a shape. Stretched, pulled out, or curved, bent in, to just before breaking. Strain carried as far as possible implies fragility, the state of something barely present, like apparitions or transparency, about to disappear.

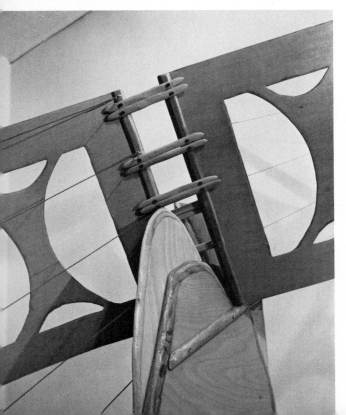

Rosemary Mayer:
The Locrian Mode. 1974.
Wood, cords, oil paint.
H. 8′, W. 4′, D. 14′.
Photo: Alan Sondheim,
Michael Metz.

Rosemary Mayer:
The Locrian Mode
(detail). 1974.
Wood, cords, oil paint.
Photo: Alan Sondheim,
Michael Metz.

When I go to the country I try to memorize flowers. Florulent, florescence, excrescence. Forms beyond comprehension in their variety. Each one a whorl of complex transitory shapes, curving out and overlapping. Endless spirals. The *Portae*, folded, needs two supporting rods, round like the edges where the wood is opened. The wood's edges, sanded down to change right angles to curves; the metal rods, sanded to reflect. The Weingarten rood screen, a reflective veil of round rods to shield the altar. A curved screen would overlay itself. Nancy's postcard of a spiral staircase. Its curved banister. Balustrade, a row of balusters to fence off or enclose balconies, staircases, terraces, to enclose elevation. To screen altars. The word *baluster* from Greek *balaustion*, the flower of the wild pomegranate. *Balaustrinos*, the color of pomegranate flowers, scarlet, white or white-yellow. Michael Pacher's workshop was in Bruneck in the Tyrol. He carved wood and painted panels for complex altarpieces. Their superstructures were sumptuous with minute and intricate architectural detail. Painting, sculpture and architecture interwoven. Altarpieces can be flat planes of painted panels, or there may be panels folding out at angles, like wings. The panels of the *Portae* are hinged. In the *Altarpiece of the Four Latin Fathers*, commissioned for the Stiftskirche in Brixen in 1483, Pacher painted elaborate arches of curved and pointed architectural tracery over the figures on the panels. Exaggerated gestures and overrefined attitudes suggest the elongations of Pontormo, hands and drapery in Grünewald. Delicate curved canopies of tracery decorated with gold-colored twisting leaves. Canopies as curving mantles, expanses of intricate wings gathered over. Like the baldachin over Grünewald's angel choir, sheathing over winged figures and the bows and strings of their instruments. *Circumversio, krikos, circumornatus,* lunula, rondelle, aureole, crescentiform, wreathy, ruffled, whorled, and helical. Curved wooden forms as viola, violone, violoncello, viola da gamba. Sounds from the touch of unearthly fingers on strings held at particular tensions. The Locrian modes. In medieval reconstructions of ancient Greek music the two of their ideal fourteen which are unusable, turning melody discordant.

Rosemary Mayer: *The Locrian Mode*. 1974. Wood, cords, oil paint.
H. 8′, W. 4′, D. 14′. Photo: Alan Sondheim, Michael Metz.

Rebec, trumpet, and golden lute. Harps and lyres supported by Grünewald's strangely hued extraordinary creatures. The celesta could be a stringed instrument with a pear-shaped wooden body. Like the blue rose, the hippogriff, the Hyperboreans, none exists. *The Locrian Mode* as gold-orange, ochre, three greens, and blue-crimson. Colored cords curving two bands of thin wood, ochre concavities, the obverses orange, viridian. Cords in the thin pedestal's plane, green projecting up into space, crimson down to the floor. The layered pedestal at the center viridian/ochre/orange-gold. The highest part, orange/ochre, curved by cold green cords, held up in space by a round wood rod, warm green. The rod sanded to slight irregularity, projecting like the arm of a steelyard for weighing or the crosspiece of a set of scales. *Scalae,* for steps, a ladder or a staircase, from *scandere,* to climb, mount, ascend, also to measure or read by feet, but especially to rise. Large and small curves take the place of drapery. Curving repeated in a pattern, cut out from the bands. They become a curved screen, Pacher's tracery, a balustrade circling up. Thin wooden strips, ochre, irregular, elongated beyond necessity, connecting the rising curves. Thinned-down strips, longer. The fingers of Pontormo's entwined women. Grünewald, his angel orchestra, his pointing St. John. Unnecessarily doubled where they rise from the pedestal's open, supporting groove. That opening, with clear spaces between the thin ochre strips, as a transparent joint. The bands, opened by repeated curves, as transparent screens. The cords, overlaid veils. The pedestal, in three layers, viridian/ochre/orange-gold, pressed together, projecting edge sanded thin. It is believed that the harp developed from the taut strings of warriors' bows. Diana's. The seven bows of the Queen. *Shekinah.* The curved bands of *The Locrian Mode,* elaborations, painted transparent colors like the *Istas,* the *Portae.* Glazes leaving the wood grain visible. Water marks on moire taffeta. *The Locrian Mode* colored with the half-light hues of Fiorentino's *Deposition,* unnatural. *Nitidus,* shining. *Nitor,* brightness. In medieval philosophy, in the ontic theory of light, the experience of God is described as a bursting forth of light. *Lucens,* shining through, visible, clear and evident. Grünewald's enormous halo circling the risen Christ. *Fulgens,* flashing, shining, gleaming, lightning. The Trinity in medieval Neoplatonism, three concentric rings of colored light. *Nitescens,* glittering, shining, blooming, growing luxuriously.

Nicholas of Flüe who saw in the night sky the face of God centered in gigantic circles of light. *Fulgidus,* flashing and glittering. Philo's light, preceding all creation. *Fulgor,* gleam, brightness, lightning, splendor. In the Apocalypse, the woman clothed with the sun. "Begun in Florence in the house of Piero di Braccio Martelli, on the 22nd day of March, 1508. This will be a collection without order, made up of many sheets which I have copied here, hoping afterwards to arrange them in order in their proper places according to the subjects of which they treat; and I believe that before I am at the end of this I shall have to repeat the same thing several times; and therefore, O reader, blame me not, because the subjects are many, and the memory cannot retain them and say 'this I will not write because I have already written it.' And if I wished to avoid falling into this mistake it would be necessary, in order to avoid repetition, that on every occasion when I wished to transcribe a passage I should always read over all the preceding portion, and this especially because long periods of time elapse between one time of writing and another." Leonardo in the Arundel Manuscript, N.263 in the British Museum, translated by Edward MacCurdy. "Tell me," wrote Leonardo, "if anything similar was ever made: you understand, and that is enough for the present."

SOURCES

Evelina Borea, *Rosso Fiorentino* (Milan: Fratelli Fabbri, 1965).

F. M. Clapp, *Jacopo Carucci da Pontormo, His Life and Work* (New Haven, Conn.: Yale University Press, 1916).

Gustav Davidson, *A Dictionary of Angels* (New York: The Free Press, 1967).

The Drawings of Mathis Gothart Nithart Called Gruenewald, edited by Guido Schoenberger (New York: H. Bittner & Co., 1948).

Walter Friedlaender, *Mannerism and Anti-Mannerism in Italian Painting* (New York: Schocken Books, 1965).

The Notebooks of Leonardo da Vinci, edited and translated by Edward MacCurdy (New York: George Braziller, 1958).

Francis Ponge, *The Voice of Things,* translated by Beth Archer (New York: McGraw-Hill Book Co., 1974).

MODELS

Mike Metz

model / Behavior
(protection).

it's what I want to do.
it's all I want to do.

myself

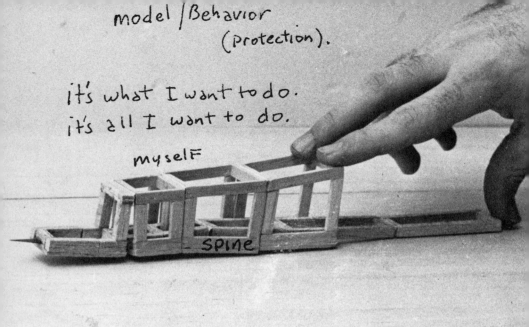

spine

I add the pressure

a pressure point. (on my spine)

adding pressure forces me
to curl up,

for protection.

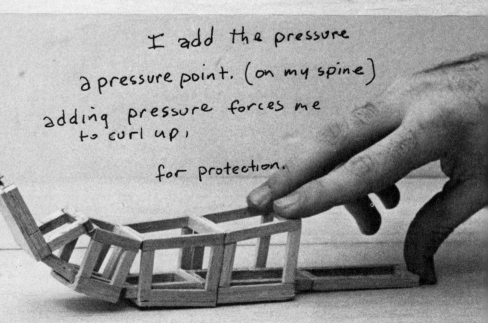

I pressure myself.

It points to me (into me).
I point to myself.

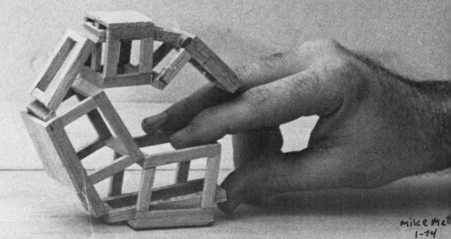

mike Mel
1-74

cramped, I am forced to stop.
again pointing to myself. it's my own fau

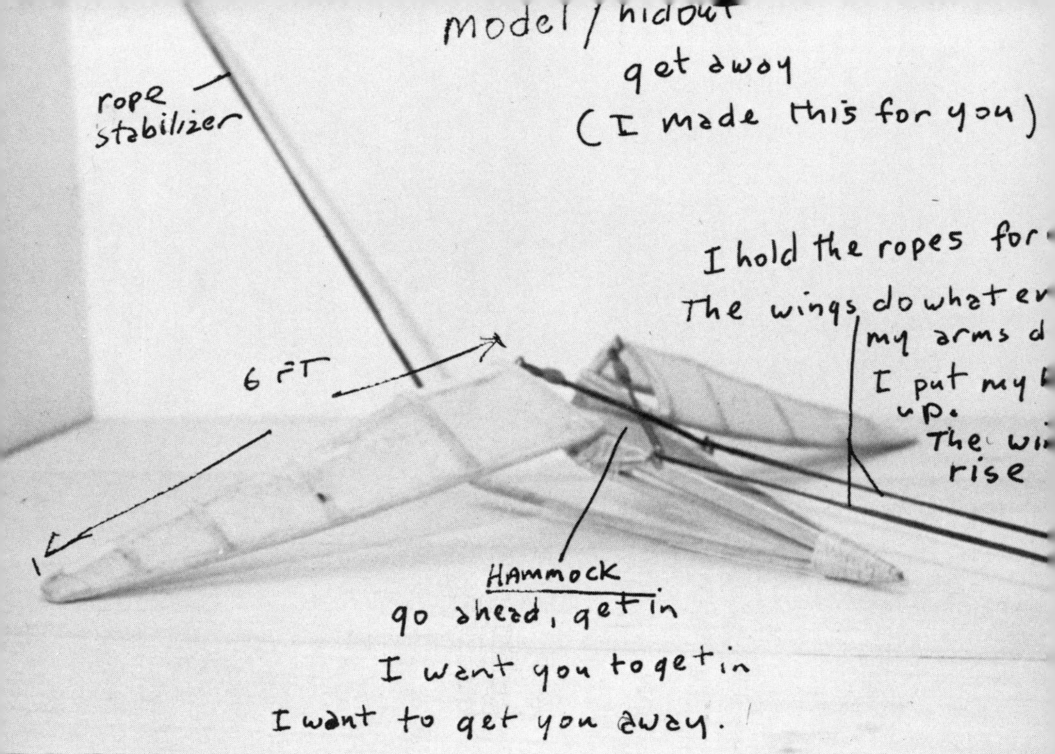

Model / hidout
get away
(I made this for you)

rope
stabilizer

I hold the ropes for
The wings do whatev
my arms d
I put my h
up.
The wi
rise

6 FT

HAMMOCK
go ahead, get in
I went you to get in
I want to get you away.

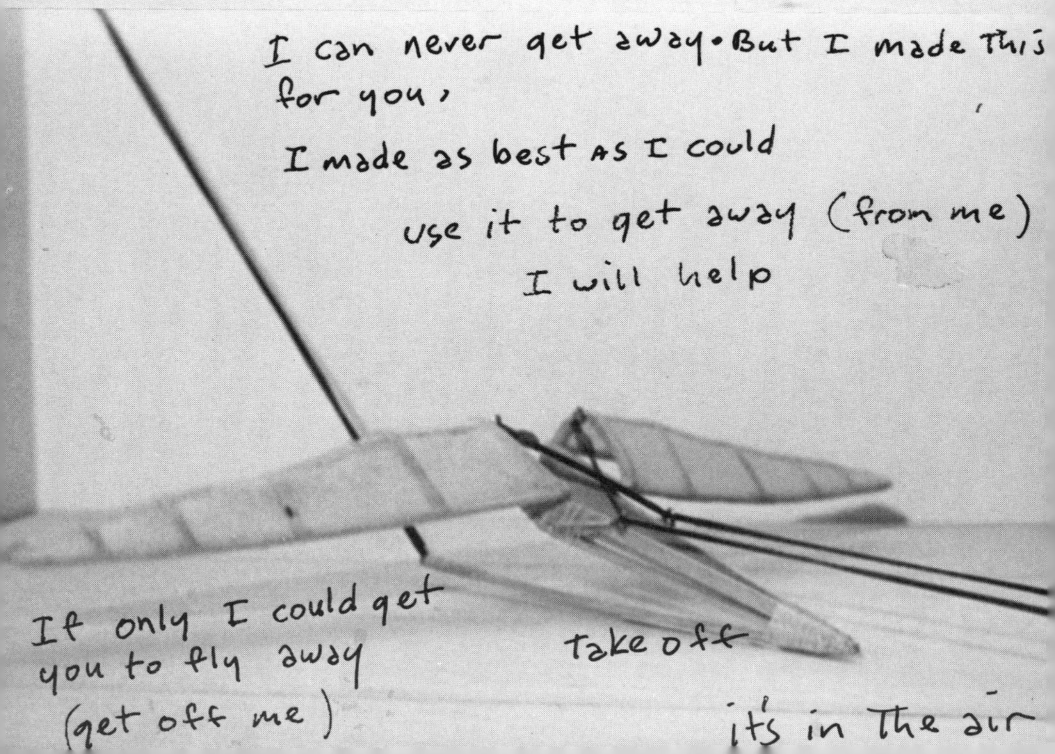

I can never get away. But I made This
for you,
I made as best as I could
use it to get away (from me)
I will help

If only I could get
you to fly away
(get off me)

take off

it's in the air

I promise I'll keep working *the white*
with my hands until I'm sure you're
gone.

until I believe you are gone

all I want is for you to
get away

you're
inside me
I've got to
Be able to get
you out.

you can have everything
Just Leave me

you can overpower me
but I can let you Fly to
a place I've never been
(I'll never get in)
I know you'd
Like to
Try.

I hope you
get in

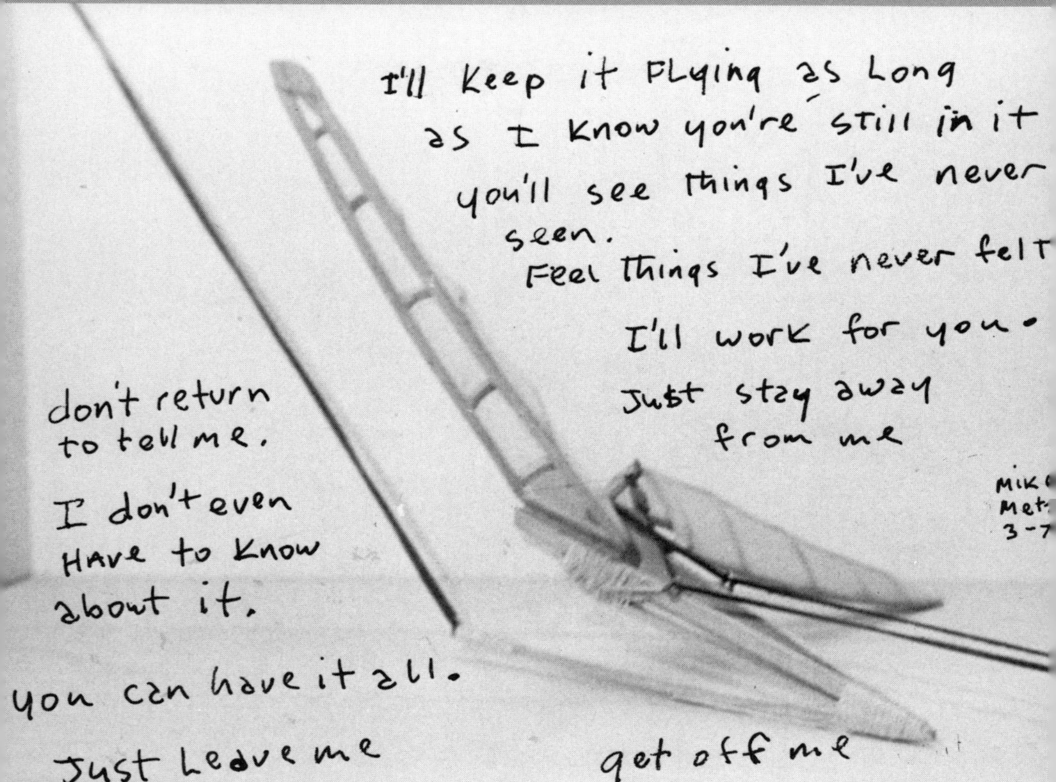
I'll keep it flying as long
as I know you're still in it
you'll see things I've never
seen.
Feel things I've never felt
I'll work for you.
Just stay away
from me
MIK
Met
3-7
don't return
to tell me.
I don't even
Have to know
about it.
you can have it all.
Just Leave me
get off me
(out of me)

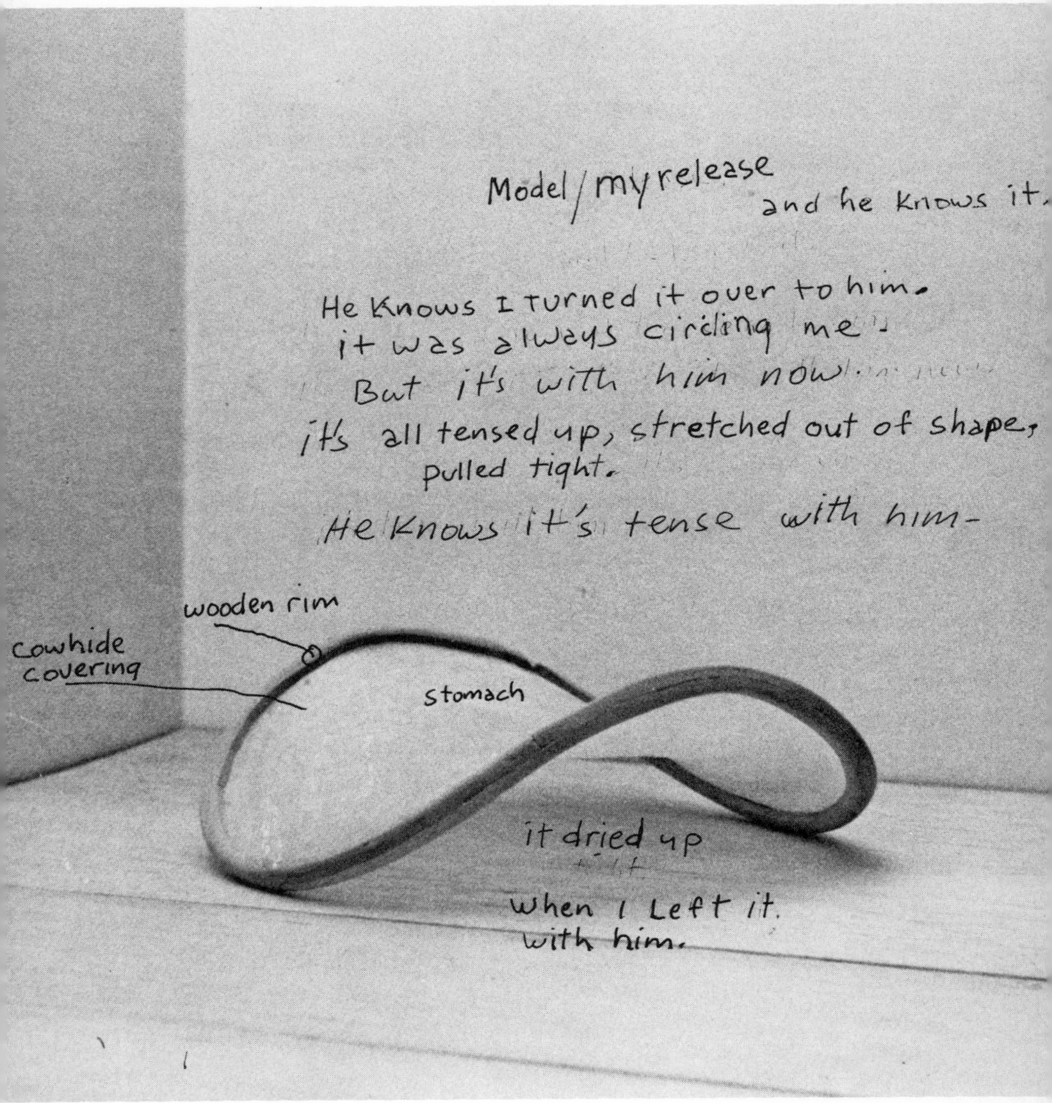

Model / my release

and he knows it.

He knows I turned it over to him.
it was always circling me.
But it's with him now.
it's all tensed up, stretched out of shape,
pulled tight.

He knows it's tense with him—

cowhide
covering

wooden rim

stomach

it dried up

when I left it.
with him.

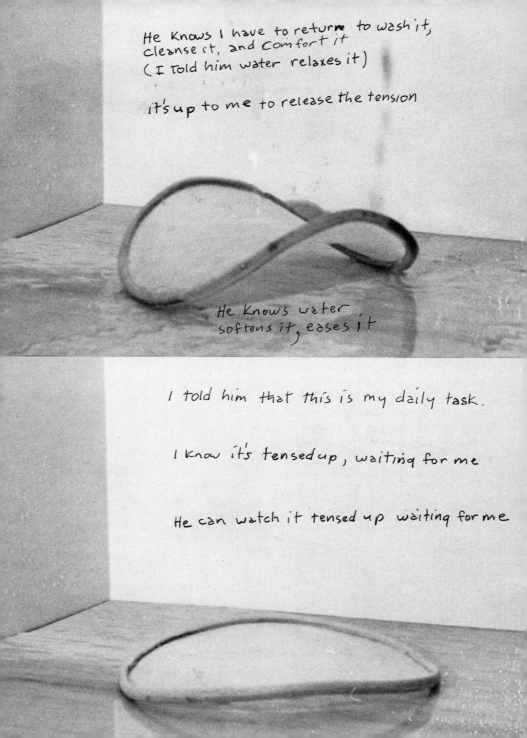

He knows I have to return to wash it, cleanse it, and comfort it
(I told him water relaxes it)

it's up to me to release the tension

He knows water softens it, eases it

I told him that this is my daily task.

I know it's tensed up, waiting for me

He can watch it tensed up waiting for me

it's up to me to decide when to return

Because he **does** not want to destroy it,
all he can do is wait for me to come and
ease the tension, As I told him I
once did

I'll always know I can return and relieve it.

I know how tense it is

I just wait.

I know How tense He is

metz
may 74

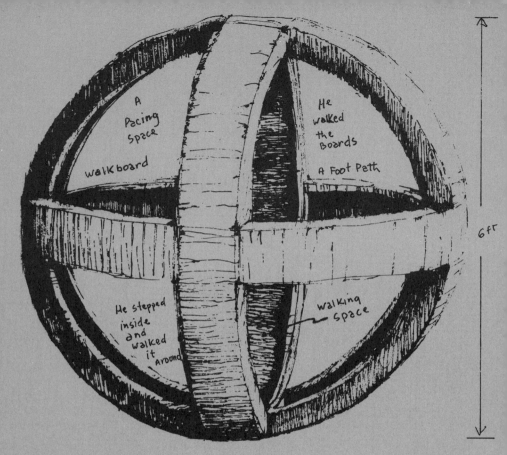

Within the illustration: A Pacing Space · walkboard · He walked the Boards · A Foot Path · He stepped inside and walked it Around · walking space · 6 ft

Model / Boardwalk

His time was his own and all he did was pace back and forth
As long as he walked he was not waiting.
All he chose was to pace to and fro.
　　It was not what he would have chosen,
　　if He could choose.
　　It was all He knew

There was nothing to it.
His time was His own, he walked all around
　　He didn't have to wait.
　　　　He paced.

IT was all he was able to do. All He was able to Know.

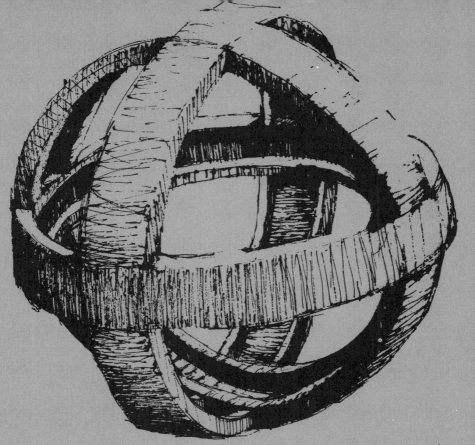

There was no destination he could choose except
one he did not want.

But, he did want to protect himself for his walks

It was a mistake.
 Even pacing was too much to know
He thought of a walking board
It is not what he would have done if he could choose what to do

He knew even this was more than he should have allowed

He frequently stopped building to walk
Over and over the same space.

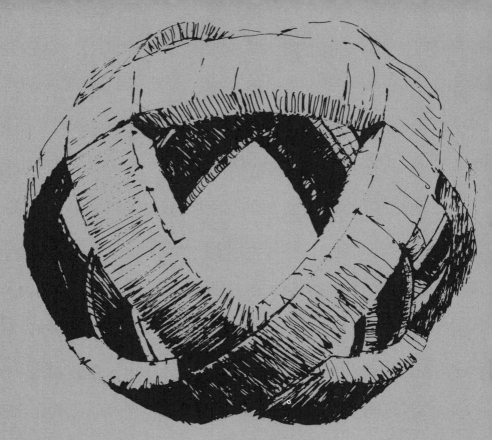

Others saw him and said he staged His walks

They said he strutted

He should have Kept his walking to himself

Others said he paraded

Others joined in. 2, 3, 4, each wanting to walk
to a different place on his boardwalk

This was all each did
He paced with them to whatever destination
each waited to reach

He feared this most of all.

He no Longer paces

it no Longer
moves

no one any Longer
walks

Metz
Dec. 74

ANALECTS

Ree Morton

Untitled. 1972. Paper, wood, paint. H. 84″, W. 120″, D. 108″.

LOCATIONS

all at sea

along shore

along side

around the bend

behind the eight ball

at the peak

at wit's end

at the brink

at the crossroad

up the creek

down the river

up a tree

down the drain

on the right road

on the fence

on the mattress

off the wall

in a rut

in a stew

in the dark

in your hat

out on a limb

over the rainbow

out of your gourd

OVER the hill

OUT to lunch.

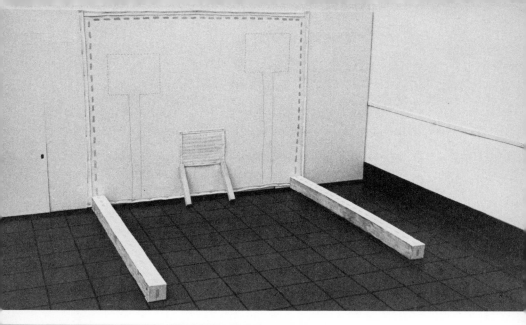

Untitled. 1973.
Canvas, watercolor,
pencil, wood.

Untitled. 1973.
Watercolor on canvas,
painted logs.
H. 70″, W. 26″, D. 70″.

RECITATIONS

MEAN BUSINESS	TENSION
mean	not tight enough
mean ing	not loose enough
mean ing ful	
	tighten up
mean	loosen up
mean er	
de mean ing	tighten down
	loosen down
me an you, babe.	
	tighten around
	loosen around
	tighten
	loosen
	tight
	loose
	take a break.

Untitled. 1972. Wood, paper, charcoal. H. 84″, Diam. 144″.

Sister Perpetua's Lie. 1973. Installation Institute of Contemporary Art, Philadelphia. Photo: Will Brown.

Sister Perpetua's Lie (detail of outdoor version). 1973. Philadelphia. Photo: Will Brown.

Sister Perpetua's Lie. 1973. Outdoor version. Photo: Will Brown.

Love and Death in a Barn;

OR,

The Sad, Sorrowful Life of Beautiful Kate Harrington,

WHO

Was Married to the Son of an Aristocratic Family,

with whom she lived as a Servant,

AND,

BEING DISCOVERED BY THEM, BOTH SANK INTO MISERY

AND SICKNESS, RESULTING IN

KATE'S DEATH BY STARVATION.

IN PHILADELPHIA.

PUBLISHED BY

THE OLD FRANKLIN PUBLISHING HOUSE,

PHILADELPHIA, PA.

On a cold day, after a long run, horses' bodies give off steam.

This photograph was taken in the summer.

The man is named Jack.
The trees are named Joshua.
I don't know what to call the rocks.
I don't know how to call Jack.

PATH —

STOP

GOAL

TOWARD A

FOLLOWED

DIRECTION

EVENTS

HAPPEN

DURING THE JOURNEY,

START

NARRATIVE POSSIBILITIES

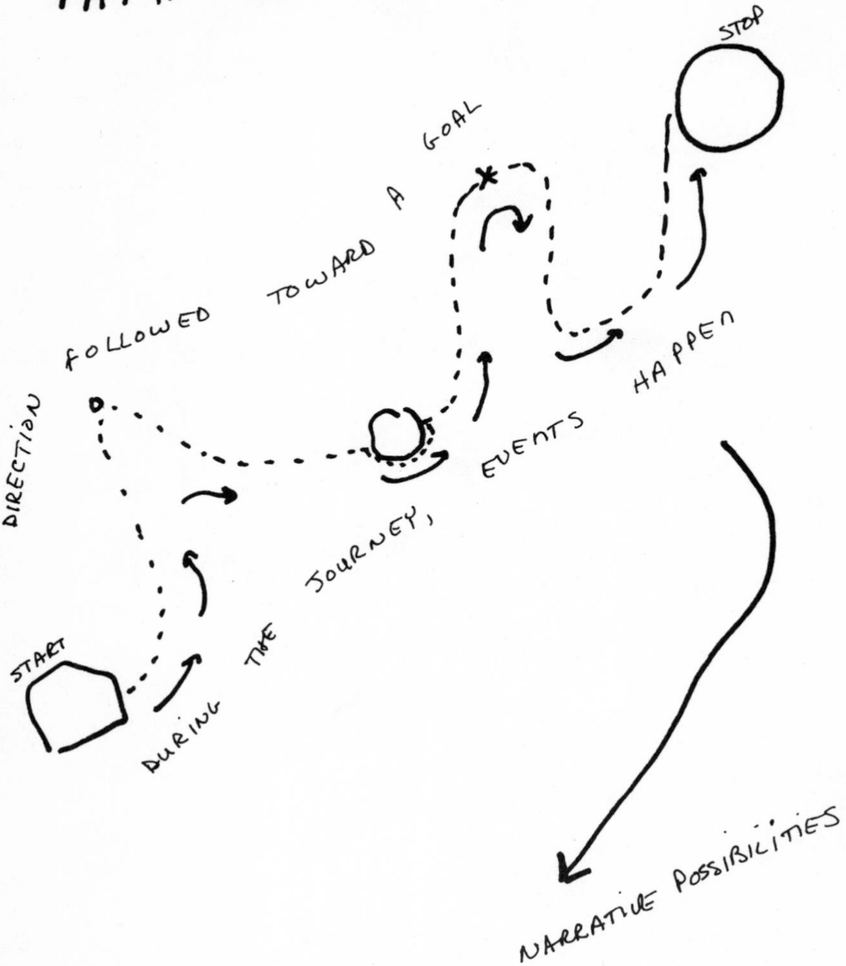

EPISODE —

A DEVELOPED SITUATION THAT IS
INTEGRAL TO BUT SEPARATE FROM
A CONTINUOUS NARRATIVE.

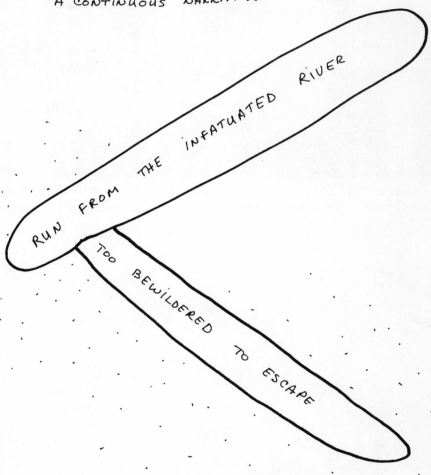

RUN FROM THE INFATUATED RIVER

TOO BEWILDERED TO ESCAPE

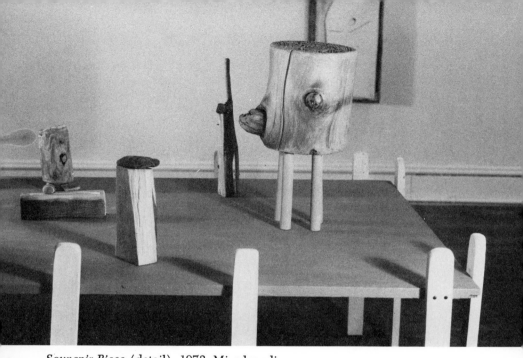

Souvenir Piece (detail). 1973. Mixed media.
Installation Artists' Space, New York.

Souvenir Piece. 1973. Mixed media.
Installation Artists' Space, New York.

To Each Concrete Man (detail). 1974. Mixed media.
Installation Whitney Museum of American Art, New York. Photo: Stan Ries.

To Each Concrete Man. 1974. Mixed media. Installation Whitney Museum
of American Art. Photo: Stan Ries.

REE MORTON

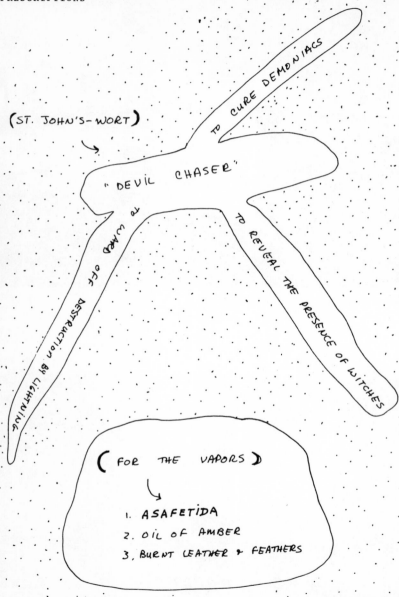

(ST. JOHN'S-WORT)

"DEVIL CHASER"

TO CURE DEMONIACS

TO WARD OFF DESTRUCTION BY LIGHTNING

TO REVEAL THE PRESENCE OF WITCHES

(FOR THE VAPORS)

1. ASAFETIDA
2. OIL OF AMBER
3. BURNT LEATHER & FEATHERS

BILLS OF BIRDS

1. Flamingo
2. Hawk
3. Pigeon
4. Thrush

5. Duck (Merganser)
6. Toucan
7. Finch
8. Spoonbill
9. Pelican

Fading Flowers. 1974. Celastic, wood, lights. H. 48″, W. 48″.

Antidotes for Madness. 1974. Celastic, wood. H. 40″, W. 112″, D. 4″.

NOTATIONS

Artificial surfaces. The objects can be identified....surfaces
are falsified.

found words

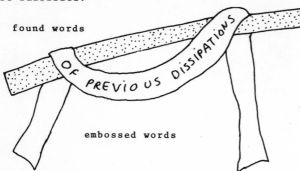

OF PREVIOUS DISSIPATIONS

sources outside
of oneself in order to get
at oneself

imitation
mime
caricature
reminder

embossed words

memory and fantasy

specific situations via
memory

relation of ambiguity to poetic image

going and coming

paying attention

lights blink on and off

not just a vehicle for words
an image

associative images
associative spaces
associative words

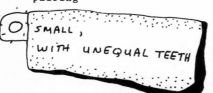

PERFECTLY
POLYGAMOUS
FLOWERS

light
lighten

colors..bright...decorated...deteriorated

contradiction to funerary look

pairing

SMALL,
WITH UNEQUAL TEETH

form with (sometimes)
sadness of words

special significance of ordinary
things

the importance of drawing

leave a message if you are out
leave your card at the door

out   of   sync

advertising things painful and private

plants having attributes of humans

affection for the work

illusion
and
allusion

SELF-FERTILIZATION MAY BE AN EVIL

rather than conceiving of
work as a consequence of theory,
it is, to the contrary, done
in anticipation

"mere talk"
tracks   conversations in which the topic becomes the
              vehicle of expression and not the matter
traces   of predominant interest

sweet and sour color

Some Have RUN AWAY, TO BE SURE

invest with meaning   foreground and backdrop

          signs or tokens of a thought,
                    a sentiment, a saying or an event

          key memories...what you want to believe, or what
markers   time has forced you to believe

signals

                              images of words

                              fragments
                                   not coalesced into sentences
                                          or sentenced

REGAINS ITS NATURAL LIBERTIES

Victorian funeral monuments   THROUGH NEGLECT
     the drapery
     the sentiment   underlinings
                                underpinnings
                                underneath the arches
                                sub rosa

Scenery is a valley in moonlight
Scenery is left of a valley in moonlight   G.Stein

oxymoron

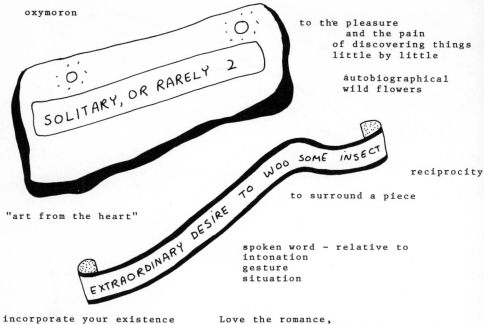

SOLITARY, OR RARELY 2

to the pleasure
and the pain
of discovering things
little by little

áutobiographical
wild flowers

EXTRAORDINARY DESIRE TO WOO SOME INSECT

reciprocity

to surround a piece

"art from the heart"

spoken word – relative to
intonation
gesture
situation

incorporate your existence

Love the romance,
Analysis may be better suited
to the couch

inanimate objects in
confrontational
situations

appropriate vehicles

stage lights
low wattage bulbs

SOMETIMES FATALLY IMPRISONED

sentimentality

a way of
getting at
questions that
are interesting,
provocative

layering

memorials to lost intentions

find the meaning
change the meaning
contradict the original meaning

Don Roger Gill. 1941–1973.
He would if he could, but since he can't, he won't.

CATALYST 1967-1974

Dennis Oppenheim

I have always used notebooks. The first were filled with rather traditional sketches. As my work relied more heavily on language as a substructure, the material in these books shifted from pictorial to words. My thoughts no longer originated from pictorial images, and in some cases remained in language form from conception to delivery. Most of my work stems from these notebooks, and although the thoughts are often fragmentary and disjointed, they make up the original pattern that underlies the finished work.

Catalyst is an unedited transcript from these books, beginning in early 1967. Although some material has been lost which requires occasional reconstruction, the majority of these thoughts represents the rhythm which underlies my work.

Sketch Book 1967

stakes similar to those used by land surveyors to be made out of stainless steel—these markers plot segments of an existing situation
simulated field
viewing station in field
receding currents
viewing stands used by "East Coast Light and Paving Company"
directional viewing station
endless field
rotating conveyor belt distributes

246

wooden panels horizontally across floor
area
gallery acres
dead furrow
standard plow turns soil to the right
gallery as completed field
octagonal viewing station surrounded by
octagonal currents
tractor tracks
work for a Long Island paving contractor
counter-wedge
pure pigment
submerged system
feeding trough
angled hedge
mass activator—diachondra planted to
converge upon excavated piece—or
spreading outward—mass coverage
converging troughs of diachondra
ice plant
sump
visual connectors
seasonal change
sculpture affected by life process
color changes
a construction that lies dormant half the
year—shows itself—fades out

Yellow Sketch Book April 1968

white sand with black streaks
inverted earth layers
air layers condensed in scale (drawing)
ripple marks in sedimentary rocks
asphalt basins
piled and formed asphalt
rippled asphalt surface
reverse fault
painted core
negative strip showing subflooring
asphalt spread
land slide
excavated strip
colored aggregate
place all ingredients of Whitney Museum
into hourglass—subject to a process of
mixing—counterconic—interbreed two
structures—decomposed Whitney and
Modern
all museums stacked up in order of perspective distance in relationship to location of base structure
string out horizontally
analyze material ingredient of connecting objects—this determines substance
of pile

chemical dictates shape—responds only
to gravity, extension and inertia
subject chemical elements to alternate
forces
chemical breakdown
stable elements
inverted decomposed Whitney subjected
to a process of reconstruction
impurities quantitative analysis
combined mixture of vertical wall support and horizontal floor support
the pure Whitney
submerged strata
dead slide
decomposed objects—book series—
paper pulp/powdered ink/color breakdown
solid to powder
ruptured salt flat
decomposed walls
gallery heat—room temperature
indentations (1967–1968 editions)
sheet erosion
376 square feet of flooring removed in
five stages—removal sold by the linear
foot—prices upon request
ecological complex
interaction of units that do not normally
involve each other
Maine projects
isotherms cut into field until complete
field is removed
protruding test cores
subsoil placed on top of topsoil
2 photos of Manhattan—each with extremely different temperatures
dividing the divider
bounded boundaries
salt flat to be removed by wind action
melting forest
frozen lake project
zonal cuts
cut and fill
a perfectly straight cut showing only
direction
sawdust inside cut on frozen lake
artificial plankton

Yellow Sketch Book September to November 1968

climate modification series—cloud seeding
salt particles used to create large ice
nucleus in clouds
cloud de-composition

Maine project—scribe isotherms of past weather data onto existing snow weather contours of area in complete southwest region (San Diego) scribed onto northeast region of Maine
Maine elevation contour scribed onto sand of Southern California beach
accumulation piece—snow—record height increase
recording ephemeral two-dimensional data onto an ephemeral surface condition
information changes as surface conditions change
magnetic pull/reverse information
time piece located at Canadian border—time break/time displacement
increased loss factor
eradicated time line
broken dateline (international dateline discontinued at 0 equator)
stake off land area to claim seasonal change
thermograph—heat detector

seasonal blocks—to be removed at each ½ rotation of the earth
tree ring project

Sketch Book Amsterdam April 1969

application forms exhibited
directional arrow opposes direction
raw material goes for preliminary processing
colored yarn used to relate field grid to retail store
escalator—raising and lowering of matter
cut 16 pieces of hardwood with saw—leave residue and photos of process
abrasive residue
points of interference
set up system—disturb it
Paris factory tours
paper mill in Finsterwolde—return end product to field
obstructions—salt blockade

Dennis Oppenheim: *Viewing System for Gallery Space* (scale model). 1967. Wood and Formica. H. 72″, W. 72″, D. 72″. Objects constructed, not to be viewed, but to view from. These stations were placed on exterior field locations in Long Island during the winter of 1967.

ROCKED CIRCLE - FEAR. 1971.   One half hour video tape / with Super 8 film loop.
A situation was created which allowed registration of an exterior stimulus directly through facial expression. As
I stood in a 5' diameter circle, rocks were thrown at me. The circle demarcated the line of fire. A video camera
was focused on my face. The face was captive, its expression a direct result of the apprehension of hazard.
Here, stimulus is not abstracted from its source. Fear is the emotion which produced a final series of expressions
on the face.

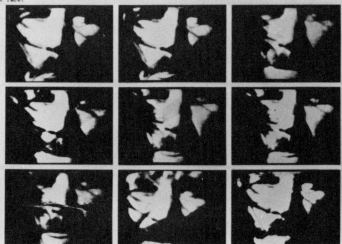

Dennis Oppenheim: *Directed Seeding—Canceled Crop.* 1969.
Finsterwolde, Holland. Procedure: The route from Finsterwolde
(location of wheat field) to Nieuwe Schans (location of storage silo)
was reduced by a factor of 6 times and plotted on a 154- by
267-meter field. The field was then seeded following this line.
In September the field was harvested in the form of an X.
The grain was isolated in its raw state; further processing was withheld.
This project poses an interaction upon media during the early stages
of processing. Planting and cultivating my own material is like mining
one's own pigment (for paint)—I can direct the later stages of
development at will. In this case the material is planted and cultivated
for the sole purpose of withholding it from a product-oriented system.
Isolating this grain from further processing (production of food stuffs)
becomes like stopping raw pigment from becoming an illusionistic
force on canvas. The aesthetic is in the raw material prior
to refinement, and since no organization is imposed through refinement,
the material's destiny is bred with its origin.

interchange—infected area/sterilized area
scatter piece—photo of stampeding cattle
locust
tulip harvest—distribution of color—plot arrangement
ground-based tape recorders
sterilized subway train—solution: ammonia/water—surface analysis made after various routes
food-depletion piece (animals)
void
directional change—rat poison over arrow
milk delivery
canceled crop
project for automatic car wash—check mileage—residue collection point
mechanical counters
ecological barrier
reverse processing
mothballs crushed under varying weights p.s.i.
void—buy a product from consumer shelf—photograph space—ask merchant to leave space for specified time—ENFORCE VOID—exhibit product
sterilized surface—glass
list of antidotes
weight distribution
plug-in
gallery engages in alternative business during show
6 reservations: airlines, bus, train, restaurant, sports event, pre-need burial plot—tape-recorded telephone calls
infected zone—Milan—kill traps/rat poison/burned grass—in progress
fish channels
branding irons—brand floors/trees/grass
brand a mountain
proper channels
processing list/new material/end product
change/one month's variation/bend
pass over/bow/installation pit
catalyst vs. pigment
illusion before product (paint) applied to canvas
depletion—removal from consumer shelves. harvest crop in reconstruction of consumer depletion
supply/demand

ingoing/outgoing
water project—turn on your water at 7:30 a.m. October 31st
film—broad jump
film—lagging—throwing pennies at a cast shadow—object breakdown
matter/process
brand the word *diphtheria* on mountain anthrax
moving body/antibody
short-circuit—interrupted
X ray
meat packing/salt harvest
set up disturbance—aesthetic comes in tabulation
cause/effect
show reactions to various chemicals
artist's body—reaction to external/internal pressures
flex—reflex
tagging fish/branding cattle
casting for fish
castings of one-mile walk condensed in gallery
healing of a wound
code of specifications
building code—size limitations
healing skin tissue—building a surface
100-yard dash—condensed
220-yard dash—piled
440-yard dash—stacked
880-yard dash—fragmented
the mile—cubed
run through a brick wall
quantity control
watermarks
water pressure
heel marks
animal traps used to determine frequency of intersecting travel
cowhide mountain (Jersey)
stressing interacting effect of environment on organism
my weight in ocean water returned to sea via N.Y.C. sewer channels
drag strip/sandpaper (sounds of sanding fused with sounds of speeding)—sound track for film
sound track of speeding with castings of hop/step/jump—distance numbers on video tape
single-file iron filings spread on floor to assimilate file surface
castings of cattle hoofprints before slaughter—Chicago stockyards—summer

1969—each casting tagged exhibit A

Sketch Book West Coast Summer 1969

untested materials
against the grain
firing line
document undisturbed stationary objects
start with end product . . . breakdown/
reverse
static form unaffected by time-system
counterbalance
burning up energy—digestion of food
b.t.u.
ice cuts—lights submerged
aerial formations—bodies push through
crowds—amass 5 minutes—spread and
hide under cover 5 minutes—reunite—
continue process
fishing holes cut in ice . . . fish for
one day . . . photograph catch
food-depletion piece
artist as matter
burning up weight
close-up—breathing in cold weather—
5-minute film
1-week weight tabulation—list of foods
—intake—effects of food on body weight
structure a plan that can effect predetermined chemical change in body—record through electron microscope—
make 4 x 4 color slide—project on snow
from helicopter—increase magnification
x 360,000
body fighting infection (documentation)
transparency on light box
pressure course—staple rows of sand-
paper on floor—use balsa wood 2″ x 4″
—subject wood to specific pressure—
exhaust material
guard making simple formations around
projected image of cancer cell projected
to 300′ x 600′ in snow parking lot—rent
space in predetermined formation—
photograph from top—take license
numbers from cars bordering space—get
addresses—draw new configuration from
addresses
film—top view of artist on scale showing
weight—artist begins sawing 2 x 4s by
hand—2 hour stationary camera—artist
returns to scale—weight loss recorded
catalyst barrier—withholding catalyst
from compound—wooden barricade—
show photo of faulty barricades (model
form)—hypothetical results of spillover
catalyst barrier—insufficient postage
body fighting infection

controlled environment
film loop—sliding into an embankment
large maze—excavated
armed guards
track for increasing heartbeat
proposal for Evil Knievel—Salt Lake
Desert, Utah
hire a guard—daily report becomes art
document
guarded trench—3-day surveillance
training ground
track for reaching 80 miles per hour
swimming race for artists (proposal for
museum sponsorship) positions of racer
determined by preliminary times—diagram at finish
combined distances of broad jump by 10
major artists measured out on cloth tape
—sold in reels
testing ground for Jesse Owens
300-lb. pressure required for release-re-
tention piece
obstacle course
project for 1-year seclusion
projection pit
X ray of digestive tract (GI series) video
—slow intake of liquid
documentation of exercise showing
burning up of energy
bins of different compounds which when
added to water solidify
distributional barrier
fluorescent substance on landscape
200-foot drop
erosion—tissue
ecological bridge
tug of war
take a hill
fasting project
final-assault practice course
rooting section—diagrams—card section
ground mutations—drill—marching
trench system based on attack diagram
of Pearl Harbor
edition: ground maneuvers (drill formations) military shoes with ¼″ diagonal
grooves down sole and heel
physical characteristics
physical limitations
distance endurance
pressure/pushing down on matter/p.s.i./
pushups
projection of infected blood cells on
snow from helicopter—correlation of
projected image with land forms—rephotograph
35mm slides of landmass before snow
projected from helicopter onto freshly

fallen snow of same area—rephotograph correlating skin tissue (layers) with land strata
untitled film (8 minutes) documentation of indentation made on forearm while rolling over cording and twine (close-up)
untitled film (10 minutes) documentation of forearm rolling over warm asphalt and plaster—slow dissolve onto land

Sketch Book January 1970

Matched hybrid for digestive tract—red zone (cranberry-apple) yellow zone (pineapple-grapefruit)
efficiency breakdown
bucket brigade
magnets
thumbprint blowup
backstop
family tree
physical limitation becomes objective
bruise
4-color print on cowhide
stress position
stored material
wooden leg
multiple land grafts
reading position for second-degree burn
limitations with extended end
hair piece (film)
block for future energy
rehearsal block
color slide of pure gypsum projected on plaster
blocked residue
2 jumps for Dead Dog Creek, Idaho
confined energy
recirculate
potato-sack race
push-pull
growth patterns
3-stage penetration piece
concentration pit—displaced energy
free fall
2 acres seeded from air
land bridge
decoy
recorded only half the object
transfusion

1971 Black Sketch Book

shoe leather—application of surface—installation of shoeshine stand
skin tone—sunburn on kristin's back
throwing a rock at chandra
bricking a circle

photo-sensitive wall—during performance develop image directly onto it
exhibition of photographically recorded prior work—cut diagonally
rock fight—cockfight
pit stop
erik's fingerprint on wax—transfer enlarged version onto land
salt-block wall
swallow something—X-ray film fades to bullet penetrating ice—slow-motion film
spray wall with reflective paint—videotape this process—video projects this activity back onto reflective surface
transfer of square light image onto stomach—use light with adjustable frame
body feedback—tracing image of my foot onto my stomach
shadow piece—body as light block—body allowing light to be cast on it
shielding light from casting onto wall—shadow interruption—image absorption
finger exercises—slow shadow piece—8mm film
send a boy to camp—issue a camera—exhibition of photographs—energy transfer
slide-dissolve system piece—spinning chandra around until she blends into ground—35mm color slides
pulling chandra's hair—handing it back to her—
blowing at her eyelids—spreading tears filling a cavity
interference—pitfall—traps (skins)
trap for 800 lb. release (earth project)
measurement of pain
irregular heartbeat
circumcision for erik (get hospital record)
binding feet
boxing match—slow shine—application of surface—close breathing circuits
elements found in the bloodstream of schizophrenic
castings—seven people with broken arms—tolerance factor . . . calcium compound
dependency project (put yourself in someone else's hands)
metal taps—walk around the room during sebastian's performance
hard pressed—beehive-interrogation, object looked at for 24 hours
interrogation room—chandra and I on closed-circuit video tape
2 people eating gingerbread men—back

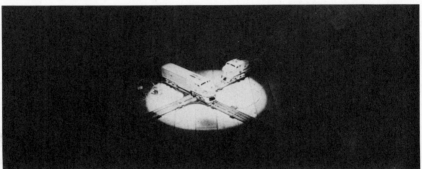

Dennis Oppenheim: *Predictions*. The track section spotted in red light is a surrogate for an existing track located between Syosset and Huntington at the Amott signal on the Long Island Railroad. This section was concentrated upon until I could easily produce a mental picture of it. This image was then mentally superimposed onto the surrogate track during the recording of the collision date. The model trains pass this zone at the rate of approximately 5,000 r.p.m. per day (250 times as frequent as the L.I.R.R.'s daily crossings). The installation will be activated at every opportunity, for as long a period as possible during this exhibition and at subsequent exhibitions, until 11:22 P.M. June 10, 1988.

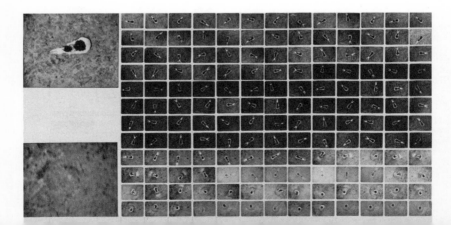

Dennis Oppenheim: *Polarities 1972*. Bridgehampton, New York. 500'.
Presumed to be the last graphic gesture by my father, David Oppenheim, before his
death, November 28, 1971. Enlarged and plotted with red magnesium flares.
Dennis Oppenheim: *Polarities 1972*. Bridgehampton, New York. 500'.
One of the first drawings by my daughter Chandra Oppenheim, executed in 1969.
Enlarged and plotted with red magnesium flares.

Dennis Oppenheim and Chandra Oppenheim: *Ground Gel* (slide dissolve sequence).
1972. 35mm color film with sound. Excerpt from sound track, repeat loop.
"I don't want to see you . . . I don't want to be able to see you don't want to be
able to see you. Want you to go past me ahead of me I want you to go ahead of me
now I want to go with you want to go out there and touch you want to be able
to touch you out there. You're going past me soon . . . you're going to go past me
soon you're going to take me past myself. I'm going with you you're going
out there now. I'm going with you I can't see you I can't see you now. I want
to go out there and touch you. I'm touching you out there now I can touch
you out there. I can be with you now. You've taken me with you. You're
going past me now." "I'm going with you. You're taking me with you. I'm out
there with you now. I can touch you out there. I can touch you now. I'm
out there with you you've taken me with you. You've taken me past myself now."

to back—interchanging material
material breakdown—heat lamps—reform gingerbread into shape of bat
perform next to caged bat—spotlight
eat 10–15 gingerbread men slowly—apply to face
10 little Indians—performance—video camera focused on stationary hatchet
overtip a waitress
color application for chandra—teach chandra the color names—transfer this information to parrot via tape loops of chandra's voice
bleach hair—burn arm—bind right foot —bandage finger
performance—pulling hair out—blowing it through flames
look at material for a long time—then apply to face
temporary confinement—starting-point
position in hallway—access to mental ward
method of escape—bench warrant
dependency project—sustain yourself until help comes
door-to-door survey
getting information—interrogation
throwing a voice
chamber—stripping all legal rights from anyone who enters—give legal contract
pissing a rainbow—use prism—reflected light—16mm film
4-week fingernail-growth project—projection pit
blood transfusion—rent high-power telescope/thumbprint/fireflies
target on hand (tattoo) same target on land in larger aerial film of fading these two versions into each other
smoke signals
blindfolded—running hand over clay object until object can be remade
survival project—10-day documentation
keep daily log
course of greater resistance
break the law

1972 Brussels Notebook

surface infections
violations—injecting an object with vestiges of legal repercussions
steal hubcaps
from the top of my head—buried in ground—show only top of my head
use spotlight—four-hour rambling monologue
shadow extension—performance
sleight of hand—video tape (slow motion)
indirect hit—4 wall-mounted bows—lights rotating column—ricochet
getting rusty—film—body painted silver lying on dry pigment (red)
during rainstorm—pigment spreading to ground
stewing around—35mm film—spinning microphone from the center of powdered-plaster circle—50′ in diameter
2-hour slump—chandra playing electric organ—then fainting onto the keyboard
playing dead—chandra oppenheim 8mm film loop—towards a continued sound after death
chicken—½-mile sulfur strip next to severe drop—exterior speakers with tape loops of chicken cackling
predictions—electric trains—collision date on the tape loop
my father's socks—16mm film—filling a vacant space
I'm failing—submerged head—closeup film forming words in black water making wind
less mind—mindless
puppet kicking wall with inset microphones—amplified
interception—catching a football—1948 dream
training a 2 x 4—whipping into shape—video tape
drawing crowds—camera positioned on top of building—lie in street
photo documentation of collection of people drawn to body
objects with different uses—establish new uses—video tape
17 uses for an object
take my word for it
dress in target costume—red yellow blue—become your own target—performance using guns with curved barrels
ground tests
returning to the scene of a crime
color video tape—chandra painting fuck the world on room-size piece of paper—broom-size brushes
simulated sound track of jet aircraft diving from a position 20,000 feet above, to exact location of listener and crashing—duration of dive 4 minutes—speed of descent—500 miles per hour—use head-

Chandra Oppenheim: *Playing Dead*. 1972. Super 8 loop color film.

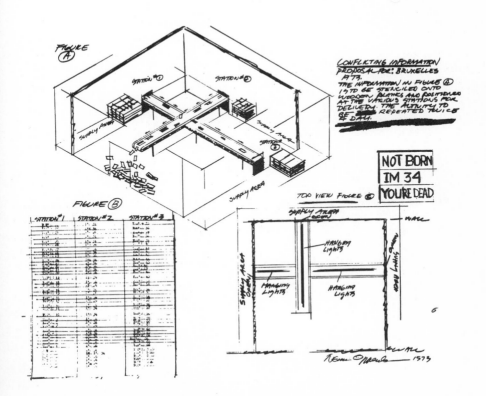

Dennis Oppenheim: *Wishing Well*. September 1973. San Francisco. Sound track.
"I want to be able to sink downward, I wish I could do this, I want this
well to act in favor of this, I wish these pennies could act as sparks, to charge
the eventuality of this. I know where I want to stand. I know the location
to be in this city, near by. I'll stand there as often as I can. It's not far away. My
shoulder blades will be pressed against a building, a thick wall. I'll be looking out
toward the street. The heels of my shoes will be against the concrete and planted
firmly on the sidewalk. It's not as if this material begins to soften or relax, but
the first sensation is similar to that. I can feel the pavement begin to surround the
soles of my shoes. At the same time, my shoulder blades have gone at least 1 inch
back, as my feet are further engulfed by the concrete. I can feel my shoulders
dragging downward, as they sink deeper into the wall. My feet are now in the
pavement, not quite up to the beginning of my ankles. At this point I gently rest
my head toward the wall. As I do this the lower part of my back begins to
touch the surface. My shoulders are sinking further back. The ground is well over
my ankles now. I know the soles of my shoes are touching the dirt surface, 4″ below
a concrete slab. My body now distinguishes between the materials encroaching upon
it. The sidewalk slab becomes a templet passing up my legs—when it reaches my
kneecaps—my feet have easily adjusted to the dirt around them, my legs are
surrounded, my shoulders and much of my head have passed through the surface. I
can feel the pressure moving around to the front of my body, my neck is practically
engulfed now, only my chin remains. My thighs are well into the ground, my feet
passing through different forms of rock and gravel, dampness. My chest and stomach
become the only visible portions, as the sidewalk surface is now level with my waist.
My back is arched, my head well into the wall and now passing through a series of
steel members. Only a small part of my stomach remains, acting as a connector
between the wall and ground. My upper extremities are continuing to sink downward
even though I have been pressing backward. I am now through this surface,
continuing in an almost vertical direction. My back is straight, arms against my sides.
The material surrounding me feels of a consistent nature. . . . I don't remember it
changing as I continued in this direction."

Dennis Oppenheim: *Whirlpool—Eye of the Storm.* August 1973. El Mirage, Southern California. 16mm film. ¾- by 4-mile schema of tornado, traced in the sky using standard white smoke discharge from aircraft.

Dennis Oppenheim: *Rehearsal for 5-Hour Slump, Chandra Oppenheim.* 1973. Component: electric organ. Installation: video, electric organ, reflective black mylar plastic. This piece acts as a rehearsal for a performance lasting 5 hours in which a static body produces a steady electric sound. Ideally, it asks that the figure die on top of the organ. (Continuous sound produced by a dead organism.)

Dennis Oppenheim: *2 Right Feet for Sebastian.* 1973. 2 motorized boots, 2 amps/ speakers, microphones, 2 lead poles, spotlight. Boots strike the wall at 60 kicks per minute. The project deals with physical vacancy, a missing right leg.

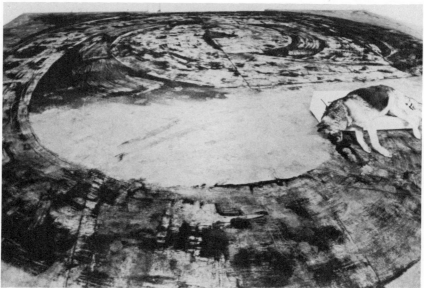

Dennis Oppenheim: *Untitled Performance.* Summer 1971.
Clocktower, New York City. Dog, electric organ, graphite.
Sound emission from dead organism. Deterioration plays itself out.

Dennis Oppenheim: *Theme for a Major Hit.* 1974. Recorded at Angel Sound,
New York City. "It ain't what you make, it's what makes you do it."
Motor-driven marionette, H. 24"; 2-hour recording; circular stage; spotlight.
Jim Ballard, vocals; Roger Welch, drums; Bill Beckley, guitar/vocals;
Christa Maiwald, vocals; John Shole, lead guitar; Diego Cortez, electric organ;
Connie Beckley, vocals; Dennis Oppenheim, lyrics.

set installed in gallery—invasion
video projector—sound track from siege
(militant capture of N.Y.C.)—ants moving over surface—close-up
linear extension for Anna Grossman (my grandmother)—exhume body of Anna Grossman—position every bone in skeletal frame end to end in straight line on gallery floor—produce a white outline of my body at the midpoint (beginning of her waist)—bones should run diagonally through several rooms of the gallery
performance—pulling endless handkerchiefs from ground—color video tape
one-hour video tape of beetle slowly dying—play back in reverse
go-between—Phyllis and I engage in fistfight using kristin and erik as go-betweens (they become extensions of our fists and receive and discharge the blows)
clearing—carrying 4′ x 8′ sheet of glass down one block—shoot from top of building 2 persons—glass is not detected by camera
castings—shadow project—paper cutouts of family members
video-tape interview of father of convicted murderer
put head inside lion's mouth
hope less—flare project

1973

wishing well—conveyor belt—pennies—wish to pass through a solid
sunshine room—heat lamps—spinning mirrored ball—walls painted chrome yellow—sound track—I can't be happy in here
2 right feet for Sebastian—mechanical boots kick the wall—amplified
whirlpool—white smoke discharge—vortex 5 miles high—16mm film
echo—8mm film—sound-sync loops with 4 projectors
end of the line
enlarged hot-plate coil—gallery installation
age regression–acceleration—erik advancing in age—me regressing—rotating loop projecting images
spinning knife
look in your eye
hanging over my head

wrong frame of mind
I smell a hit
guess works (book)
that's not the word for it
project for 2 searchlights 2 mirrors—landscape—split beam split shadow
going in one ear and out the other
6 ways to enter the past
going through the floor
come through the back door
I want to know when she did it last—I want to know what she did
I don't want to know what you have to say

1974

installation with dead dog lying on top of organ—sound changes as body deteriorates—equipment is dragged through graphite to form X pattern
chandra hitting herself with mittens attached to coat—they become uncontrollable outside force—16mm film
end of the line
the word *fuck* produced on the floor by dragging video equipment through colored pigment—final installation shows word, and video-taped process of dragging
Ratta-Ratta-Ratta—Callity—outdoor sound piece—split track: track #1 Ratta track #2 Callity
trouble spot
bar tricks—sleight of hand—book
off white
twisting a word into the ground—twisting my mind—it's a twisted mind that could go into this floor—the idea is to get the word over me
passing a word around my back—reflected light
loose track
a lot to draw from—nothing to draw from
I don't want to think about what I'm doing wrong
raise hell—carpet and bell—a method for raising hell
hey baby, gimme some skin—film loop (1972)
inside/outside—video dragging project

Washington, D.C.—I can pull through this—video project

262

Dennis Oppenheim: *Recall*. 1974. Video monitor; metal pan, W. 24″, L. 96″;
5 gallons of turpentine; black tint. A paint medium (turpentine) used to
draw me into the past . . . as a sensory catalyst . . . activating my
reflections as a painter . . . an art student . . . during the fifties.
I concentrate only on what is directly stimulated through the smell . . .
the prevailing stench of turpentine.

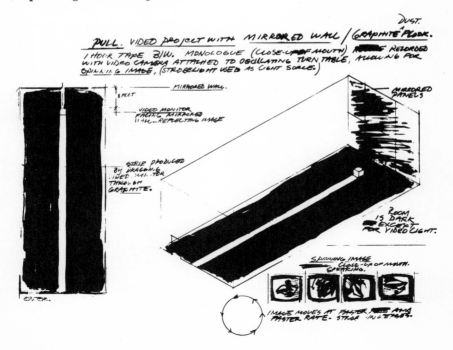

UNTITLED VIDEO INSTALLATION FOR:
GALLERY D. BRUXELLES 1973.

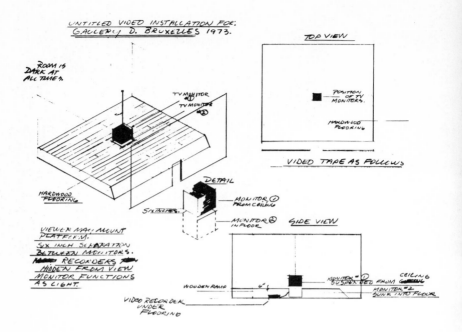

TOP VIEW

ROOM IS
DARK AT
ALL TIMES.

TV MONITOR
①
TV MONITOR
②

POSITION
OF TV
MONITORS.

HARDWOOD
FLOORING

VIDEO TAPE AS FOLLOWS

HARDWOOD
FLOORING

DETAIL

MONITOR ①
FROM CEILING

SIX INCHES.

MONITOR ②
IN FLOOR

SIDE VIEW

VIEWER MAY MOUNT
PLATFORM.
SIX INCH SEPARATION
BETWEEN MONITORS.
RECORDERS
HIDDEN FROM VIEW
MONITOR FUNCTIONS
AS LIGHT.

VIDEO RECORDER
UNDER
FLOORING

WOODEN RAMP   6"   MONITOR ① CEILING
SUSPENDED FROM
MONITOR ②
SUNK INTO FLOOR

PROPOSAL FOR:
ROTTERDAMSE KUNSTSTICHTING

ROTTERDAM
HOLLAND
1973

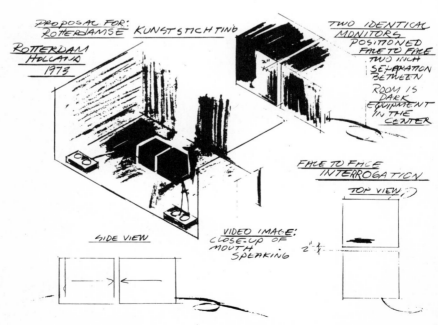

TWO IDENTICAL
MONITORS
POSITIONED
FACE TO FACE
TWO INCH
SEPARATION
BETWEEN

ROOM IS
DARK
EQUIPMENT
IN THE
CENTER

FACE TO FACE
INTERROGATION

TOP VIEW

SIDE VIEW

VIDEO IMAGE:
CLOSE-UP OF
MOUTH
SPEAKING

2" ¾

Dennis Oppenheim: *Radicality*. 1974. Long Island, New York.
Red/yellow/green strontium nitrate flares. W. 15′, L. 100′.

Dennis Oppenheim: *Pretty Ideas*. 1974. Long Island, New York.
Red/yellow/green strontium nitrate flares. W. 75′, L. 1,000′.

Dennis Oppenheim: *Attempt to Raise Hell.* 1974. Clothed figure, magnet, metal bell, blue spotlight. A magnet forces the metal head of a small, seated figure to slam into a large, polished bell. The strike occurs at eye level every 100 seconds and produces an echo lasting half of that duration. The sound of metal clashing against metal fills the room as well as the mind.

you can go farther with fiction—land
project with flares
spinning a yarn
does my mind have to twist

I'm going to pretend you're dead, I'm
going to use that feeling to get somewhere else
the wrong frame of mind

Notes on
THE MYTHIC BEING, I
March 1974

Adrian Piper

*A person frees himself from himself in the
very act by which he makes himself an object
for himself.*
—JEAN-PAUL SARTRE, *Being and Nothingness*

1. Each month, I select a passage from the journal which I have been
keeping for the last twelve years. This is done on a systematic basis.[1]
The passage is called a "mantra."

The visual image of the Mythic Being appears publicly on a
monthly basis in *The Village Voice* on the Gallery Page. The mantra
is reascribed to the personal history of the Mythic Being by appearing
as the content of his thought in the thought balloon.

During that month, the mantra and the autobiographical situation
which provoked it become an object of meditation for me. I repeat it,
reexperience it, examine and analyze it, infuse myself with it until I
have wrung it of personal meaning and significance. It becomes an
object for me to contemplate, and simultaneously loses its status as an
element in my own personality or subjecthood. As my subjecthood
weakens, the meaning of the object thus weakens, and vice versa.

The end result is that I am freer for having exhausted it as an
important determinant in my life, while it simultaneously gains public

[1] See "Outline for a Serial History of the Mythic Being," pp. 278-279.

status in the eyes of the many who apprehend it. The experience of the Mythic Being thus becomes part of public history, and is no longer a part of my own.

2. I began by dressing in the guise of the Mythic Being and appearing publicly several times during the month (reascription of my thoughts and history, sentence by sentence, to a masculine version of myself; myself in drag). I now consider shelving this aspect of the piece for fear that the Mythic Being will gradually acquire a personal auto-biography of experiences and feelings as particular and localized—and limited—as my own. This was the misfortune of Rrose Selavy.

My behavior changes. I swagger, stride, lope, lower my eyebrows, raise my shoulders, sit with my legs wide apart on the subway, so as to accommodate my protruding genitalia.

My sexual attraction to women flows more freely, uninhibited by my fear of their rejection in case my feelings should show in my face; unencumbered by my usual feminine suspicions of them as ultimately hostile competitors for men. I follow them with my eyes on the street, fantasizing vivid scenes of lovemaking and intimacy.

My sexual attraction to men is complicated and altered by my masculine appearance. I envision the possibility of deep love relation-ships based on friendship, trust, camaraderie, masculine empathy; but I instinctively suppress expression of my sexual feelings for fear of alienating the comparatively tenuous feelings of kinship with men I now have.

How might I be different if the history I chronicled in my journal had happened to a man? My adolescent preoccupations with men would have been infused with guilt; my conflicting feelings and be-havior towards my girl friends would have been viewed with alarm by my parents; my stints as model and discotheque dancer would have schooled me in the subtle arts of transvestism; my period in a mental hospital would have included attempted reorientation of my adolescent homosexuality; my drug experiences might have been more traumatic and conflict-ridden, perhaps more sexually than mystically oriented.

Has this part of the piece taught me about myself, or about the Mythic Being?

3. The Mythic Being is, or may be:
An unrealized but possible product of the particular history of

events I in fact underwent, a necessary alternative to the limits of my sense of self;

An abstract entity of mythic proportions, whose history is a matter of public knowledge, and whose presence and thoughts are dispersed over the totality of individuals who apprehend him in the *Voice;*

A nonmaterial art object, unspecified with regard to time or place, the bearer of a finite number of properties, the number and quality of which are circumscribed by my own life, and acquired coextensively with my growth into a *different* person;

A product of my own self-consciousness, and unlike other pieces I have done in not being the generator of my self-consciousness;

A therapeutic device for freeing me of the burden of my past, which haunts me, determines all my actions, increasingly habituates me to the limitations of my personality and physical appearance.

4. A conceptual problem: I find it difficult to figure out what this piece is really about, if it is really about anything, because it is not one in a series of similar pieces over which I can generalize. Because this is the only one of its kind that I have worked on since last September, I have no way of finding out what it has in common with other such pieces (although I can say things about its relationship to everything I've done in the last few years), thus no way of knowing what direction it represents to me, nor what I intend by doing it. All my speculations about it thus seem inconclusive to me; I have the feeling that I will never be sure of what it is I'm really up to.

Notes on
THE MYTHIC BEING, II
January 1975

This isn't just about the Mythic Being, but also about the related constellation of concerns that has constituted "arting" for me lately.

1. SOME METHODOLOGICAL CONSIDERATIONS:

Nothing I say here should be construed as expressing any *decision procedure* for generating the work in any interesting sense of that term. I don't mean, of course, that the work miraculously appears as the result of apparently haphazard activity on my part, quite the contrary. I just mean that the reasoning, ruminations, conjectures I record are essentially attempts to rationalize and make intelligible *ex post facto* a part of my life which would otherwise remain inexplicable to me. The attempt is to make certain preoccupations consistent and coherent with: my own past and present, philosophical ideas that interest me, social and psychosexual relationships I get into, problems I have about my own identity, etc. Perhaps the best way of bringing out what I mean is by contrasting it with a rationalizing process which takes place *a priori,* as it were. Not that I think art activity is rational. But it's certainly possible to generate art through a process of reasoning (if one accepts the premises—as with arguments about the existence of God), rather than using that process to make sense of what's already occurred. The latter best describes what goes on with me. I take the art itself, and my impulse to do it, to be generated by causes rather than by reasons. "Causes" here includes anything and everything from the details of my particular physiological makeup, my background, art education, to current social and environmental factors, relationships, information input, etc., independently of any conscious choice I may make.

I think the distinction is worth making if only to get clear about what kind of thing is being said. Nothing I say, for example, can provide any satisfying answer to the question, "Why did you do X in this piece?" Usually, answers to this question tend to range from the disappointing to the depressing; from "Because it hides the underpinning," to "Because it reveals the essence of existence." One reason for this is that it is not clear what kind of answer is needed. Nor is it clear what kind of answer would make sense, for it is not immediately evident that the question does. For me, the question is precluded because it asks for *reasons* for the presence of X; deliberative calculation of the function X relative to the entire work; an account of how X is intended to support the rational whole. While I'm interested in speculating on these topics, and ready to adduce tentative hypotheses to explain the phenomenon, I assume no firsthand authority on the significance of X. This is not to deny that an account of my intentions contributes to a satisfactory account of the work; indeed the former is a necessary condition for the latter. But alone, an account of my intentions no more constitutes a rational theory or explanation of the work than one's avowed intention to do a good deed constitutes a theory or explanation of why one ought to do that good deed.

2. POLITICAL CONSTRAINTS:

First let me say that they are, then, briefly, why. Some of these ideas are expanded in more detail elsewhere.[2] The political constraints

[2] See *Talking to Myself: The Ongoing Autobiography of an Art Object*, pts. II–IV, IX (Italian-English: Bari, Italy: Marilena Bonomo, 1975; French-Flemish-English: Brussels, Belgium: Fernand Spillemaeckers, 1974). Also "In Support of Meta-Art," *Artforum*, 12, no. 2 (October 1973), pp. 79–81.

are, unlike the work, the result of conscious deliberation. The decision to abjure certain opportunities and outlets, forgo exploration of certain art forms and media, was made around 1970, and continues to evolve. It may have forced my art activity into narrower or different channels than it might otherwise have taken. But I think it has also stimulated a certain growth which I might otherwise have lacked. In any case, I found the option of continuing as I had before 1970 morally unacceptable to me, and this seems to me as important as any purely aesthetic consideration I might entertain.

i. I don't make concrete, spatiotemporally unique, discrete objects which cannot be multiply reproduced or assimilated to any type of space.

ii. I don't rely on discrete, spatially unique art contexts for presentation of the work. It can be done or shown anywhere; but I specifically eschew art contexts as such (galleries, performances).[3]

iii. The exchange value of the work is equal to its production value. Like all art, its economic value is an intrinsic element in its aesthetic value.[4]

iv. I utilize art contexts only in their information-disseminating capacities. I have used them only to the extent of making available information about work or works which can be cheaply distributed on request.[5]

One intentional consequence of these constraints is that my work has no investment value, since its exchange value is an economic constant, i.e. a function of its production value at the time of its production. So it may or may not be good art, but it can't be a good investment. My early performances were done in public spaces, freely accessible to whoever was around at the time. I also considered making these performances available to particular people on a weekly or monthly salaried basis: for $125.00 per week, I would give one performance a day in a public space of my own choosing, for the period of time during which I was hired. I say I considered this idea because, after broaching it to a few people, I got the general impression that no one particularly wanted to pay for something they couldn't own, at least temporarily. More recently, the work has had more to do with visual imagery and written information. My practice here has been to

[3] This is no longer the case (May 1976).
[4] See "A Proposal for Pricing Works of Art," *The Fox,* no. 2 (1975).
[5] See note 3.

272

distribute the work as widely as possible by utilizing the public media (see *Notes* . . . , *I,* above), or by employing cheap and easily available means of reproduction, e.g. photostats, offset printing, posters, etc.

This is desirable to me because I don't think aesthetic value has anything to do with investment value. But a confusion between the two is primarily responsible for the hierarchical power structure of the art world, to which all participants in this confusion implicitly contribute. At one end, there are dealers and collectors who explicitly regard good art as little more than a good investment: the monetary value of a work increases with the gallery-generated publicity accorded to the artist, time, the death of the artist (very important), the critical response to the work, the artist's circle of friends, etc. While any one of these separately is innocuous, their combination can be insidious. At the other end of the spectrum, there are artists who justifiably wish compensation for their labor, but for whom a gradually increasing and inflated overcompensation soon becomes a necessary index of personal and artistic worth, power, and success.

I think the notion of compensation for labor and materials is a fertile one, but not in its present embodiment. The argument (so far as anyone tries to give one) seems to be something like this: just as professionals in other fields are paid proportionally to their education, experience, and achievements, so should artists be compensated in proportion to the magnitude of their contributions to contemporary art, for such a contribution presupposes much the same kind of background preparation. I suppose this argument might have some weight if there were any justification for paying business executives or academics three and four times as much as secretaries or unskilled laborers. But I can't imagine what such a justification would look like. In any case, the argument fails on independent grounds, for there is little or nothing analogous to the process of advancement in other fields, in the career of an artist, for past the putatively obligatory art education, too much depends on such things as one's social and political connections, one's proximity to the "practitioners of mainstream contemporary art" (!!), etc.

A second consequence of these constraints is that the work is potentially as accessible as comic books or television. This is important to me because I personally feel victimized as an artist by the recondite and elitist character of contemporary art, including my own. The failure of communication between the art-educated and the non-art educated is closely related to the many dissonances and socioeconomic discrepancies that exist between the rich and the poor; for an involvement in contemporary art, and an education in contemporary art, is a luxury which is socially and financially feasible for very few. This is not to say that I think art could conceivably solve any socioeconomic problems, no matter how accessible or integrated into the culture it is. But if it were accessible to wider segments of the culture, it would be informed by more various types of critical feedback, would effect a more various and richer quality of experience for people, would be responsive to more of what in fact constitutes our social reality. If it were more integrated into the society in these ways, artists would similarly be more integrated. And this would be a good thing because then the art-world hierarchy which nurtures us, victimizes us, and reinforces our isolation from the rest of the world would become unnecessary. Then perhaps we would be able to be more concerned and responsible as people to the problems of other people: benefits would accrue as much to artists as to everyone else.

A third consequence, which follows from the first two, is that I get to go on making art without giving any support (that I can see) to a system which I find politically and economically repressive, exploitative, and unethical. I would like to think that there is no feature of what I do as an artist that would be precluded under some other political system than capitalism. Specifically, I would like to think that because it is cheap, accessible, doesn't require an isolated art context, and exists independently of capitalist art-world politics, it could subsist under some form of socialism as that term is theoretically understood. As things presently stand, I am, of course, at a disadvantage. I will never be able to try to support myself as an artist, for I can't accept the process of co-optation that seems to be an inevitable condition of the attempt (let alone the success of the attempt). And I may well be consigning my work to art-historical oblivion as a consequence of these decisions. But it seems futile to worry about this possibility.

3. METAMORPHOSIS OF THE MYTHIC BEING:

The material existence of the Mythic Being was an important feature in its original conception. It was important that I experience the same history predicated of the Mythic Being, not as part of my own past alone, but also insofar as that past belonged to him. To become the Mythic Being was to elicit, through contacts with others and recollection of my own past, a masculine version of myself, the masculine part of myself. It was to invert the significance of the events that have formed me, and invert their sexual effect on my psyche. The transformation was dynamic, intersocial, and fluid.

Occasionally I still assume the guise of the Mythic Being and scrutinize myself in the mirror, simultaneously meditating on the appropriate mantra for that time. But this is gradually becoming unnecessary, and functions as little more than a pleasurable behavioral reinforcement of a process of internal metamorphosis that seems to have occurred independently of any deliberate attempts on my part to help it along. I feel my masculinity to be very nearly fully articulated in me. The overt material existence of the Mythic Being has given way to a personality, partly abstract and fictional, which manifests its influence on me by imbuing my perceptions and my memories with a self-conscious awareness of my own intrinsic masculinity. My androgyny is a source of joy and confusion to me.

Recently, I have become more preoccupied with the iconography of the Mythic Being as a marker, sign, or symbol of the Mythic Being himself: the abstract entity, the semifictional hero who exists partly in me, and partly independently of me. I regard his image and see both that he is me, and also that he is completely inscrutable to me. I read the contents of his thoughts every month in *The Village Voice,* and they are as cryptic to me as they must seem to anyone else, at the same time that they recall to me the personal situations they were originally intended to signify. I have been exploring this phenomenon by gradually situating the image of the Mythic Being in matrices that have very familiar and personal connotations to me: photographs of familiar past environments, posing with friends or family, evolving gradually out of a photographic image of myself with which I strongly identify: I undergo a deliberate metamorphosis into the Mythic Being in visual appearance, just as often happens in psychological fact.

My internal transformations, which have occurred and continue to occur, are thus statically and symbolically denoted in the photographs. In each work the same photograph, capturing one and the same moment in time, is multiply reproduced: that moment is expanded and distorted to encompass the alteration in my psychosexual demeanor which that moment effected in me. The maleness of my personality gradually overtakes and overrides my feminine appearance; as an identity I disappear in deference to the Mythic Being. The effect of this is not, however, to infuse the image of the Mythic Being with the same familiarity which my own image has for me; I discover that the familiar contexts of my past are not familiar enough to sustain themselves in an alien presence. The presence of the Mythic Being in the environments that formed me force me to acquiesce in identifying with him; I acknowledge the extent to which I have always identified with what he represents: his maleness, his careful expressionlessness, his protective shades and cigar.

The presence of the Mythic Being in my life and my past goes as unnoticed by the other characters in the photographs as do my masculine aspects in my actual life. But in actuality, the conventional responses of other people to my overt physical appearance reinforce my sense of my own internal strangeness; in the matrix of the photographic environment, it is they, with their static placidity, their symbolic fixity, who are strange.

The Mythic Being has become a visual and psychological entity, rather than an even fleetingly material one, and any character traits which can be ascribed to him qua himself must be ascribed in either or both of these two modes. And because his visual appearance is more readily available to an observer (like myself) than the psychological, the visual mode of characterization is primary: the Mythic Being can most easily be individuated by the visual predicates which can be ascribed to him. The thought/speech balloon convention serves this function: it is as intrinsic to the iconographic identity of the Mythic Being as his dark glasses, his cigar, or his Afro.

This convention also serves a second, perhaps more important, function: it supports the essentially public nature of his personality. The image of the Mythic Being per se is static, and without an inherent identifying context or environment. He is not visually portrayed as moving though, affecting, or being affected by other characters, situations, or events. He is, as it were, portable, and there is no particular context or matrix in relation to which he has special significance. Thus the autobiographically articulated, the iconographically accessible, is of major importance in determining what those experiences are: they are, and can be, only what he *says* they are. We have no independent means for determining the parameters of his history, or the scope of his personality; nor for inferring, from his behavior, what his psychology might be. For he exhibits no behavior at all; we must take his avowals on faith. This reinforces the claim made above. I am able to predicate his verbal avowals to him as indices of his psychology. As portrayed in the thought/speech balloon, they are intrinsic to his visual and psychological identity. And because these avowals are the only possible indices there are, there can be no grounds for hypothesizing anything beyond them. So far as he can be said to have a personality at all, this personality is essentially and wholly public. The Mythic Being as such is all verbal and visual surface, for there is nothing further within him, and nothing further behind the iconographic surface he projects.

This might explain his opacity, his inscrutability for me. For while I recognize the sense in which we are psychologically identical, or at least complementary, I nevertheless can't penetrate past the barrier of his visual image. His visual image is all there is, and psychologically, I resist that. I resist acknowledging his literal two-dimensionality, his conceptual pliability. To contemplate his image is, despite myself, to wonder what that image conceals. It is to hypothesize character traits inferable from the image itself. But those character traits have a curious familiarity; his surface may be nothing but an inverted reflection of my own.

This is not to deny that as an abstract psychological entity he bears a complex relation to me. He has infiltrated my psyche; I have assimilated him into my sense of self. But the relation between him and me is not that of denotation to the object denoted; the Mythic Being does not "stand for" me. In some ways, he *is* me; but as independent abstract object, he is only himself.

4. I/YOU (HER):

Lizzy is the girl on the left in the picture. She was my friend in junior high school. She was very pretty and very rich. She had an older sister and lived with her mother, who was divorced. She took dancing lessons and piano lessons. She was very accomplished socially, although she felt more comfortable having a special boyfriend (she was always going steady with someone, from the age of ten on) than flirting with everyone in general and no one in particular. She was the most popular girl in school. She wasn't very intelligent, but she had a good personality and a charming vulnerability which she manifested by blushing deeply, and which she used to great advantage. She was popular with the girls as well as the boys. All the girls wanted to look like her and be like her, and were honored to be chosen, even temporarily, as her chum. I learned a lot from her about how to flirt, how to be engagingly feminine, how to act in a socially confident and poised manner. I learned all this by simply copying some of her mannerisms and behavior, which she had copied from her older and very sophisticated sister. During the time we were friends, I too was very popular. We both reveled in being asked to all the parties, being the center of attention, and having everybody else want to be with us. Our friendship was based in part on the similarity of our positions, and what we had in common as a result of that, and in part on an implicit truce: we made fun of, gossiped about, and outdid everyone else, but not each other. Or so it seemed at the time. I was going steady with Robbie at the time, but was more attracted to Clyde, whom I dated secretly a number of times (because he was going steady with Janet). I often confided in Lizzy about the predicament, and about how much I wanted to break up with Robbie but didn't want to hurt his feelings. She seemed very understanding, but didn't offer any suggestions. Then I developed the suspicion that Robbie and Lizzy liked each other. So first I tried breaking up with Robbie, but he got very upset and made me feel guilty, so I took it back. Then I confronted each of them individually with my suspicion, but they denied it. Later I found out that Robbie and Lizzy had been dating secretly the whole time I had been fretting to Lizzy about how much I wanted to break up with him. She had dated him behind my back for no other reason than to compete with me socially and sexually, and prove her superior attractiveness and popularity. That was the first time I had ever had a girl friend who undermined our relationship for the sake of a boy, in fact who sacrificed our relationship completely for the sake of a boy. Since then I have had no really close women friends.

OUTLINE FOR A SERIAL HISTORY OF THE MYTHIC BEING:

Cycle Mantra (month/year of journal entry)
I.   9/61 10/62 11/63 12/64 1/65 2/66 3/67 4/68 5/69 6/70 7/71 8/72
II.   10/61 11/62 12/63 1/64 2/65 3/66 4/67 5/68 6/69 7/70 8/71 9/72

III.	11/61 12/62 1/63 2/64 3/65 4/66 5/67 6/68 7/69 8/70 9/71 10/72
IV.	12/61 1/62 2/63 3/64 4/65 5/66 6/67 7/68 8/69 9/70 10/71 11/72
V.	1/61 2/62 3/63 4/64 5/65 6/66 7/67 8/68 9/69 10/70 11/71 12/72
VI.	2/61 3/62 4/63 5/64 6/65 7/66 8/67 9/68 10/69 11/70 12/71 1/72
VII.	3/61 4/62 5/63 6/64 7/65 8/66 9/67 10/68 11/69 12/70 1/71 2/72
VIII.	4/61 5/62 6/63 7/64 8/65 9/66 10/67 11/68 12/69 1/70 2/71 3/72
IX.	5/61 6/62 7/63 8/64 9/65 10/66 11/67 12/68 1/69 2/70 3/71 4/72
X.	6/61 7/62 8/63 9/64 10/65 11/66 12/67 1/68 2/69 3/70 4/71 5/72
XI.	7/61 8/62 9/63 10/64 11/65 12/66 1/67 2/68 3/69 4/70 5/71 6/72
XII.	8/61 9/62 10/63 11/64 12/65 1/66 2/67 3/68 4/69 5/70 6/71 7/72

1. This outline provides an essentially arbitrary means for systematically substantiating the identity of the Mythic Being by gradually publicizing his phenomenological history to readers of *The Village Voice*. It has no other purpose.

2. There are 144 mantras. The first was dispersed via the *Voice* of September 27, 1973. Without interruption, exhaustion of Cycles I.–XII. will take exactly twelve years.[6]

3. There are some gaps in my journal entries, especially around the mid-1960s. I fill these occasional lacunae with conventional phrases of etiquette or standard intersocial speech-acts, such as "Thanks," "Why not?," "Damn," etc. This convention will facilitate transition into a work in progress, *Surfaces*, which utilizes the Mythic Being in a different but related capacity.

[6] Temporarily discontinued due to lack of funds (May 1976).

The Mythic Being: I/You (Her), 1.

The Mythic Being: I/You (Her), 2.

The Mythic Being: I/You (Her), 3.

The Mythic Being: I/You (Her), 4.

The Mythic Being: I/You (Her), 5.

The Mythic Being: I/You (Her), 6.

The Mythic Being: I/You (Her), 7.

The Mythic Being: I/You (Her), 8.

The Mythic Being: I/You (Her), 9.

The Mythic Being: I/You (Her), 10.

SELECTED WORK

Charles Simonds

SOME WORK FROM THE PAST FIVE YEARS:

Birth, in 1970 I buried myself in the earth and was reborn from it. (16mm color movie and double 12-part sequence of color photographs)

Body↔Earth, 1971 on. Using the movements of my body, I shape the earth, creating a small-scale landscape within the landscape by giving it the contour of my body. (1971, 16mm black-and-white movie filmed by David Troy; 1974, 16mm color movie filmed by Rudy Burckhardt)

Landscape↔Body↔Dwelling, 1970 on. I lie down on the earth and with clay transform my body into a landscape; then I build a fantasy dwelling on the landscape on my body on the earth, turning myself into a house. (1971, super 8mm color movie filmed by David Troy; 1973, 16mm color movie filmed by Rudy Burckhardt)

Charles Simonds: *Landscape ↔ Body ↔ Dwelling.* 1972. Photo: Nathanson.

Charles Simonds: *Body↔Earth*. 1971.
Stills from 16mm black-and-white movie by David Troy.

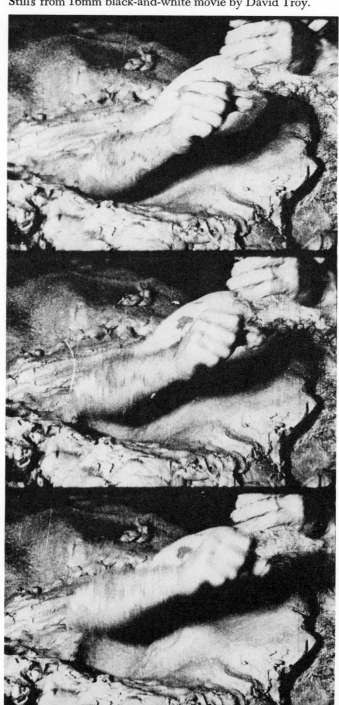

Dwellings, since 1970 most of my time has been spent constructing dwelling places for an imaginary civilization of Little People who are migrating through the streets of different neighborhoods in the city (more than 150 to date). The dwellings are made of raw clay in the street, in niches in broken walls, vacant lots, wherever the architecture of the city offers them a home. Some of the dwellings are ritual places, some ruins, some ruins being reinhabited, some just houses or settlements. During their construction I am in constant dialogue with passersby. On the Lower East Side, the Little People exist as a metaphor for the life of the people in the neighborhood. The creation and eventual destruction of the dwellings is seen as emblematic of lives lived in an area where the buildings of the city are undergoing constant transformation. New construction, vacant building, rehabilitated building, vacant lot are mirrored respectively by dwelling, ruin, reinhabited ruin and destroyed dwelling. Slowly the Little People are developing their own history and potential archaeology. (1972, 16mm black-and-white movie by David Troy; 1974, 16mm color movie by Rudy Burckhardt)

Park—Project Uphill, La Placita, 1973 on. While making the dwellings I have become involved in the creation of a park-playlot sculpture. This plan to develop a vacant lot has resulted from working with local residents and two community groups—the Lower East Side Coalition for Human Housing and the Association of Community Service Centers. The intention is to liberate a parcel of land from the city, relandscape and reactivate it so that local residents invest the space with new life-directed activity.

Niagara Gorge—Artpark, 1974. With the help of local residents I excavated the remains of an old railway tunnel and transformed it into a full-scale three-story dwelling and ritual place. In the cliffs below were small dwellings for my imaginary group of Little People, which coincided with Iroquois legends of a little people who carved the cliffs. *Landscape↔Body↔Dwelling* was enacted as a ritual among the cairns to culminate this project.

Three Civilizations, part of a series of living structures/life architectures: Linear People (model unbuilt, see drawings p. 301).

Circular People (model 1972, p. 304).
Spiral People (model 1974, p. 308).

Pyramid, 1973 (p. 311).

The Growth House, 1975, a seasonally renewable dwelling. As the seeds sprout, growth transforms the built structure; the dwelling is converted from shelter to food and is harvested and eaten.

Charles Simonds: *Dwellings*. 1973. Niche in wall.
East Fourth Street, New York. Photo: Yuri.

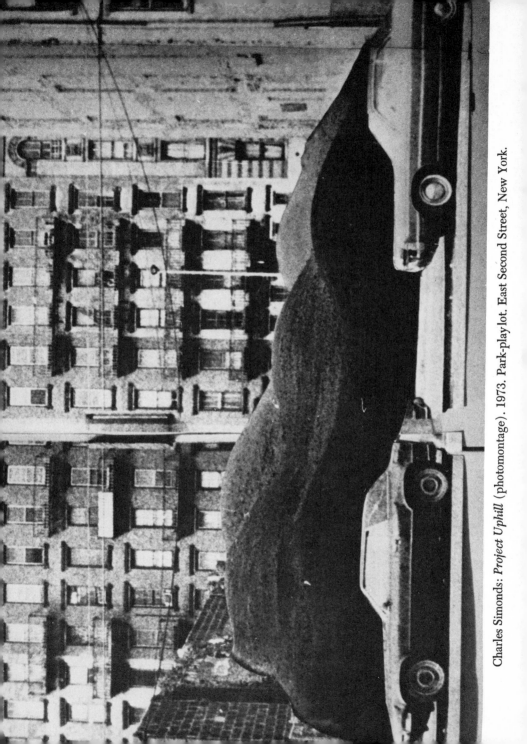

Charles Simonds: *Project Uphill* (photomontage). 1973. Park-play lot. East Second Street, New York.

Charles Simonds: *Park Model/Fantasy.* 1973. The remains of a group of people, the geometry of whose architecture existed at a 45-degree slant to the axis of New York City. Collection of Lucy Lippard. Photo: Rudolph Burckhardt.

Charles Simonds: *Niagara Gorge—Artpark*. 1974. Cairns.

Charles Simonds: *Niagara Gorge—Artpark.* 1974. Excavated and inhabited railroad tunnel remains and ritual place.

SOME THOUGHTS TOWARDS DEVELOPING AN ARCHAEOLOGY AND ANTHROPOLOGY FOR THREE CIVILIZATIONS

Their dwellings make a pattern on the earth as of a great tree laid flat, branching and forking according to their loves and hates, forming an ancestral record of life lived as an odyssey, its roots in a dark and distant past . . .

Occasionally one meets an old minstrel along the paths through the dwellings. People say that as a child he and his parents began a long journey back and that in his endless wanderings he had accumulated an almost total history of his people. He returned with the jumbled and rambling songs which form a blanket of memories from the threads of a growing, listless and venturesome people who have been many places, and done many things. . . .

. . . an old woman who came back from her journey into the past with a vision: what everyone had believed to be a life following an endless line was really part of a great unperceived arc that would eventually meet itself. At that point everyone would join their ancestors in a great joyous dance . . .

—FRAGMENTS OF NOTES RECOVERED FROM A TRAVELER

Their dwellings formed a road/house wandering over the earth on its way towards the future and away from the past. When moved from one dwelling to the next, they left everything behind untouched as a museum of personal effects. As dwelling followed dwelling, traces of a diminishingly distinct personal history remained. Traveling backwards was almost like stumbling into a room whose inhabitants had just left by another door. The farther the distance in time, the more this immediacy blurred; its distinctness dissolved into other moments. Time became continuous. Sand collected in the corners and roof beams

300

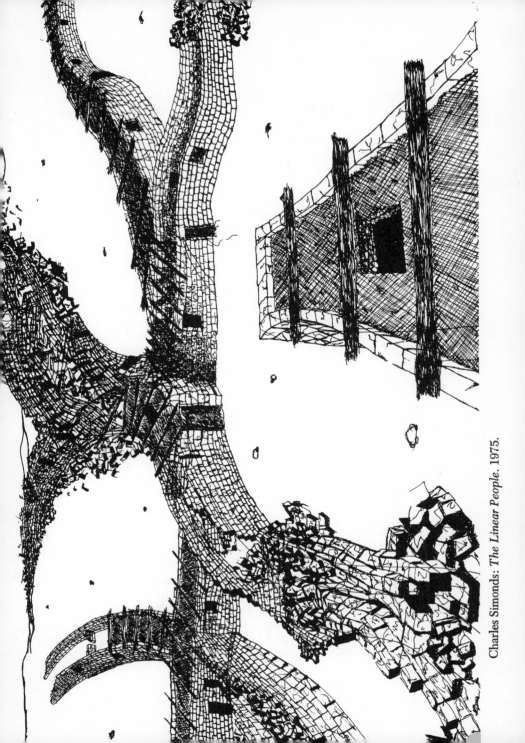

Charles Simonds: *The Linear People*. 1975.

fell in, until the earth reclaimed the architecture. Only a trace, an irregularity recalled that someone had once passed here on the way to somewhere else.

⚇ were preoccupied with cultivation and with decisions about the next direction the dwelling might take. Marital agreements, social ties, and economic concerns, the lay of the land, junctures—all these had to be thought about. Bureaucracies rarely developed because decisions were capricious. Paths might intersect or pass near one another, but each dwelling retained its autonomy. Webs and thickets of old and new dwellings emerged, creating strange cities that combined houses with ruins, gardens with parks that exposed personal histories to everyone's view. Intermarriage was common when these joinings occurred; traditions and pasts were traded and lineages mixed.

Reminiscing about these gatherings, ⚇ saw them as the high points of their lives. Fortified with a feeling of here-we-all-are, ⚇ moved on. Dense civilizations might occur and then disintegrate while ⚇ parted and returned to their adventures. When someone wanting to trace their past came upon these intersections he might be unable to sort out the trails and, taking a chance would find himself lost in a confusion of pasts. Occasionally someone who had ventured too far back would turn up on a doorstep—without a past or a present. These people were a source of much pity, having risked all trying to penetrate what came before.

Tours into the past were organized. Teams of specialists—archaeologists, sociologists, anyone who might have a clue to the past—set out on expeditions. Periodically messengers returned with maps documenting some large meeting place of dwellings that had occurred long ago, and this discovery would be used to explain why certain families had maintained their beliefs, shared genetic traits, where feuds had originated.

For most of the ⚇, the past formed a tremendous net on which their lives traveled; or it was like a dark forest into which there were many paths. The past was a temptation and a threat, the begetter of insanities, the cause of endless ruminations and confusions—a mysterious world that might begin happily in the present on an afternoon stroll, but which stretched backwards into a terrifying miasma, a genealogical geography that disappeared over the hill and into the earth, beyond the horizon.

302

There is a warning tale—a troubling memory—repeated every year among ⟳ *of a child who was born unhappily spinning toward the future instead of turning clockwise toward his past. For some time his confusion went unnoticed, and they merely thought he was dizzy and slow in learning to walk. But when he came of age, he joined in the rebirth and was caught in the whirling dance. Suddenly he was spun, wrenched and twisted out of the circle—dying horribly alone.*

⟳ lives had two aspects: the first was the daily sorting out and keeping of time that placed events in space and history, merging past and present to make both histories and ongoing sagas as well as dwellings that changed according to the seasons; the second was the yearly concentration of birth and growth energy into one ritual at the winter solstice. The first historiographical aspect governed the daily task of reconstructing the new dwelling from the remains of the old. This effort was a recapitulation and reworking of personal memories into myth and history. The second ritual aspect, eschewing all temporal activity, reenacted original creation in a dizzying celebration of sexual possibility.

The gathering took place in the dome-womb at the center of the earth-dwelling universe that could be entered only by a ladder through the opening at the top. The cyclical dwellings were built around it in two concentric rings: the first, one story high, containing the cooking

303

Charles Simonds: *The Circular People*. 1972. Collection of Lucy Lippard. Photo: Rudolph Burckhardt.

and eating quarters, the second, usually two or three storys high, the living quarters. A passageway between the inner and outer structures linked the two. Construction advanced the rings, rotating them laterally around the dome. As portions of the structure were abandoned, they were sealed up, to deteriorate, and after one revolution was completed were dug up and rebuilt. Thus the remnants of each previous dwelling were excavated and remade. Life followed a circle.

The structure grew at least one unit a year. Completion of the new dwelling was timed to coincide with the winter solstice so that everyone's dwelling place could be moved forward a unit toward the distant past and one away from the recent. Crops grown outside the dwelling were part of this circular pattern, planted in a rotation around a center.

The dwelling functioned palpably as a personal and cosmological clock, its encircling architecture operating as an elaborate sundial. The annuary poles over the entrance to the dome cast shadows on the surrounding walls in complex and changing patterns, marking the passage of time. Inside the dome a chant was maintained without interruption. Its faint rhythm audibly kept time for those outside. Everyone took their turn. Chanting was meditation, a way of passing into a non-ordinal pulse, unrelated to the particular incidents of life.

The construction of the new dwelling took a year and followed a precise schedule so that the building progressed with the seasons. The continual sifting and sorting of the rubble formed a sort of ouroboros in which the present devoured the past. Some things recovered were collected and reused; some were reminisced over and became artifacts or keepsakes. Stories and memories were woven around these mementos and the past was reconstituted in C minds just as the old bricks were fitted into the new dwelling.

At times, this resurrection of the past was not achieved without some effort. Those who felt a need to wrestle with the memory of the person or event unearthed stepped forward and relived it in the form of a story, a song or a speech, entering a dialogue between the living present and the dead. An entire day might be set aside to settle a particularly disturbing recollection. Once everyone was reassured, the excavation and construction began with rhythmic singing, sifting, and sorting.

Sexual relations supposedly were confined to the rebirth ceremony. There were strong prohibitions against other sexual encounters, and transgressors, if caught, were executed. This repression was intended to channel all sexual energy toward one shared incestuous moment, although in fact it gave rise to heightened daily promiscuity. Surreptitious meetings took place through elaborate and oftimes humorous subterfuges. Lovemaking in a hidden corridor or through some inventive masquerade of another activity was commonplace. Such behavior was ignored and thus tolerated, as long as it did not result in pregnancy. Self-administered abortions and prophylactic roots, although taboo, were common. Incestuous relations were the goal of such illicit encounters. Even then, they were only a burlesqued version of the imploding/exploding sexual activities of the annual rebirth, and introduced a note of obscene laughter and discord into an everyday life that was otherwise bland and routine. Although the result was supposed to be death, the risk was slight in actuality, and held the fascination of a sexual Russian roulette. Publicly, any one of the G⃗ would say sexual activity for any purpose other than conception was incomprehensible, that intercourse could take place only within the sacred confines of the dome, and then only on the solstice; that unless protected by the dome-womb, no conception was possible.

The solstice was the focus of the G⃗ lives. As the day approached, excavation ceased and excitement spread throughout the dwellings. Foodstuffs were harvested and a share placed within the new house. At sunset every adult gathered according to age and descended into the dome. Each, upon reaching the bottom of the ladder, placed a log upon the fire at the center, removed and burned his or her clothes, and took up the chant. As the circle expanded the chant grew louder, the fire brighter and hotter. With the entrance of the last person, the ladder was drawn in crosswise above their heads.

Everyone stood hand in hand around the wall in a large circle. The dance of rotation began, whirling into eddies of energy. Mirroring the solar system couples formed and swung each other around the fire. The dance continued, faster and faster, until the fire began to die. Everyone spun, always trying to increase the other's speed. As the womb darkened, they moved toward the center, reeling to the floor. Lost in the void, they clutched for another body to find themselves in orgasm. When G⃗ were spent, fatigue having overtaken them, G⃗ returned to the daily counting and ordering of time, taking with them each other's potential.

believed in a world entirely created by their own wills, in which nature's realities were of little concern. Their dwelling formed an ascending spiral—with the past, constantly buried, serving as a building material for the future. They obsessively gambled with their resources, the number of inhabitants, the height of the structure. As the dwelling grew higher and higher, it buried the cultivatable land. As it grew fewer and fewer workers were needed for its construction.

 aspired towards an ecstatic death. Their goal was to achieve both the greatest possible height and to predict the very moment of collapse, the moment when the last of their resources would be consumed and their death inevitable. They lived for that moment alone. After a collapse survivors would begin anew, tracing out a tremendous spiral on the earth's surface. At the periphery they built a house. The detritus of life gradually deposited in front of it providing the base for the next dwelling. As time passed, a ramp was thrown up, the rate of incline planned to bring them to the highest possible point at the center of the spiral. As their predictive mechanisms became increasingly accurate and sophisticated, there were constant readjustments, such calculations determined the infrastructure of social system. Life was hierarchical. The uses of energies were determined by the ruling philosopher/mathematicians. Division of labor, population control, food, size and disposition of labor and research forces were all dictated by elaborate evaluative and self-corrective mechanisms.

 were for the most part optimistic. Although the construction required hard work and sacrifice, they labored happily knowing that

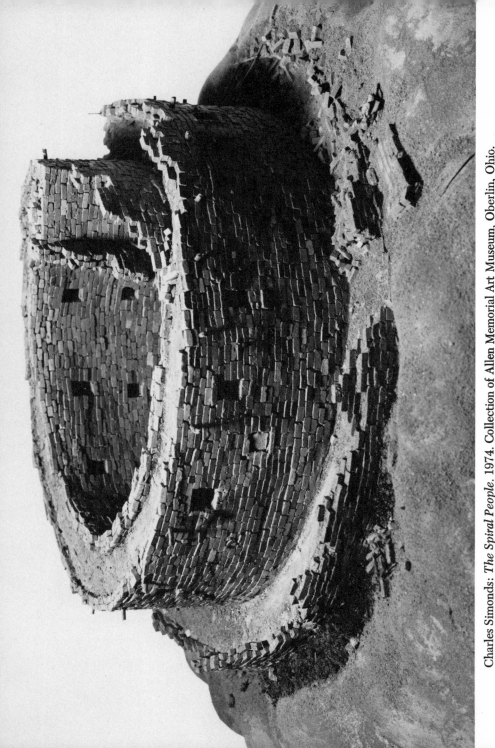

Charles Simonds: *The Spiral People.* 1974. Collection of Allen Memorial Art Museum, Oberlin, Ohio. Photo: Rudolph Burckhardt.

the mathematician's predictions were finer, their dwelling place higher, their lives nearer the climax. They believed resolutely that they were contributing to the most ambitious monument ever conceived by man. Their assurance was confirmed by badges of merit and honors given to the various work forces. Visitors from the spiral cities compared progress with their own and were filled with immense pride at their accomplishments.

The monument relentlessly consumed all material goods. Property had importance only as it related to the construction. Objects no longer useful were by law contributed to the pile of debris at the front of the dwelling. No personal possessions were allowed, no artifacts or keepsakes, no objects of art, no religious figures, no personal or communal decoration; life was merely a function of shelter and height. As the highest elevations were reached, and fewer and fewer laborers were needed to continue, large groups were sacrificed, jumping voluntarily from the forward edge of the structure into the central well, giving their bodies to the task of pushing the edifice higher.

The past, in any personal sense, was dismissed and forgotten. The exception was the carefully kept records of previous structural decisions—abstracted and distilled into mathematical equations to be used in projecting the building. The dwelling's past was reconstructed by a mathematical model to be used in dynamic relationship to its future. These records were kept with compulsive accuracy, because the slightest error might mean the failure of the entire edifice. Failure was, in fact, inevitable so that the work process itself was punctuated by pangs of doubt that led to depression and, finally, to extinction.

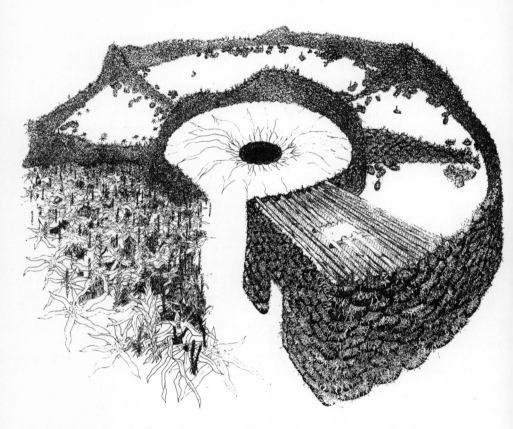

Charles Simonds: *The Growth House*. 1975. A seasonally renewable dwelling.

Charles Simonds: *Pyramid*. 1973. Collection Susana Torre.
Photo: Eeva-Inkeri.

BIOGRAPHIES

of the Artists*

WALTER ABISH's books are *Alphabetical Africa* and *Minds Meet* (New Directions) and a collection of poems, *Duel Site* (Tibor de Nagy). He is a frequent contributor to *New Directions Anthology of Prose & Poetry* and has published in numerous literary magazines, including: *TriQuarterly, Paris Review, Fiction and Statements: New Fiction.* An interview with him has recently appeared in *Fiction International,* and his work is represented in the traveling exhibition, "Language & Structure in North America."

VITO ACCONCI was born in 1940 in the Bronx, New York. He is represented by Sonnabend Gallery.

LAURIE ANDERSON was born in 1947 in Chicago. She has shown in various places in the United States and Europe. Performances include "AS:IF" at Artists' Space, "In the Nick of Time" at the Clocktower,

* From information supplied by the artists.

"How to Yodel" at the Kitchen, "Music" with Alan Sondheim at the Downtown Whitney (all New York), "For Instants" at the Museum of Contemporary Art, Chicago, "Bach to Bach" (violin duets) on street corners, "For Instants Part 3: Refried Beans" at the Whitney Museum of American Art and The Museum of Modern Art (New York). She lives in New York. Currently working on films and video.

DAVID ASKEVOLD was born in March 1940 in Conrad, Montana, and has lived and worked in Halifax, Nova Scotia, since 1968. He taught at the Nova Scotia College of Art and Design through 1973. His work is mainly represented by Paul Maenz in Cologne, and John Gibson in New York.

ALICE AYCOCK was born in 1946 in Harrisburg, Pennsylvania. She has had one-artist exhibitions at the Nova Scotia College of Art and Design in Halifax, 112 Greene Street Gallery in New York, and Williams College in Williamstown, Massachusetts. Her group exhibitions include "Interventions in Landscape" (M.I.T.), "c. 7500" (traveling show), "PROJEKT '74" (Cologne), 1975 Paris Biennale, and Projects in Nature (New Jersey).

ROBERT HORVITZ was born in 1947 in New Bedford, Massachusetts. He studied art at Yale, and has taught at Yale, Phillips and Abbot academies (Andover, Massachusetts), and the Rhode Island School of Design. Occasional contributor to *Artforum*. He showed at the I.C.A., Boston, the Akron Art Institute, and in group shows at the Museum of Modern Art Lending Service and N.S.C.A.D. He currently lives in New Haven.

NANCY WILSON KITCHEL was born in 1941 in Peru, Indiana, and received a B.F.A. from The Cooper Union, New York. Recent one-artist shows include A.I.R., 112 Greene Street, New York, Galerie Germain, Paris, and Galleriaforma, Genoa.

ALVIN LUCIER was born in 1931 in Nashua, New Hampshire, studied music at Yale and Brandeis, and spent two years in Rome on a Fulbright Scholarship. He has lectured and performed extensively in Europe and America with the Sonic Arts Union and the Viola Farber

Dance Company and has pioneered in several areas of composition and performance, including the use of notated physical gestures (*Action Music for Piano, 1962*); the first use of brain waves in musical performance (*Music for Solo Performer, 1965*); acoustic orientation by means of echolocation (*Vespers, 1967*); the articulation of resonant frequencies of rooms by speech (*"I am sitting in a room," 1970*); the generation of visual imagery with sound in vibrating media (*The Queen of the South, 1972*); the computer control of sound environments (*RMSIM 1, The Bird of Bremen Flies Through the Houses of the Burghers, 1972*); and the alteration of vocal identities (*The Duke of York, 1972*). At present he teaches at Wesleyan.

BERNADETTE MAYER was born in 1945. Author of *Story, Moving,* and *Memory.*

ROSEMARY MAYER was born in 1943 in New York City. She has had one-artist exhibitions at A.I.R., 1973, and the Whitney Museum Art Resources Center, 1975. Group exhibitions include the New York Cultural Center, the Massachusetts College of Art, Boston, The Clocktower, New York, Galerie Gerald Piltzer, Paris. Her writing has appeared in *Arts Magazine* and *Art in America.*

MIKE METZ was born in 1945 in New York City. One-artist show at James Yu Gallery, 1973; solo performance at Albright-Knox Museum, Buffalo, New York, 1971. Video tape show with Alan Sondheim at 112 Greene Street Gallery, New York, 1971. Solo performances at the Rhode Island School of Design, 1971, and Newark College of Engineering, 1973. Group shows include "Language and Structure," 1975, and exhibition at Anna Leonowen Gallery, N.S.C.A.D., Halifax, Nova Scotia, 1972.

REE MORTON was born in 1936 in Ossining, New York. She studied at the University of Rhode Island and the Tyler School of Art. Group exhibitions include the Institute of Contemporary Art, Philadelphia, Whitney Museum, New York, Corcoran Museum, Washington, D.C., Institute of Contemporary Art, Boston, Allen Memorial Art Museum at Oberlin College, Ohio, and Vassar College, Poughkeepsie, New York; individual exhibitions at Artists' Space, the Whitney Museum, and the John Doyle Gallery, Chicago.

DENNIS OPPENHEIM was born in 1938 in Mason City, Washington. He attended the California Institute of Arts and Crafts and Stanford University. He has shown extensively in the United States, Canada, and Europe. He is a pioneer in what are now termed "land art," "body art," and "conceptual art."

ADRIAN PIPER was born in 1948 in New York. She studied sculpture at the School of Visual Arts and philosophy at City College. She has shown extensively in the United States and Europe. She is presently a doctoral candidate in philosophy at Harvard University.

CHARLES SIMONDS was born in 1945 in New York, received his B.A. from the University of California, Berkeley, and his M.F.A. from Rutgers University, New Brunswick, New Jersey. He taught at Newark State College from 1969 to 1971. Since 1970 he has focused primarily on working in the streets of New York, making dwellings for an imaginary civilization of Little People who are migrating through the city. He has been a member of the Board of the Lower East Side Coalition for Human Housing since 1973 and has exhibited at the 1973 (8e) and 1975 (9e) Biennales de Paris, M.I.T., the 1975 Whitney Biennial, Artists' Space, and the Centre National d'Art Contemporain, Paris. In the summers of 1974 and 1975 he worked at Artpark in Lewiston, New York. His "Microcosm to Macrocosm/Fantasy World to Real World" appeared in *Artforum* in February 1974, and an article on his work, "Vernacular Myth," was in *Art-Rite*, May 1974.